STRUCTURAL BUDGET DEFICITS IN THE FEDERAL GOVERNMENT

Causes, Consequences, and Remedies

Edited by

Khi V. Thai
Associate Professor
University of Maine

UNIVERSITY
PRESS OF
AMERICA

LANHAM • NEW YORK • LONDON

British Cataloging in Publication Information Available

Library of Congress Cataloging-in-Publication Data

Structural budget deficits in the federal government.

  Includes bibliographies.
  1. Budget deficits—United States. I. Thai, Khi V.,
1941-
HJ2052.S74   1987   339.5'23'0973   86-33961
ISBN 0-8191-6138-1 (alk. paper)
ISBN 0-8191-6139-X (pbk. : alk. paper)

All University Press of America books are produced on acid-free
paper which exceeds the minimum standards set by the National
Historical Publication and Records Commission.

To Xuan, Xuan-Thu, and Edward

iii

iv

Acknowledgements

The editor is pleased to acknowledge his debts. I am grateful to the various authors and publishers for their permission to reprint and particularly to those government officials who produced excellent research reports reprinted in this book.

Special thanks are also extended to Michael Gemignani, Dean of the College of Arts and Science, and G. Thomas Taylor, Chairman of the Department of Public Administration, University of Maine for funding typing expenses of this manuscript; Kathryn Godwin, Director, and Charles E. Morris, Research and Development Coordinator of the Bureau of Public Administration for helping printing the final draft of the book; Margaret Coleman and Joyce Grondin for typing this manuscript; and Arthur W. Ellingwood, Patricia A. Fowler, Charles D. Morgan III, David Sullivan, and Nancy Teachout for proofreading the book.

I would also like to thank my wife Xuan and my children Xuan-Thu and Edward for their patience, perseverance, and unwavering support at home.

TABLE OF CONTENTS

Preface

The Federal budget deficit, which has emerged as a prime issue in the 1980 and 1984 presidential elections, looks like a familiar problem but is really a new one. The deficit is likely to keep widening for years to come even if the economy continues to grow toward full employment. In its 1984 report, the President's Private Sector Survey on Cost Control, commonly known as the Grace Commission, projected a deficit of $2 trillion and a national debt of $13 trillion by the year 2000 if fundamental changes are not made in federal spending and taxing. The nation has been and continues to face a built-in or structural deficits, which persist despite the cycle of the economy, and which will be the central policy issue in the political arena.

Indeed, there is strong interest in partitioning the budget deficit into a cyclical component, measuring the automatic responses of budget receipts and outlays to economic fluctuations, and a cyclically adjusted or structural component, measuring discretionary fiscal policy and other noncyclical factors affecting the budget. As the concept of structural deficit is relatively new, despite many articles and symposia dealing with the budget deficit, no single comprehensive book is fully devoted to the structural component of the budget deficit.

With the passage of the Deficit Control Act of 1985, known as the Gramm-Rudman Act, the federal budget deficit was thought to be resolved. Unfortunately, one of the most important provision of the act, the automatic budget-cutting procedure, was ruled unconstitutional by the Supreme Court in summer, 1986. This court decision brought to an end any hope of a balanced budget by 1991. As a consequence, the budget deficit of fiscal year 1986 reached another record high at $220.7 billion as reported by the office of Management and Budget (New York Times, October 29, 1986). Thus, the annual budget deficit of the Federal government continues to be the center of attention in the policy arena in years to come. Many policy makers, budget experts and laymen believe that the federal budget deficit can be reduced by cutting expenditures, increasing taxes or a combination of both. In reality, it is not easy to do so. Why? This book is mainly devoted to this question.

This book is of the interest of appointed and elected officials, and interest groups not only in the United States but also in other industrial as well as developing countries because almost all countries around the world have the problem of budget deficit. It is also used as a complimentary text in public budgeting, economics and public finance courses offered in the departments of political science, public administration, economics and business administration.

Currently in the markret, no book is fully devoted to the structural budget deficit. There are some proceedings such as Control of Federal Spending (The Academy of Political Science, 1985), What Should Be Done About the Federal Deficit? The Donald S. MacNaughton Symposium (Syracuse University, 1984), The Economics of Large Government Deficits, (Federal Reserve Bank of Boston, 1983). These proceedings contain excellent papers. However, they cover mostly the federal budget deficit without paying enough emphasis to the structural component of the deficit.

PART I.

OVERVIEW OF STRUCTURAL BUDGET DEFICITS

IN THE FEDERAL GOVERNMENT

2

BK Title

CHAPTER 1

INTRODUCTION

The passage of the Deficit Control Act of 1985, known as Gramm-Rudman law, was thought to be the last hope for balancing federal budget. Unfortunately, one of the most important provisions of the act, the automatic budget-cutting procedure, was ruled unconstitutional by the Supreme Court in summer, 1986. This court decision has led to a question: Will the federal budget be ever balanced? The fact that the fiscal year 1986 ended with a deficit of $220.7 billion as reported by the Office of Management and Budget (New York Times, October 29, 1986) proves the failure of the Gramm-Rudman law.

This book is concerned with the seriousness of enormous federal budget deficits which have hovered at about $200 billion a year in the past several years and are likely to persist at least in the remaining years of this decade. the deficits persist although the economy continues to grow toward full employment. Therefore, many economists and budget experts believe that the nation has been facing a **structural budget deficit** - one that will persist despite the business cycle of the economy. This editor believes that the current continuing deficit is similar to a time bomb. The time for its explosion is the economic recession which is cyclical in the history of American economy. The success of "Reaganomics" in spurring growth has opened a unique opportunity for balancing the federal budget because the current economic expansion is so strong that taxes can be gradually increased and government expenditure can be gradually cut without causing a major economic slowdown. The time to act is now. If no action is taken to reduce the gigantic deficits, an unavoidable economic recession in the American economy may occur and would bring serious economic hardship to the nation.

In exploring the causes and consequences of structural budget deficits and suggesting some remedies to cure the deficits, this book is an attempt to keep public policy analysts, policy makers and particularly the public aware of the potential danger of the current and future state of budget deficit. The reasons for an early action are numerous. Firstly, fiscal changes are required now in order to have even a moderate effect in later years. The longer the time period for adjust-

3

ment to fiscal changes, the smoother and more efficient the adjustments will be. This applies particularly to social programs: abrupt and sharp budget cuts will intensify the shock for recipients. Moreover, the current strong economic performance offers policy-makers a unique opportunity to reduce the "red ink".

Secondly, any spending reduction usually has cumulative effects. That is, the savings would be small at first; but later in the projection period, they grow rapidly. Conversely, the longer the delay in change in fiscal policies, the harder the expenditures are controlled due to the compounding effect of annual expenditure increases.

Thirdly, although a slight decline in the budget deficit occurred in 1984, this decline was less than normally expected during an economic recovery. Even worse, the budget deficits rose again in fiscal years 1985 and 1986 despite the continuing strong performance of the economy.

Finally, enacting measures to reduce the deficit would be politically difficult in any year, and especially so in election years. President Reagan is in the best position to act now because he is no longer under re-election pressure.

This book consists of twelve chapters which are grouped in four parts. The first part of the book will:

- explore the definition of relatively new terms structural budget deficit, traces the trends of cyclical and structural deficits, analyzes the patterns of revenues and public expenditures, and considers the extent, or seriousness, of deficits from the perspective of federal financial liabilities and obligations (K. Thai, "Structural Budget Deficits: Concepts and Facts").

- identify the causes of the deficit, and highlight fiscal theories regarding the size of government and the consequences of budget deficits (L. Cao and K. Thai, "Structural Budget Deficits in the Federal Government: A Theoretical Perspective").

- review empirical studies, point out some serious statistical problems of these studies, and simulate several scenarios in which the budget deficit may be reduced (D. Nguyen and J. Olson, "U.S. Budget

4

Deficits: Empirical and Policy Issues".

The second part of the book is to examine expenditure restraint alternatives. The question facing policy makers is not whether the federal budget should be restrained, but rather "by how much?" and "by what means?" G. Mills, in Chapter 5, reviews the context for the debate over federal spending cuts and, through budget data, proves that instead of considering structural reforms, Congress tends to exercise spending restraint through an ad hoc rules-of thumb or across-the-board fashion.

Chapter 6 is devoted to a major spending category, social security outlays. Although the social security system is currently in a healthy financial condition due to continuous increase in social security taxes or contributions, the long-term problem of this system may emerge again. Thus, a major part of a 1982 study of the Congressional Office is reprinted here. It analyzes two major ways in which outlays for benefits could be reduced relative to current law over the long run: lowering the levels of initial retirement and disability retirement age. Changes in benefit indexation procedures are also considered to stabilize trust fund balances over the long run.

Another major spending category is defense outlays which are the topic of discussion of Chapter 7. The author, Fred Thompson, contends that "no matter what happens to the Grace Commission's proposals, defense outlays defense outlays will increase in real terms for the next several years." The reason is that defense spending is governed by too many rules and not enough policy direction. This situation cannot be corrected by the imposition of more rules: further congressional attempts to manage the Department of Defense will merely exacerbate an already bad situation.

After more than five years being implemented, the "Reaganomics" has produced a clear evidence: large structural budget deficits cannot be reduced by economic growth. As will be explained in Chapter 3, while it is impossible to cut federal expenditures, federal budget revenues must be increased. Increasing taxes, however, would not be an attractive policy option because this would accentuate the existing inequities, and economic losses and efficiency of the present tax system. Therefore, the third part of the book is devoted to the current tax reform efforts.

Chapter 8 is a reprint of a study of the Joint Economic Committee's Subcommittee on Goal and Intergovernmental Policy. After addressing basic principles of taxation including revenue generating, economic stabilization, fairness, efficiency, simplicity, compliance, federalism, and predictability, the study discusses the question of whether a consumption tax should be adopted and then analyzes three tax reform proposals -- the Bradley-Gephardt Fair tax, the Kemp-Kasten FAST tax and the Treasury tax simplification proposal.

Chapter 9 contains a reprint of a Treasury report to the President regarding the shortcommings of the federal tax system. Then it summarizes the content and impacts of President Reagan's tax reform proposal, describes political pressure against it, and traces the evolution of this tax reform proposal until passage of the 1986 tax law. Although it was too early to assess impacts of the new tax law, the author pointed out some of its implications.

The last part of the book covers three basic possible reforms related to the American government structure and Constitution: federal budgeting and accounting system, and reforming the current budget process (Chapter 10), budgetary process (Chapter 11), and proposed constitutional amendment which would give the President the power to line-item veto budget (Chapter 12).

Although this book contains several proposed alternatives to reduce federal budget deficits, budget deficits will never be ended.

7 - 28

CHAPTER 2

STRUCTURAL BUDGET DEFICITS: CONCEPTS AND FACTS*

Khi V. Thai

U.S.
322 6

I. INTRODUCTION

The budget deficit in the federal government has been a prime issue in the last two presidential election campaigns and will continue to be a problem for years to come. Traditionally, Americans are in favor of a balanced budget, less taxes and less government; and budget deficits usually led to legislative reforms. The Budget and Accounting Act of 1921, for example, was partially a reaction to budget deficits caused by the lack of an executive budget. By the late 1930's, after many years of continuous budget deficits caused by President Franklin D. Roosevelt economic and social programs during the Great Depression, the Americans again were concerned with the impacts of budget deficits and national debt. The issue of balancing budget was raised; and the February 1940 issue of <u>Congressional Digest</u> was devoted to the question: Should a Joint Committee of Congress be appointed to balance the Federal budget? The public attention to Federal budget deficits subsided due, in part, to critical events around the world in the next thirty years or so, such as World War II, the Korean War, and the Vietnam War; and in part to high economic growth of the nation.

Suddenly, the public antipathy against high taxes and big government were stronger in the late 1970s and early 1980s than ever before. Spurred by the passage of Proposition 13 in California in 1978, the tax revolts and spending limitation movements have successfully imposed limits on state and local taxes and expenditures over half the states. This movement was also reflected in the 1980 election campaign when President Reagan vowed to cut taxes and reduce expenditures in order to balance the federal budget.

---

* This chapter is a revised version of the author's article of the same title, published in <u>International Journal of Public Administration</u>, Vol.8, No. 1 (1986): pp. 7 - 32.

Additionally, there have been attempts to require, by constitutional amendment, a balanced budget at the federal level. Almost enough state legislatures (thirty two at the time of this writing) have endorsed a balanced budget amendment to meet the two-thirds requirement specified in the U.S. Constitution for calling a constitutional convention to propose such an amendment. The U.S. House of Representatives and Senate have worked on a similar measure.

Recently, however, the movement seemed to fade away. In the November 6, 1984 election, voters in four states, Michigan, California, Nevada and Oregon, rejected major tax limitation measures, and efforts to impose milder restraints on state spending failed in Louisiana and Arizona. The drive for a constitutional convention to propose a balanced budget amendment was stalled as the courts struck proposals mandating such a convention from the November 6, 1984 ballots in Montana and California.(1) In conjunction with the above setbacks, during his campaign President Reagan abandoned his balanced budget goal and vowed to <u>reduce</u> the budget deficit to an "acceptable" level over several years. The setbacks of the tax and spending limitation and balanced budget movement resulted from the strong performance of the economy. Coincidentally, supported by a stiff decline in oil prices, President Reagan's tax reduction appears to be a spectacular success: the economic growth has reached the highest level since World War II, and inflation has been pushed to lows not seen since the 1950s.

Despite some recent setbacks of the tax and spending limitation movement, however, huge budget deficits are still a concern of a majority of Americans. A recent survey of <u>U.S.</u> <u>News</u> <u>and</u> <u>World</u> <u>Report</u> shows that 83.8 percent of the surveyed population are worried by rising budget deficits (49.3 percent are worried very much, and 34.5 percent are somewhat worried).(2) The focus of this study is to define structural budget deficit, a relatively new term, trace the trend of federal budget deficits of the United States, analyze the patterns of revenues and public expenditures, and discuss the implications of budget deficits from the perspective of federal financial liabilities and debt payments.

II. STRUCTURAL BUDGET DEFICITS: DEFINITION AND TRENDS

In the Donald S. MacNaughton Symposium on "What

Should Be Done About the Federal Deficits?", organized at Syracuse University in May 1984, Senator David Patrick Moynihan distinguished four different types of budget deficits. The first type, wartime deficit, is caused by war-related expenditures. The budget deficit during World War II reached 21.9 percent of GNP (Table 2). The second type, business-cycle or cyclical deficit, is a consequence of economic recession which causes a reduction in revenues and an increase in expenditures. The third type, full-employment deficit, is "a Keynesian concept of a budget which would spend that amount of money which would be received as revenue, under conditions of full employment. The difference between outlays and income is the full-employment deficit".(3) The fourth type, "revenue reduction deficit", is brought about for the purpose of reducing the size of government by first reducing the resources of government.(4)

Excluding wartime deficits, there is currently strong interest in two types of deficits: cyclical and cyclically adjusted or structural. According to Richard and Peggy Musgrave, the concept of structural deficit "applies to the deficit which would prevail if income was at full employment, with a corresponding level of full employment revenue being obtained. The deficit remaining under such circumstances is referred to as structural, while the excess of the actual over the full-employment deficit is referred to as cyclical".(5)

In many circumstances, a budget deficit may consist of cyclical and structural components. For illustration, Figure 1 presents a situation where public expenditures are measured on the vertical axis, equal to OE. As shown by the line EE', public expenditures are independent of the level of income Y, as measured on the horizontal axis. Tax revenues, TT', is a function of Y, reflecting a given tax rate t. Assume that the budget is in balance as the economy performs at a particular employment level, say Y_1. If the economy reaches the full-employment level, say, Y_f, the budget shows a full employment surplus of F_1F_2. A budget deficit can occur in at least three simplified circumstances.

1. If income falls from Y_1, to, say, Y_2, and there is no change in fiscal policy, tax revenues decline (4) and the budget changes from balanced to a deficit of D_1D_2 (Figure 1), which is a cyclical deficit. This has occurred without any change in the other two fiscal

9

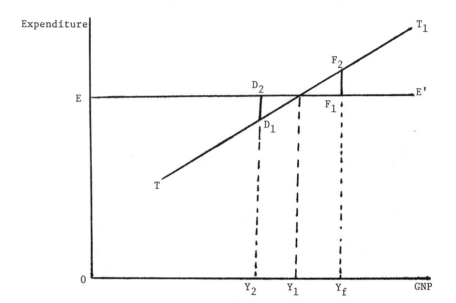

Figure 1

parameters, public expenditures and tax rate. Since
the government does not react to the economic decline,
it is said that fiscal policy has been passive.

2. Assume that there is no change in income and
tax rate, but that public expenditures are raised to E_1
(Figure 2). As a result, income rises from Y_1 to Y_2,
and so do the tax revenues. However, in the short term,
this rise is less than the increase in public
expenditures. The budget then shows a deficit of D_1D_3.
This budget deficit is different from the deficit in
the previous case because of the difference in
circumstances surrounding it. While the first case
depicts a passive fiscal policy, the second involves an
active or expansionary fiscal policy, that is, spending

10

increase. In other words, with increased public expenditure, the full employment surplus changes to a deficit of F_2F_3, which is equal to D_2D_3. This budget deficit of D_1D_3 consists of two components: D_1D_2, which is called <u>cyclical</u> because the income has reached the full-employment level yet, and D_2D_3, which is called <u>structural</u>, because this budget deficit is due to the policy change.

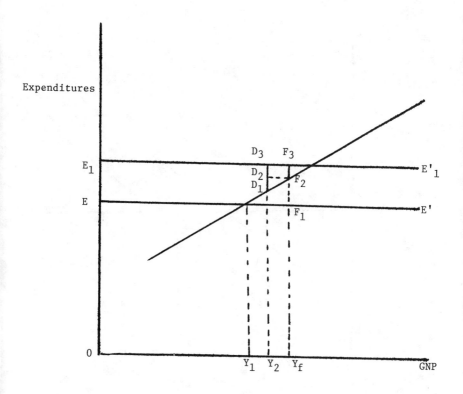

Figure 2

3.   Assume that there is no changes in income and public expenditures, but that tax rates are cut similar to the Tax Reduction Act of 1981. Thus tax revenues shift from TT' to T_1T_1' . As a result, income rises from Y_1 to, say, Y_2 (Figure 3), and so do the tax revenues, from R_1 to R_2. The budget again shifts from balance to a deficit of D_1D_3. Similar to the second case, with tax cuts, the budget deficit consists of two components: <u>cyclical</u> D_1D_2 and <u>structural</u> D_2D_3 .

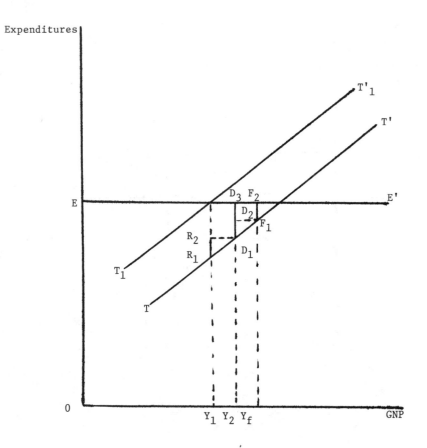

Figure 3

The above illustrations are in the simplest forms since they exclude "multipliers" or the built-in effects of fiscal policy, behavioral relationships between consumption investment, and liquidity preferences. Moreover, two of the three variables (income, tax rate, and public expenditure) are kept constant at any given time. In fact, these variables do not remain constant throughout any fiscal year.

The concept of structural budget deficits as illustrated above helps to indicate what portion of the actual deficit reflects the business cycle, and what portion is caused by fiscal policy. There is, however, a major issue involved in calculating structural deficits. It is the issue of the determination of income levels, termed by the Congressional Budget Office as a "benchmark measure" of income (6) or an income benchmark. Two observations should be mentioned in this vein.

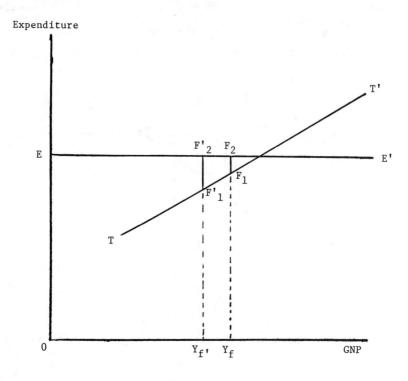

Figure 4

First, the full-employment income Y_f is always at a level where tax revenues are less than public expenditures. If Y_f is set at a lower level, say Y_{f1} (Figure 4), the structural deficit F'_1F_2 becomes larger than F_1F_2. Thus, the lower the full-employment income level is set for calculation, the larger the structural deficit.

Second, assume that the full-employment income level remains unchanged. The actual level of income can vary between Y_1 and Y_f (Figure 5). If the benchmark level is set at Y_1, the budget deficit will be D_1D_4. If the income benchmark is set at Y_2, instead of Y_1, the budget deficit will be $D'_1 D'_4$. In other words, if the income benchmark is set at Y_2, instead of Y_1, the budget deficit becomes smaller, changing from D_1D_4 to $D'_1 D'_4$, which is equal to D_2D_4. This is due to a smaller cyclical deficit, as the higher income level reduces the cyclical deficit by D_1D_2. The structural budget deficits at both income levels Y_1 and Y_2 remain unchanged, that is, $D_3D_4 = D'_3D'_4$ (Figure 5). Thus, the higher the income benchmark, the smaller the

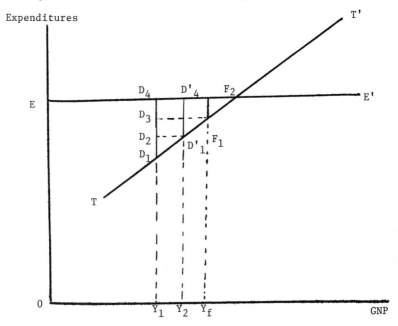

Figure 5

14

cyclical component of the deficit.

There is widespread agreement among economists that the actual budget deficit in the United States consists of both components: cyclical and structural. Many people tend to think that the structural budget deficit was caused by the Reagan fiscal policy. The reason is that the budget deficit has jumped up from $78.9 billion or 2.6 percent of GNP in fiscal year 1981 to 127.9 billion or 4.1 percent of GNP in 1982, and has been lingering around $200 billion in fiscal years 1983 to 1985, and would be around $230 billion in fiscal year 1986. These figures represent record-high deficits in the U.S. peacetime budget history (Table 1).

According to a well-known deficit measuring model, however, structural budget deficits have existed since 1962 (Table 2). The data in use is based on the full employment or standardized-employment economy at 6 percent unemployment. This mismatch between tax revenues and public expenditures cannot be blamed solely on the cycle of the economy. The budget deficits have been built-in from the past. With or without Reagan fiscal policy, structural budget deficits have already existed. This situation merely became worse when President Reagan tried to reduce the size of government by successfully cutting taxes, but failing to reduce public expenditures for a variety of reasons, as will be explained in chapter 3. Therefore, while total budget receipts as a percentage of GNP declined in 1982, 1983, and 1984, total budget outlays continued to increase in 1982 and 1983. Although outlays declined from 24.3 percent of GNP in 1983 to 23.1 percent in 1983, they bounced back to 24.0 percent in 1985 (Table 1). Without being cyclically adjusted, the budget deficit reached a record high of 6.3 percent of GNP in 1983. On the full employment structural deficit basis, budget deficits under the Reagan administration, except its first two fiscal years 1981 and 1982 have been the largest since 1956 (Table 2). It is noted that Table 2 contains the Johnson administration period which marked the spending pressure caused by the Vietnam war and the great society programs.

III.PATTERNS OF BUDGET RECEIPTS AND OUTLAYS

As seen in Table 1, for the period before 1980, budget receipts were 6.8 percent of GNP in 1940, jumped to a wartime high of over twenty percent in 1945,

15

TABLE 1. Budget Receipts, Outlays and Surplus or Deficit(-)
1940-1991 (In Billions of Dollars and as a Percentage of GNP)

Fiscal Year	GNP	Budget Totals (including off-budgets)					
		Receipts		Outlays		Surplus or Deficit (-)	
1940	95.8	6.5	6.8%	9.5	9.9%	-3.0	-3.0%
1945	212.4	45.2	21.3	92.7	43.6	-47.5	-22.4
1950	266.9	39.4	14.8	42.6	15.9	-3.1	-1.2
1955	387.6	65.5	16.9	68.4	17.7	-3.0	-.8
1960	507.7	92.5	18.2	92.2	18.2	.3	.1
1965	673.6	116.8	17.3	118.2	17.6	-1.4	-.2
1970	990.5	192.8	19.5	195.6	19.8	-2.8	-.3
1975	1,523.5	279.1	18.3	332.3	21.8	-53.2	-3.5
1980	2,667.6	517.1	19.4	590.9	22.2	-73.8	-2.8
1981	2,986.2	599.3	20.1	678.2	22.7	-78.9	-2.6
1982	3,141.5	617.8	19.7	745.7	23.7	-127.9	-4.1
1983	3,320.9	600.0	18.1	808.3	24.3	-207.8	-6.3
1984	3,695.3	666.5	18.0	851.8	23.1	-185.3	-5.0
1985	3,936.8	734.1	18.6	946.3	24.0	-212.3	-5.4
1986	4,192.2	777.1	18.5	979.9	23.4	-202.8	-4.8
1987	4,538.1	850.4	18.7	994.0	21.9	-143.6	-3.2
1988	4,902.9	933.2	19.0	1,026.8	20.9	-93.6	-1.9
1989	5,268.9	996.1	18.9	1,063.6	20.2	-67.5	-1.3
1990	5,623.4	1,058.1	18.8	1,093.8	19.5	-35.7	-.6
1991	5,955.2	1,124.0	18.9	1,122.7	18.9	1.3	*

Notes: Data for fiscal years 1986-1991 are estimated.

Source: Office of Budget and Management, Historical Tables--Budget of the United
States Government, Fiscal Year 1987, pp: 1.1(1), 1.1(2), 1.2(1),
and 1.2(2).

16

TABLE 2. Federal Budget Surpluses or Deficits (-):
Structural and Current
(In Billions of Dollars and as a Percent of GNP)

Fiscal Year	Actual		Structural	
1956	3.9	0.9%	5.8	1.4%
1957	3.4	0.8	2.7	0.6
1958	-2.8	-0.6	-4.8	-1.0
1959	-12.8	-2.7	-0.8	-0.2
1960	0.3	0.1	4.8	0.9
1961	-3.3	-0.6	-0.1	0.0
1962	-7.1	-1.3	-4.1	-0.7
1963	-4.8	-0.8	-0.3	0.0
1964	-5.9	-0.9	-6.6	-1.0
1965	-1.4	-0.2	-6.9	-1.0
1966	-3.7	-0.5	-14.4	-2.0
1967	-8.6	-1.1	-24.6	-3.2
1968	-25.1	-3.0	-20.2	-2.4
1969	3.2	0.3	-4.0	-0.4
1970	-2.8	-0.3	-10.9	-1.1
1971	-23.0	-2.2	-16.8	-1.5
1972	-23.4	-2.0	-15.6	-1.3
1973	-14.9	-1.2	-13.5	-1.0
1974	-6.1	-0.4	-9.1	-0.6
1975	-53.2	-3.5	-44.4	-2.7
1976	-73.7	-4.3	-37.9	-2.1
1977	-53.6	-2.8	-42.7	-2.1
1978	-59.2	-2.7	-45.3	-2.1
1979	-40.2	-1.6	-36.3	-1.5
1980	-73.8	-2.8	-60.5	-2.2
1981	-78.9	-2.6	-55.6	-1.8
1982	-127.9	-4.1	-88.9	-2.7
1983	-207.8	-6.3	-129.5	-3.7
1984	-185.3	-5.0	-171.3	-4.6
1985	-212.3	-5.4	-202.7	-5.1

Source: Office of Budget and Management, Historical
Tables – Budget of the United States
Government, Fiscal Year 1987, pp. 1.1 (1) –
(2); and Thomas M. Holloway, "The Cyclically
Adjusted Federal Budget and Federal Debt:
Revised and Updated Estimates", Survey of
Current Business, Vol. 66, No. 3 (1986), p.
14.

declined to 14.8 percent by 1950 and never reached 20 percent of GNP again until 1981, except fiscal year 1969 (at 20.5 percent of GNP). Budget receipts reached 20.1 percent in 1981, then declined drastically to 18.0 percent of GNP in 1985. This decline was attributed to President Reagan's tax cut policy as analyzed in detail later in this section.

On the spending side, budget outlays were 9.9 percent of GNP in 1940, then jumped up to 43.6 percent in 1945, and remained consistently below 20 percent until 1975 (except in 1953, 1968, and 1972). Since 1975 outlays have been lingering between 20 and 24 percent of GNP. Although President Reagan has tried hard to reduce government spending, budget outlays remained constant. As analyzed in detail later in this section budget outlays have been lingering above 20 percent of GNP because of increases in defense spending and interest payments.

1. Patterns of Budget Receipts

Table 3 shows two major sources of budget receipts, personal income taxes and social security taxes and contributions. Personal income taxes were 13.6 percent of budget revenues in 1940, jumped up to 40.7 percent in 1945 and reached 48.2 percent in 1982. They declined significantly to 44.8 percent of budget revenues in 1984 and bounced back to over 45 percent of budget revenues in 1985 and 1986. However, due to the 1986 tax reform (see Chapter 9), this source of revenue would decline significantly in the next five years.

Meanwhile, social security taxes and contributions were 27.3 percent of budget revenues in 1940, declined to 7.6 percent in 1945, gradually increased from 1946 to 1970, increased tremendously in the 1970s, from 20.9 percent of budget revenues in 1969 to 30.0 percent in 1979 (9), and continued to increase in the early 1980s. In total, personal income taxes and social security taxes and contributions currently contribute over 80 percent of revenues to the annual budget since 1982.

Excise taxes, once the most important source of budget revenues, declined from 30.2 percent of budget receipts in 1940 to 4.9 percent in 1985 and are projected to decline to 3.0 in 1991.

Corporate income taxes, another important source of budget receipts since World War II, have gradually

TABLE 3. Budget Receipts: 1940-1991
As a Percentage of Budget Composition and GNP ( )

Fiscal Year	Personal Income Taxes	Corporation Income Taxes	Social Security Taxes and Contributions	Excise Taxes	All Other Receipts	Total Receipts
1940	13.6 (0.9)	18.3 (1.2)	27.3 (1.9)	30.2 (2.1)	10.7 (0.7)	100 (6.8)
1945	40.7 (8.6)	35.4 (7.5)	7.6 (1.6)	13.9 (2.9)	2.4 (0.5)	100 (21.3)
1950	39.9 (5.9)	26.5 (3.9)	11.0 (1.6)	19.1 (2.8)	3.4 (0.5)	100 (14.8)
1955	43.9 (7.4)	27.3 (4.6)	12.0 (2.0)	14.0 (2.4)	2.8 (0.5)	100 (16.9)
1960	44.0 (8.0)	23.2 (4.2)	15.9 (2.9)	12.6 (2.3)	4.2 (0.8)	100 (18.2)
1965	41.8 (7.2)	21.8 (3.8)	19.0 (3.3)	12.5 (2.2)	4.9 (0.9)	100 (17.3)
1970	46.9 (9.1)	17.0 (3.3)	23.0 (4.5)	8.1 (1.6)	4.9 (1.0)	100 (19.5)
1975	43.9 (8.0)	14.6 (2.7)	30.3 (5.5)	5.9 (1.1)	5.4 (1.0)	100 (18.3)
1980	47.2 (9.1)	12.5 (2.4)	30.5 (5.9)	4.7 (0.9)	5.1 (1.0)	100 (19.4)
1981	47.7 (9.6)	10.2 (2.0)	30.5 (6.1)	6.8 (1.4)	4.8 (1.0)	100 (20.1)
1982	48.2 (9.5)	8.0 (1.6)	32.6 (6.4)	5.9 (1.2)	5.3 (1.1)	100 (19.7)
1983	48.1 (9.7)	6.2 (1.1)	34.8 (6.3)	5.9 (1.1)	5.0 (0.9)	100 (18.1)
1984	44.8 (8.1)	8.5 (1.5)	35.9 (6.5)	5.6 (1.0)	5.2 (0.9)	100 (18.0)
1985	45.6 (8.5)	8.4 (1.6)	36.1 (6.7)	4.9 (0.9)	5.0 (0.9)	100 (18.6)
1986	45.5 (8.4)	9.1 (1.7)	36.1 (6.7)	4.5 (0.8)	4.8 (0.9)	100 (18.5)
1987	45.4 (8.5)	10.2 (1.9)	35.6 (6.7)	4.1 (0.8)	4.7 (0.9)	100 (18.7)
1988	45.6 (8.7)	10.8 (2.1)	35.9 (6.8)	3.6 (0.7)	4.0 (0.8)	100 (19.0)
1989	45.7 (8.6)	11.2 (2.1)	36.0 (6.8)	3.3 (0.6)	3.8 (0.7)	100 (18.9)
1990	45.6 (8.6)	11.3 (2.1)	36.3 (6.8)	3.1 (0.6)	3.7 (0.7)	100 (18.8)
1991	45.9 (8.2)	11.2 (2.1)	36.3 (6.8)	3.0 (0.6)	3.6 (0.7)	100 (18.9)

Notes: Data from 1986 to 1991 is estimated.
Sources: Office of Management and Budget, Historical Tables--Budget of the United States Government, Fiscal Year 1987, pp. 2.2(1), 2.2(2) and 2.3(2).

TABLE 4. Impacts of ERTA, TEFRA and DRA
Budget Receipts (By Fiscal Year, In Billions of Dollars)

	1982	1983	1984	1985	1986	1987	1988	1989	1990
ERTA	-42	-93	-141	-169	-208	-244	-270	-299	-335
TEFRA		16	34	37	48	58	58	54	53
DRA			1	9	16	22	24	26	30
Net result	-42	-77	-106	-123	-144	-164	-188	-219	-272
Budget deficits	128	208	185	222	194	198	183	173	171

Source: Congressional Budget Office, The Economic and Budget Outlook: Fiscal Years
1986-1990 (February 1985), p. 154.

declined from 35.4 percent of budget receipts in 1945
to 12.5 percent in 1980, and again declined
significantly in the period of 1981 - 1986. This trend
would be reversed afterward due to the 1986 tax reform.
While the decline in corporate income taxes in 1981
could be attributed to economic recession, the Economic
Recovery Act of 1981 contributed to the fall in the
ratio of corporate income taxes to budget revenues.

In general, budget receipts as the share of GNP
declined during the 1982- 1984 period. This decline was
caused by the fall in personal and corporate income
taxes as a result of the Economic Recovery Act of 1981
(ERTA). This act was projected to have reduced budget
receipts by $335 billion by 1990. The Tax Equity and
Fiscal Recovery Act (TEFRA) of 1982 and Deficit Reduction Act (DRA) of 1984 have somewhat offset revenue
losses caused by ERTA (Table 4). Had the tax reduction
law not been enacted, a budget surplus would be
projected for 1989. That, however, would have required
taxpayers to bear a tax load of 23.6 percent of GNP,
much more than in any post-war year.(10)

Researchers, economists, political scientists, and
policy makers alike believe that cutting the budget
deficit requires additional tax revenues. Many argue
that the current tax system needs to be reformed.
Many tax reforms have been proposed, including the 1985
proposal of President Reagan. After almost two years of
work, the Congress passed a compromise tax bill in late
1986. One of the many impacts of this new tax law would
be a shift of about $120 billion in taxes from
individuals to corporations over the next five years.
It would not raise budget revenues to reduce structural
budget deficits. The above analyzed patterns of budget
receipts may have some implications for tax policy.
Should the declining trend of excise taxes be reversed?
Should the continuing increase in social security
taxes and contributions be stopped or even reversed?
Should new sources of revenue such as a national sales
tax or user charge and fees be raised? Of course, the
data on the revenue sources contained in Table 3 do
not show shortcomings of the current tax system which
has been criticized by many tax experts as unfair and
insensitive to investment.

2. Patterns of Budget Outlays

As Americans do not like "big government," budget
outlays, which have been the central focus in budget

decisions, become more important now, in a period of huge structural deficit, than ever before. Therefore, budget outlays are analyzed at length here. In order to highlight major categories of federal spending, four categories of budget outlays were considered: defense, payments for individuals, net interest, and all other. Defense outlays consist of all defense-related activities such as procurement, military personnel, military construction, research, development, test and evaluation, family housing, and atomic energy defense activities. Payments for individuals are spending programs designed to transfer income to individuals or families such as medical care, food stamps, social security benefits, public assistance, and assistance to low-income students. Net interest is interest payments to the public on the public debt. Actually, the net interest does not reflect the true cost of interest payments of the federal government, because a portion of the federal debt comes from federal trust funds. "All other" is a category composed of the federal nondefense grants to state and local governments other than grants defined as payments for individuals, all federal loan activities, most of federal spending for foreign assistance, farm price supports, medical and other scientific research, federal direct program activities and undistributed offsetting receipts.

In Table 5, payments for individuals have become the largest spending category of the federal budget since 1975 (actually since 1971, if the budget outlays of every year were shown in this table). Until 1965, payments for individuals shared between 1 to 5.1 percent of GNP, or between 2.4 to 32.2 percent budget outlays. After 1965, this category shared a larger portion of budget outlays and GNP. In 1985, the federal government spent almost half its budget (45.5 percent, equal to 10.8 percent GNP) for payments for individuals despite President Reagan's efforts in cutting many programs under that category. Some analysts argue that the drastic growth of payments for individuals was rooted in the Great Depression and New Deal programs. Under the New Deal theory, the government provides for Americans in times of need through the establishment of social security, mass public employment, and other economic reconstruction programs. (11) The New Deal theory, stemming from the Keynesian economic theory, led to "Great Society" programs under the Johnson administration. Consequently, the share of the payments for individuals jumped from 28.0 percent of the total

22

TABLE 5. Budget Outlays: 1940-1991
As a Percentage of Budget Composition and GNP ( )

	Defense	Payments for Individuals	Net Interest	All Other	Total Outlays
1940	17.5 (1.7)	17.5 (1.7)	9.5 (0.9)	55.5 (5.6)	100 (9.9)
1945	89.5 (39.1)	2.4 (1.0)	3.4 (1.5)	4.7 (2.0)	100 (43.6)
1950	32.2 (5.1)	32.2 (5.1)	11.3 (1.8)	24.3 (3.9)	100 (15.9)
1955	62.4 (11.0)	20.9 (3.7)	7.1 (1.3)	9.6 (1.7)	100 (17.7)
1960	52.2 (9.5)	26.2 (4.8)	7.5 (1.4)	14.1 (2.5)	100 (18.2)
1965	42.8 (7.5)	28.0 (4.9)	7.3 (1.3)	22.9 (3.9)	100 (17.6)
1970	41.8 (8.2)	33.1 (6.5)	7.4 (1.5)	17.7 (3.6)	100 (19.8)
1975	26.0 (5.7)	46.2 (10.1)	7.0 (1.5)	20.8 (4.5)	100 (21.8)
1980	22.7 (5.0)	47.0 (10.4)	8.9 (2.0)	21.4 (4.8)	100 (22.2)
1981	23.2 (5.3)	47.7 (10.8)	10.1 (2.3)	19.0 (4.3)	100 (22.7)
1982	24.9 (5.9)	47.8 (11.4)	11.4 (2.7)	15.9 (3.7)	100 (23.7)
1983	26.0 (6.3)	48.9 (11.9)	11.1 (2.7)	14.0 (3.4)	100 (24.3)
1984	26.7 (6.2)	46.9 (10.8)	13.0 (3.0)	13.6 (3.1)	100 (23.1)
1985	26.7 (6.4)	45.0 (10.8)	13.7 (3.3)	14.6 (3.5)	100 (24.0)
1986	27.1 (6.3)	45.5 (10.6)	14.6 (3.4)	12.8 (3.1)	100 (23.4)
1987	28.4 (6.2)	46.2 (10.1)	14.9 (3.3)	10.5 (2.3)	100 (21.9)
1988	29.1 (6.1)	47.3 (9.9)	14.1 (3.0)	9.5 (1.9)	100 (20.9)
1989	30.3 (6.1)	48.3 (9.7)	12.8 (2.6)	8.6 (1.8)	100 (20.2)
1990	31.5 (6.1)	49.6 (9.6)	11.5 (2.2)	7.4 (1.6)	100 (19.5)
1991	32.6 (6.2)	50.4 (9.5)	10.3 (1.9)	6.7 (1.3)	100 (18.9)

Source: Office of Budget and Management Historical Tables--Budget of the
United States Government: Fiscal Year 1987, pp. 6.2 (1) - 6.2 (9).

23

budget outlays in 1965, or 4.9 percent of GNP, to 33.1 percent of the 1970 budget, or 6.5 percent GNP. Since payments for individuals are open-ended, (i.e., eligibility for benefit levels is normally established through automatic formulas rather than through annual appropriations of budget authority), they have become a built-in component of budget outlays. It is hard to reduce these payment outlays without drastic changes in legislation. Increases in the payments for individuals are primarily caused by the cost-of-living adjustments as required by current legislation.

Programs under the category of payments for individuals should be overhauled from concepts to implementation. The military retirement system, for example, is a true "scandal" as declared by David Stockman, the Director of Office of Management and Budget in early 1985. Currently, the average military officer retires at age 46, after serving the military for 24 years. He now collects $21,915 a year and continues to do so, plus automatic cost-of-living increases, for 32 years, that is, for a third longer than his term of active duty. In 1983, the last year for which data were available, 22 percent of military retirees were in their 30s, 68 percent in their 40s, and only 10 percent were 50 or older.(12) Without policy change, this type of payment will become an unbearable burden for taxpayers in the year 2000, when two-thirds of all American men over 65 will be veterans.(13)

Parallel to veterans benefits and services, social security and medicare will be another unbearable burden for taxpayers in the year 2000, with a growing aged portion of the population due to advanced medical technology. Advanced medical technology makes medical care more expensive and helps the Americans live longer. This means that future taxpayers will bear higher costs for social security and medicare.

The defense build-up policy of President Reagan has been the primary cause of the structural budget deficit. In contrast to outlays for payments to individuals, defense outlays declined sharply from 62.4 percent of total budget outlays or 11.0 percent of GNP in 1955 to 22.7 percent of total budget outlays or 5.0 percent of GNP in 1980. President Reagan has reversed this trend during the last three fiscal years; from 1981 to 1985, defense outlays increased by 4.0 percent of total budget outlays. The pro-defense climate has accelerated defense spending growth through the acquisition of phenomenally costly high-technology and other expensive weapon systems. Due to procurement and production processes, defense outlays will increase significantly in the remaining years of this decade. The Office of Management and Budget projected an increase in the share of defense outlays of the total budget from 26.7 percent in 1985 to 32.6 percent in 1991. Defense outlays projected by the Office of Management and Budget as presented in Table 5 are understated as veterans benefits and services are classified under payments for individuals. The prodefense policy is only one major cause for defense spending growth. Actually, without the defense build-up policy, the defense costs have been a built-in factor of budget deficit because of the termination of the military draft, resulting in massive increases in pay and benefits to military personnel.

The structural budget deficit has led to a large federal debt thus resulting in growing interest payments. In contrast to the automatic tendency of the federal debt which normally grows in recessions and shrinks in economic growth, the federal debt has continued to increase during the past two years despite the strong performance of the economy, and is expected to increase in years to come. The gross debt increase has been from $1,003.9 billion in 1981 (33.6 percent of GNP) to $1,827.5 billion in 1985 (46.4 percent of GNP), and is projected to reach $2,976.7 billion by 1991 (50.0 percent of GNP). Annual net interest payments have increased from $68.7 billion in 1981 to $129.4 billion in 1985 and are expected to reach $115.9 billion by 1991. The above data are net federal debt, which is held by the public excluding interest paid to federal trust funds and understates the real debt and interest costs of the federal government. The gross federal debt, which is held by the public and federal accounts, is much larger and expected to reach $3 trillion by 1990 (Table 6). If no fiscal changes are made, the federal debt will reach $13 trillion in the year 2000 ($160,000 per current taxpayer), and the interest payments would be $1.5 trillion per year ($18,500 per year per current taxpayer).(14) Disregarding economic debates over the impact of public debt and interest payments on the macro-economic variables, the current and projected federal debt and annual interest payments become a major concern to policymakers, economists, political scientists and the public alike. Some critics argue that the federal debt

TABLE 6. Federal Debt and Annual Interest Payment: 1965-1991
In Billions of Dollars and as a Percentage of GNP ( )

	Federal Debt			Net Interest Payment
	Gross Debt	Held by the Public	Held by Federal Accounts	
1965	323.2 (48.0)	261.6 (38.8)	61.5 (9.1)	8.6 (1.3)
1970	382.6 (38.6)	284.9 (28.8)	97.7 (9.9)	14.4 (1.5)
1975	544.1 (35.7)	396.9 (26.1)	147.2 (9.7)	23.2 (1.5)
1980	914.3 (34.3)	715.1 (26.8)	199.2 (7.5)	52.5 (2.0)
1981	1,003.9 (33.6)	794.4 (26.6)	209.5 (7.0)	68.7 (2.3)
1982	1,147.0 (36.5)	929.4 (29.6)	217.6 (6.9)	85.0 (2.7)
1983	1,381.9 (41.6)	1,141.8 (34.4)	240.1 (7.2)	89.8 (2.7)
1984	1,576.7 (42.7)	1,312.6 (35.5)	264.2 (7.1)	111.1 (3.0)
1985	1,827.5 (46.4)	1,509.0 (38.4)	317.6 (8.1)	129.4 (3.3)
1986	2,012.0 (50.4)	1,714.0 (40.9)	398.0 (9.5)	142.7 (3.4)
1987	2,320.6 (51.1)	1,855.7 (40.9)	464.9 (10.2)	148.0 (3.3)
1988	2,509.0 (51.2)	1,948.7 (39.7)	560.3 (11.4)	145.1 (3.0)
1989	2,684.3 (50.9)	2,005.4 (38.3)	668.9 (12.7)	136.0 (2.6)
1990	2,841.7 (50.5)	2,050.3 (36.5)	791.0 (14.1)	125.6 (2.2)
1991	2,976.7 (50.0)	2,048.1 (34.4)	928.6 (15.6)	115.9 (1.9)

Note: Data for fiscal years 1986-91 are estimated.
Source: The calculation was based on Office of Budget and Management Historical Tables--Budget of the United States Government: Fiscal Year 1987, pp. 3.1(1), 7.1(1), 3.3(29) - 3.3(32).

and interest payments are an unbearable burden on future generations, make the fiscal choice more inflexible due to larger share of debt payments in the total budget outlays, and are unfair because in fiscal year 1985, for example, current taxpayers pay 78.3 cents and the future taxpayers pay 21.7 cents for each dollar spent for the current generation's benefits.

IV. CONCLUSION

The concept of structural budget deficit is relatively new. It is used to distinguish the effects of fiscal policies from noncyclical economic factors on the budget receipts and outlays. This article explores, at length, the concept and measurement of structural deficit, and analyzes patterns of budget receipts and outlays. The data presented in this study show that the structural budget deficit in the federal government will be out of control if no fundamental policy changes are made. If the debt burden becomes unbearable to future taxpayers, a national tax revolt of the future generations would be expected. Then the federal government would be in financial trouble. In the past, financially troubled local governments, as well as private industries, were bailed out by the federal government. Who will be able to bail out a financially troubled federal government when its liability is $13 trillion? Bankruptcy would be the only alternative. This is, however, the worst scenario. This author believes in the responsiveness of the American political system which will restrain its fiscal bias (as explained in the next article of this symposium) so that the structural budget deficit will be cut. If policymakers cannot restrain their voting bias, as suggested above, some extremely rigid fiscal measures such as constitutional amendments requiring a balanced budget or spending limits will be mandated by the public.

REFERENCES

1. U.S. News & World Report (November 19, 1984): 94.

2. U.S. News & World Report (April 1, 1985): 24.

3. Moynihan, Daniel P. "Congressional Perspectives" in What Should Be Done About the Federal Deficit?, Proceedings of the Donald S. MacNoughton Symposium, Syracuse University, Syracuse, 1984, p. 20.

4. Moynihan, Ibid, p. 20.

5. Musgrave, Richard A. and Musgrave, Peggy B. Public
   Finance in Theory and Practice Fourth Edition,
   McGraw-Hill New York, 1984, p. 602; and the illus-
   tration in Figures 1 to 4 are based on their work.

6. Congressional Budget Office, The Economic Outlook
   (February 1984), p. 105.

7. The Congressional Budget Office illustrates this
   circumstance in another way. See Congressional
   Budget Office, Ibid., pp. 105-106.

8. Congressional Budget Office, op. cit., Appendix B.
   "Understanding and Measuring the Structural
   Federal Deficit".

9. Office of Management and Budget, Historical Tables-
   Budget of the United States Government Fiscal Year
   1987, p. 2 (1).

10. This percentage is calculated by basing on Table 2
    and Table 4 as following: In 1989, the projected
    budget receipts, $996.1 billion; and the project
    revenue loss, $219 billion. Hence, without tax
    reduction, total budget receipts would be $1,249
    billion.

11. Ullman, Al, "Federal Spending and the Budget Crisis"
    in Harris C. Lowell, Control of Federal Spending
    Proceedings 35, The Academy of Political Science,
    New York, 1985, p. 39.

12. The Boston Globe, February 6, 1985.

13. Congressional Quarterly Weekly Report, 1984,
    p. 1106.

14. January 12, 1984, Letter of J. Peter Grace
    submitting the Grace Commission reports to the
    President of the United States.

CHAPTER 3

STRUCTURAL BUDGET DEFICITS IN THE
FEDERAL GOVERNMENT: A THEORETICAL PERSPECTIVE*

Khi V. Thai
Le T. Cao

I. INTRODUCTION

Enormous peacetime budget deficits have been a major policy issue in the United States. The impact of budget deficits and public debt on key macroeconomic variables such as interest rates, investment levels, and the growth rate, has been of long-term theoretical interest to both economists and political scientists. Despite the great volume of theoretical work there has been little consensus on the impacts of federal budget deficits and debt. Some economists and political scientists argue that large budget deficits raise interest rates, crowd out private investment, and slow down economic growth. Others believe that larger budget deficits generate greater savings, leading to no change in interest rates. Recent discussions have focused on whether large budget deficits impoverish future generations, an intergenerational equity problem, as explored in the previous article. Moreover, the impact of U.S. government deficits on international trade as well as debt problems of other nations, particularly Third World countries, has been another hotly debated issue.

Although empirical studies can sometimes resolve theoretical debates, the numerous empirical studies which have attempted to relate budget deficits and/or national debt to the above macroeconomic variables have also yielded conflicting results (see Chapter 4.)

This chapter explores causes of structural budget deficits in the United States, and identifies the major areas of theoretical debate regarding structural budget deficits and their impacts on certain key macroeconomic variables.

---

* This chapter is a revised version of the authors' article of the same title published in _International Journal of Public Administration_, Vol. 8, No. (1986), pp. 33 - 55.

II. CAUSES OF BUDGET DEFICITS

As explained above, budget deficits may consist of two components: cyclical and structural. The cyclical component is the result of economic recession. In times of recession, tax revenues decline due to reduced personal and corporate income, while budget outlays rise in many current social programs such as unemployment compensation, food stamps, and welfare. Thomas Holloway has developed some rough guides or "rules of thumb", to estimate some of the most important aspects of the relationship between certain major economic indicators and budget deficits in fiscal year 1984 as follows:

- Each 1-percentage-point increase in the unemployment rate increases the deficit by about $25-$30 billion,

- Each 1-percentage-point increase in the inflation rate decreases the deficit by about $7-$9 billion,

- Each $100 billion increase in current-dollar GNP decreases the deficit by about $34-$38 billion (1).

In testimony at the budget hearing of the Senate Budget Committee in Spring 1985, Congressional Budget Office Director Rudolph G. Penner forecasted a recession that could result in a ballooned 1990 deficit of $425 billion (2).

Alternatively, there are several built-in factors attributed to structural budget deficits. According to John D. Young, these factors are incremental increase due to the politics of budgeting, the growth of defense expenditure, indexing and inflation, tax reductions, and the rising cost of debt service (3). In this paper, three major reasons are explored. The first, and the most important built-in factor, lies in the political and bureaucratic system. As pointed out by Norman J. Ornstein, John D. Young, Richard A. and Peggy B. Musgrave, Kenneth A. Shepsle and Barry R. Weingast, to cite a few, there is a systematic bias in the fiscal system among voters and Congress members (4). As the tax cost is borne by all taxpayers, voting groups strongly resist any remedial measures which reduce their own benefits. Moreover, with the decline in power of political parties since the end of World War II, legislators have learned that in order to be re-elected they have to serve but their voters by blocking any fiscal measures that harm their constituents.

Those with the initiative to pursue remedial action lack the institutional power to affect these changes. The fierce struggle between President Reagan and Congress in cutting expenditures, and the failure of the military in closing bases are but a few examples. Finally, due to differences in political ideology between Congress and the chief executive, expenditure cuts are very difficult to achieve. In the past four years, as the President has wanted to raise defense spending whereas Congress has opposed his proposed cuts in domestic programs. Consequently, total budget outlays could not be reduced, and budget deficits have reached an unprecedented peacetime high (See Table 2, chapter 2).

In addition to the political system, the bureaucracy has its responsibility for structural budget deficits. The bureaucrats' central objective is to maximize the size of their agencies so as to increase their salaries as well as their power (5). Consequently, they always request and lobby for more funds and hardly support the elimination of any ineffective programs within their agencies.

Another built-in factor of structural budget deficits lies in open-ended programs such as social security payments and entitlement programs legislated by Congress.

However, the most important cause of built-in or structural budget deficit is the shift in fiscal policy from the Keynesian model to the "supply side" model (as will be explained in the next section). The current fiscal policy is to slow down the growth of public expenditure growth, or the size of government, and to reduce taxes. If tax reduction is equal to expenditure cuts, then no deficit will be caused by this fiscal policy shift. In reality, however, due to the poliltical bias mentioned above, it is easier to cut taxes than expenditures. As a result, the budget deficit rises.

III. SIZE OF GOVERNMENT

The following observation of Nobel-prize winner James Tobin reflects fully the Reagan fiscal policy:

Reaganomics in 1981 was not a wholly harmonious blend of several strands of conservative doctrine: a hawkish stance in national security

31

and foreign policy; a general laissez-faire view of government's economic role; a monetarism even stricter than the central bank's; a strong commitment to reduce the size of government, on both sides of the budget ledger; a belief that "progressive" redistribution via taxes and transfers had gone too far; and a "supply-side" faith that lowering marginal tax rates would invigorate the American economy by inducing more work, saving, investment, and enterprise (6).

Since 1981, the U.S. fiscal policy has been undergoing a reversal of its past, or a "revolution." This reversal has led to a renewal of interest in issues reminiscent of the "classical vs. Keynesian" debates of previous decades. Traditional economists, including contemporary monetarists, proponents of national expectations, neo-Ricardians, and supply-siders, believe that the economy is inherently stable. Thus government's role in the economy should be minimized, and there is little justification for governmental interference. They are preoccupied with the impacts of government expenditures and taxes on consumption, investment and interest rates, and say little of government budget deficits. The Keynesians, on the contrary, believe that the inevitable differences among expectations of households and businesses lead to market instability. Therefore, an active fiscal policy is needed to sustain the high employment of resources, and may entail budget deficits or surpluses at given times. No action taken to sustain high employment may reduce the rate of capital formation and the growth of living standards (7).

Is the current public sector really too large? If so, what is the optimal size? Leviathan theorists such as James Buchanan, Richard Wagner, Richard Rose and Guy Peters and Wallace Peterson believe that the U.S. as well as the overall Western economy is overloaded by government (8).

There exist several norms to define the appropriate or optimal quantity of public goods or size of government. Peters and Rose, for example, distinguish three situations a government may face at any time: a fiscal dividend, no dividend, or overloaded government. A fiscal dividend occurs when the national product is growing faster than budget outlays so that

32

net personal income (take-home pay) rises along with the national product. A no-dividend situation occurs when "the national product, inertia commitments to public policies, and take-home pay might each grow at such a rate that politicians would find that claims upon the national product matched what was there to be spent".(9) Finally, overloaded government occurs "when the national product grows more slowly than budget outlays and net personal income. In this situation, tax revenues are not enough to meet budget outlays if the net personal income is maintained at its previous level. According to Peters and Rose, government is eventually overloaded due to political bias or an unexpected economic recession. The Peters and Rose approach is appealing, but does not determine the optimal size of government. The second approach, Samuelson's well known efficiency condition, argues that the appropriate quantity of public goods should be up to the point where the sum of the marginal rates of substitution equals the marginal rate of transformation.(10) This approach, however, ignores the institutional difficulties in the budgetary process. A third approach defines a democratically appropriate expenditure level as the level desired by the median voter. This approach, however, ignores the intensity of preferences.

In reality, it is difficult to define an optimal size of public expenditures. Particularly, determining the appropriate or optimal size of government is even more complex with respect to transfer payments. As Musgrave has suggested, "without further empirical testing, it is difficult to say when the size of government is too large".(11) Even if it were argued that the public sector is not excessively large, tax and expenditure limitations should be called for on the grounds that the public sector is out of control due to its rapid growth and becomes inefficient. Musgrave, Aranson, Ordeshook, Courant, Gramlich and Rubinfield, consider "government failure" or inefficiency as the major cause of tax revolt and expenditure limitations.(12)

Aanalysis of tables 1 and 2 shows no relationship between the size of government and the annual rate of economic growth in industrial countries. During 1983 - 1985, Canada led industrial countries in economic growth at an annual rate of 4.5 percent of GNP, but its central government expenditure was the third largest among industrial countries (about 48.5 percent of GNP).

Italy which tied with France in the lowest rate of economic growth at about 1.2 percent of GNP had the largest size of cental expenditure at 58.4 percent of GNP. Japan had the smallest size of government but tied with the United States for the second place among industrial countries in economic growth at an annual average of 4.2 percent of GNP.

TABLE 1. Major Industrial Countries:
Central Government Expenditure, 1979 - 85
(In percent of GDP/GNP)

	1979	1983	1984	1985
Canada	40.2	47.9	48.9	48.7
United States	30.6	35.0	33.9	35.2
Japan	31.0	33.4	32.4	32.1
France	42.9	49.2	50.0	49.7
Germany, Fed. Rep. of	48.0	48.8	48.4	47.6
Italy	45.6	57.7	58.2	59.2*
Unted Kingdom	41.8	45.8	46.4	45.4

* Preliminary estimates.

Source. International Monetary Fund, <u>Annual</u> <u>Report</u> <u>1986</u>, p. 3.

IV. CONSEQUENCES OF STRUCTURAL BUDGET DEFICITS

Whether the Federal budget deficit is unacceptable is still an unsettled issue. Economists contend that the cyclical deficit, by definition, does not have an independent effect on economic activities. It decreases automatically during economic recoveries because budget receipts increase and outlays for domestic programs decrease. Their major concern is the structural deficit, the deficit component caused by active government policies. Economists, however, differ in their analyses of the impacts of structural deficits on interest rates, the crowding-out of private investment, inflation and economic growth.

1. Structural Deficits and Interest Rates

Economists' opinions are divided on the issue of the impact of government deficits on interest rates.

There are two opposite views, the first claims that government deficits raise interest rates, and the second asserts that deficits have no impact on interest rates. The major difference between these two groups of economists revolves around the effect of deficits on aggregate demand. Once aggregate demand rises, economists agree that interest rates will increase if the supply of money does not change to accommodate the increase in aggregate demand.

Using the standard life-cycle model, conventional economists make the following assumptions:

1. Economic agents always try to maximize their lifetime utility with respect to consumption and leisure. Consumption is positively dependent upon permanent disposable income.

2. People consider tax cuts as permanent and as an addition to permanent disposable income.

3. Government debt is perceived as a component of private wealth and interest payments on additional government bonds to finance government permanent disposable income.(13)

Based on these assumptions, conventional economists explain the impact of government deficits on interests rates in two different situations. If the deficit is caused by a tax reduction, private consumption increases because people consider tax cuts as permanent and additional to their permanent disposable income (assumption 2), and consumption is positively dependent upon permanent income (assumption 1). When the deficit is caused by an increase in government spending, two cases may occur. First, the additional government spending adds directly to consumption. Second as the increase in government spending is financed by debt, interest payments on bonds are perceived as additions to private permanent income (assumption 3); consequently, private consumption rises. In short, no matter what the cause of government deficits, tax reduction or government spending increase, the result is the same; total consumption rises and, hence, aggregate demand for final output increases. This, in turn, raises the demand for money and, if the money stock does not change accordingly, interest rates will rise.(14)

Using the Ricardian equivalence theorem developed

35

by Barro, monetarists, on the other hand, claim that debt-financed government deficits have no effect on interest rates because they do not increase consumption and aggregate demand. The assumptions of the Ricardian equivalence theorem are completely different from those used by conventional economists. These are:

1. Each generation derives utility not only from its own life-time consumption, but also from that of its offspring (overlapping-generations model)

2. Tax cuts are not considered by people as permanent and additonal to permanent disposable income.

3. An increase in government debt is not an increase in private wealth. It is equivalent to a future increase in taxes to retire bonds and to meet interest payments.(15)

Based on the above assumptions, monetarists explain the debt-financed deficit neutrality theorem as follows: when a government deficit occurs, whether in the form of tax cut or government spending increase, there is no increase in either consumption or aggregate demand because people do not consider tax reduction as an increase in permanent income, or government debt as an addition to their wealth. Instead of increasing consumption as maintained by conventional economists, people tend to save more to increase their bequests so that their heirs will be able to pay future taxes. If consumption and aggregate demand do not rise, interest rates remain unaltelred. Among proponents of this view are Bailey, Tobin and Barro.(16)

The strength of each view depends on the validity of its assumptions and the debate on this subject is still unsettled. Additionally, the above discussion refers only to debt financed deficits. If government deficits are "monetized", there is general agreement among economists that interest rate increases do not occur. However, in this case, inflation would accelerate. Further, the debt neutrality theorem applies only to government deficits caused by tax reductions or increases in transfer payments. If a government deficit is caused by an increase in government purchases, consumption and aggregate demand will certainly rise and cause interest rates to go up, unless government purchases are a perfect substitute for private consumption.(17)

Paul A. Volcker, the Federal Reserve Board Chairman, and Martin Feldstein, the President's Chief Economic Adviser, seemed to support the first view when claiming at the hearing before the Congress in October 1983 that the current large federal deficit contributed to the persistence of high interest rates (18). On the other hand, former Secretary of Treasury, Donald T. Regan, appeared to agree with the second view when he maintained that there was no relationship between deficits and interest rates.(19)

Empirical studies have also yielded conflicting results. A survey of recent studies conducted by the Congressional Budget Office (CBO) reported that some studies show positive and significant interest-rate effects of federal deficits. However, the CBO report also indicated that these studies were clearly outnumbered by the studies finding no significant relationship.(20) Barth, Iden, and Russek examined several other recent studies and concluded that deficits or debt did affect consumption, aggregate demand and interest rates in ways consistent to the conventional economists' viewpoint. However, these authors also cautioned that empirical results on the subject appeared to be quite sensitive to the time period examined, the choice of variables and the measurement of the deficit variables.(21)

2. Structural Deficits and Crowding-Out

The crowding-out aspect of government deficits has received widespread attention in the academic literature, as well as among the government and business communities. Crowding-out refers to "the displacement of private economic activity by public economic activity."(22) The displaced private activity may be private consumption, private investment or both. Crowding-out occurs because the economy has limited resources and the government competes with the private sector's claim on these scarce resources.

There is general consensus among economists that in a full-resource utilization and closed economy, government deficits lead to crowding-out. The crowding-out effect of government deficits in an unemployed resource situation and an open economy, however, is still open to debate.

3. Full Resource Utilization and Closed Economy

In a full resource utilization and closed economy, government deficits result in the crowing-out of private activity either directly, if government spending increased, or indirectly, if taxes are cut. Considering government spending as a perfect substitute for private spending, classical economists (Neo-Ricardians, Ultrarationalists) maintain that a government spending increase causes a one hundred percent crowding-out of private spending. Government consumption displaces private consumption and government investment displaces private investment dollar for dollar.(23)

In the case of tax reduction, the occurence of crowding-out depends on the assumption about the impact of tax cuts on interest rates. As it was discussed in the previous section, economists are divided on this matter. If the conventional economists' view is adopted, high interest rates caused by tax reduction will crowd out interest-sensitive private spending, especially investment in housing and productive facilities.

Buiter and Friedman, using the IS-LM model to examine the crowding-out effect of government deficits, confirmed the direct crowding-out caused by government spending increases, and the indirect crowding-out caused by tax reduction.(24) Keynesians, however, claim that if the government uses fiscal policy to keep aggregate demand from exceeding supply, crowding-out does not necessarily occur.

4. Unemployed Resources and Closed Economy

The Congressional Budget Office (CBO) and economists such as Friedman and Klein maintain that, in an unemployed resources economy, when the government uses fiscal policy to stimulate economic growth, crowding-out occurs first.(25) However, in the long run, some crowding-in will also take place. Crowding-in may be defined as a counterforce that stimulates private investment spending and offsets part of the original crowding-out effect caused by government deficits.

Proponents of the crowding-in concept describe this process as follows: when a government increases spending or cuts taxes to stimulate the economy, interest rates rise. Aggregate private spending, especially consumption of durable goods and investment, which depends negatively on the interest rate, declines. Crowding-out occurs and offsets some of the income-expansionary effect of fiscal policy. In the short run, government spending increases and tax incentives encourage private investment in productive capacity and thereby increase real private spending. In the long run, business expansion will result in increases in business savings and business confidence. This, in turn, will stimulate business investment. In both cases, crowding-in occurs and offsets part of the original crowding-out caused by high interest rates.(26)

Wojnilower went even farther by claiming that "government deficits may well promote rather than deter investment." He argued that a government may incur debt to finance its own investment, to finance grants-in-aid earmarked for state and local investment or to finance tax incentives that promote private capital spending. In these circumstances, government deficits raise aggregate investment instead of decreasing it.(27)

Martin Feldstein, Paul A. Volcker and Rudolph G. Penner, the CBO Director, do not appear to support the crowding-in assertion. In the hearings before the US Congress Joint Economic Committee and the Committee on the Budget House of Representatives in October of 1983, they warned that the present and prospect federal government deficits would result in crowding-out interest-sensitive private investment.(28) None of the three mentioned the possibility of any offsetting crowding-in effect.

Cross-national data do not show any correlation between a pattern of deficits and the economic performance of a country. Among seven major industrial countries during 1979-82, Japan enjoyed the highest economic growth rate (4.1 percent per year), but its budget deficit was the second largest (6.1 percent of GNP); France and Germany had the smallest budget deficit (2.1 and 1.9 percent of GNP, respectively), but their economic growth (1.7 percent, and 1.6 percent, respectively) was far behind Japan's for the same period. Meanwhile, Italy had the largest budget deficit among the major industrial countries (12.5 percent of GNP per year), and tied with Germany but had the second highest economic growth (2.1 percent of

GNP). During the period of 1983 - 85, Canada led the
seven major industrial countries in economic growth but
had the second largest budget deficits at 6.7 percent
of GNP. Japan and the United States also enjoyed high
rates of economic growth at 4.2 percent of GNP despite
large budget deficits (5.2 and 5.0 percent of GNP). The
Federal Republic of Germany had the smallest budget
deficits (1.6 percent of GNP) during 1979 - 85 but also
had a very moderate rate of economic growth (1.8
percent of GNP). Thus, economic growth does not appear
to be affected by budget deficits (Table 2).

5. Structural Deficits and an Open Economy

In the case of an open economy, if government
deficits caused interest rates to rise, as advocated by
conventional economists, high interest rates would
attrack foreign investment and induce foreign capital
inflows. These capital inflows have both favorable and
unfavorable impacts on the economy. Favorably, they
help to alleviate pressures on domestic financial
markets caused by government deficits and to offset
part of the effect of the original crowding-out. On
the other hand, the increase of foreign investment
aggravates both the country's debt burden to foreigners
and, along with these debts, the interest payment
obligation.

Finally, the increased demand for domestic
currency by foreign investors causes the exchange rate
to appreciate. A stronger currency is usually a major
cause of trade deficit. Strong currency makes imported
goods cheaper, and export goods more expensive.
Consequently, the country's export and import
competing industries will suffer depressed demand and
employment. This, in turn, offsets some of the
expansionary results of fiscal policy.

In general, regarding the crowding-out effect of
government deficits, most economists agree that
government deficits cause crowding-out, which may be
partly offset by some crowding-in resulting from
business expansion or foreign capital inflows.

Statistical data show that since 1981, government
borrowing to finance the deficit has not only been
crowding-out private investment, but has also been
relying on foreign net lending, which aggravates the
country's trade deficit. Gross private domestic
investment has decreased from 16.1% of G.N.P. (1981) to

TABLE 2. Economic Growth and National Budget
Deficits in Major Industrial Countries, 1977–1983

	Average 1968–77	1979	1980	1981	1982	1983	1984	1985
1. Real GNP (in percent)								
Canada	4.7	3.2	1.1	3.3	-4.4	3.3	5.0	4.5
United States	2.7	2.5	-0.2	1.9	-2.5	3.6	6.4	2.7
Japan	6.5	5.3	4.3	3.7	3.1	3.2	5.1	4.5
France	4.5	3.3	1.1	0.5	1.8	0.7	1.5	1.3
Germany, Fed. Rep. of	3.7	4.0	1.5	0.0	-1.0	1.5	3.0	2.4
Italy	3.8	4.9	3.9	0.2	-0.5	-0.2	2.8	2.3
United Kingdom	2.3	2.2	-2.3	-1.3	1.3	3.6	1.9	3.3
2. Budget surplus or deficit (-) as a percent of GNP								
Canada	-4.1	-3.5	-3.5	-2.2	-5.3	-6.2	-7.0	-6.9
United States	-3.0	-1.2	-2.4	-2.4	-4.1	-5.6	-4.9	-5.1
Japan	-5.6	-6.2	-6.3	-5.9	-5.9	-5.6	-5.0	-4.4
France	-2.1	-1.5	-1.1	-2.6	-2.8	-3.3	-3.4	-3.3
Germany, Fed. Rep. of	-2.0	-1.8	-1.7	-2.1	-2.1	-2.0	-1.8	-1.1
Italy	-13.0	-10.0	-10.8	-12.8	-15.1	-16.4	-15.5	-16.3
United Kingdom	-4.3	-5.3	-4.7	-2.9	-2.7	-3.2	-3.4	-2.5

Source: Internal Monetary Fund, Annual Report 1985, p.5; and Annual Report 1986, pp. 3 and 6.

41

14.2% of G.N.P. (1983). During the same period, federal debt held by foreigners had been rising, and increased by $19.5 billion.(29)

However, crowding-out is not necessarily undesirable. If government borrowing replaces the crowded-out private investment, and if government investment is as efficient as private investment, crowding-out would not cause any harm to the economy. Unfortunately, rarely is this the case. While some government borrowing is for investment, most of it is for consumption; and the productivity of government investment, according to recent studies, is considerably lower than that of private investment.(30) In this case, crowding-out reduces capital formation, impairs the country's ability to improve productivity and, consequently, reduces the country's standard of living.

6. Structural Deficits and Inflation

There is general agreement among economists that when a government deficit is "monetized," inflation occurs. However, economists have different views on the impact of debt-financed government deficits on inflation. Proponents of the Ricardian equivalence theorem maintain that debt-financed deficits do not have any impact on aggregate demand; consequently they have no effect on price level or output. These economists even claim that a "constant, positive government budget deficit can be maintained permanently and without inflation if it is financed by the issue of bonds rather than money."(31)

Friedman, on the other hand, holds that debt-financed deficits are inflationary because "what matters for prices is not only money stock but some combination of money plus the outstanding interest bearing government debt...".(32)

Empirical tests also yielded conflicting results McCallum, using a discrete-time, perfect-foresight version of the competitive equilibrium model of Sidklrauski, proved that the Ricardian equivalence theorem proponents' assertion is valid under the conventional definition of deficits, which includes interest payments, but invalid in the case that deficits are defined exclusive of interest payments.(33) Niskanen, on the other hand, used the approach developed by Borcherding, Deacon, Bergstrom

and Goodman to test the relationship between government
deficits and inflation, and came to the conclusion that
"federal deficits have significantly increased the
level of federal spending but have had no apparent
effect on the rate of inflation."(34)

V. CONCLUSION

A majority of American people believe that the
size of public expenditures has reached the so-called
"overloaded government" situation. Endorsed by this
public mood, President Reagan has tried to reduce the
size of government by cutting taxes. While he has been
successful in tax reduction, he has had a major problem
in cutting public expenditures, due to his policy for
strong defense. As a consequence, budget deficits have
reached an unprecedented peacetime high, and have been
a major concern for policymakers.

Even though economists are divided on the economic
consequences of government deficits, the majority of
them acknowledge that structural budget deficits do
have unfavorable consequences for the economy. High
interest rates, crowding out of private investment,
huge trade deficits and inflation are the frequently
cited ill-effects of government deficits. These
unfavorable consequences negate some of the stimulative
impacts of fiscal policy, and dampen economic recovery
and growth. Even Keynesians, who strongly advocate the
active use of fiscal policy to promote economic growth,
do not suggest government deficits as an appropriate
measure for fiscal policy. Apparently, current concern
is not whether the budget deficit should be reduced,
but how to reduce it to an acceptable level, and how
soon.

REFERENCES

1. Holloway, Thomas, "The Economy and the Federal
Budget: Guides to the Automatic Effects", Survey of
Current Business (July 1984): 102.

2. Boston Globe, (February 7, 1985): 50.

3. Young, John D. "Federal Budget Deficits: The
Anatomy of Causes" in What Should be Done About the
Federal Deficit? Proceedings of the Donald S.
MacNoughton Symposium, Syracuse University, Syracuse,

1984, pp. 59-70.

4. Young, Ibid; Musgrave, Richard A. and Musgrave, Peggy B. Public Finance in Theory and Practice, Fourth Edition, McGraw-Hill, New York, 1984, pp. 102 - 129; Shepsle, Kenneth A. and Weingast, Barry B. "Policy Consequences of Government by Congressional Subcommittees" in Harris, C. Lowell Control Federal Spending, The Academy of Political Science, New York, 1985, Ornstein, Norman I., "The Politics of the Budget Deficit" in What Should be Done About the Federal Deficit? op cit.

5. Musgrave and Musgrave, op cit; Fullock, Gordan, The Politics of Bureaucracy, Public Affairs Press, Washington, D.C., 1985; Niskanen, William A., Bureaucracy and Representative Government, Aldine Atherton, Chicago, 1971.

6. Tobin, James "The Fiscal Revolution: Disturbing Prospects" Challenge (January/February, 1985): 14-15.

7. For detailed review of these two schools of economic thought, see The Economics of Large Government Deficits, Proceedings of a Conference held by Federal Reserve Bank of Boston at Melvin Village, New Hampshire (October 1983).

8. Peters, Guy and Rose, Richard, "The Growth of Government and the Political Consequences of Economic Overload" in Levine, Charles H., Managing Fiscal Stress: The Crisis in the Public Sector, Chatham House Publishers, Chatham, New Jersey, 1980, Peterson, Wallace C., Our Overloaded Economy. M.E. Sharpe, Armonk, New York, 1982.

9. Peter and Rose, Ibid, p. 37.

10. Samuelson, Paul "The Pure Theory of Public Expenditures" Review of Economics and Statistics 36 (November 1954): 387-89.

11. Musgrave, Richard A. "Leviathan Cometh--or Does He?" in Ladd, Helen F. and Tideman, T. Nicolaus Tax and Expenditure LimitationsThe Urban Institute Press, Washington, D.C., 1981.

12. Musgrave, Ibid; Aranson, Peter H. and Ordeshook, Peter C. "Alternative Theories of the Growth

44

of Government and Their Implications for Constitutional Tax and Spending Limits" in Ladd and Tideman, Ibid.; Courant, Paul N., Gramlick, Edward M. and Rubinfield, Daniel L. "Why Voters Support Tax Limitation Amendments: The Michigan Case" in Ladd and Tideman, Ibid.

13. For detailed explanation, see Patinkin, D. Money Interest, and Prices, Second edition, Harper and Row, New York, 1964; and Binder, A.S. and Solow, R.M. "Does Fiscal Policy Matter?" Journal of Public Economics, 2 (November 1973).

14. Barth, James R. Iden, George, and Russell, Frank S. "Do Federal Deficits Really Matter?" Contemporary Policy Issues (Fall 1984).

15. For detailed discussion, see Barro, Robert J. "Public Debt and Taxes" in Baskin, Michael J. Federal Tax Reform Some Myths and Realities, Institute for Contemporary Studies, Washington, D.C., 1978.

16. Bailey, M.J. National Income and the Price Level McGraw Hill, New York, 1962; Barro, Robert J. "Are Government Bonds Net Wealth?" Journal of Political Economy 82 (Nov/Dec. 1974); and Tobin, James, Essays in Economics volume 1, Macroeconomics, North Holland, Amsterdam, 1971.

17. Barth, Iden, and Russell, op cit., p. 82.

18. U.S. Congress Third Quarter GNP, Hearing Before the Joint Economic Committee, Congress of the United States, 98th Congress, 1st Session (October 20, 1983) p. 10; and U.S. Congress Projected Growth of Budget Deficits, Hearing Before the Committee on the Budget House of Representatives, 98th Congress, 1st Session (October 26, 1983), p. 21.

19. U.S. Congress, Projected Growth of Budget Deficits, Ibid., p. 8.

20. Congressional Budget Office, "Deficits and Interest Rates: Empirical Findings and Selected Bibliography," Appendix A, The Economic Outlook (February 1984).

21. Barth, Iden and Russell, op. cit., pp. 82-93.

22. Buiter, William H. "`Crowding Out' and the Effectiveness of Fiscal Policy", Journal of Public Economics 7 (1977): 309.

23. For more detail, see Kopcke, Richard W. "Will Big Deficits Spoil the Recovery?" in Economics of Large Government Deficits", op cit., p. 144.

24. Buiter, op. cit.; and Friedman, Benjamin M. "Crowding Out or Crowding In? Economic Consequences of Financing Government Deficits", Brookings Papers on Economic Activity (Fall, 1978).

25. Congressional Budget Office Inflation and Unemployment: A Report on the Economy (June 30, 1975); Friedman, op. cit.; Klein, Lawrence R. "The Deficit and the Fiscal and Monetary Policy Mix", in The Economics of Large Government Deficits, op. cit.

26. Friedman, Ibid., pp. 597-99; and Klein, Ibid., p. 171.

27. Wojnilower, Albert M. "Discussion of 'Implications of the Government Deficit for U.S. Capital Formation by Benjamin M. Friedman'" in The Economics of Large Government Deficits, op. cit.

28. U.S. Congress, Third Quarter GNP , op. cit., p. 110; and Projected Growth of Budget Deficits, op. cit., p. 24.

29. Fieleke, Norman S. "The Budget Deficit: Are the International Consequences Unfavorable?" New England Economic Review (May/June, 1984).

30. Wagner, Richard E., and Tollison, Robert D. Balanced Budget, Fiscal Responsibility, and the Constitution The Cato Institute, San Francisco, 1980.

31. McCallum, Bennett T. "Are Bond-Financed Deficits Inflationary? A Ricardian Analysis", Journal of Political Economy, 92 (February 1984): 123.

32. Friedman, op. cit., p. 595.

33. McCallum, op. cit., p. 134.

34. Niskanen, op. cit., p. 591.

not

CHAPTER 4

U.S. BUDGET DEFICITS: EMPIRICAL AND POLICY ISSUES*

Dung Nguyen and Josephine E. Olson

I. INTRODUCTION

Although the U.S. economy has been experiencing a healthy recovery since the end of 1982, the historically high levels of federal budget deficits presently experienced and projected to continue for the remainder of the decade are of great concern to policymakers, politicians, economists and the general public alike. The federal deficit was approximately $172 billion in fiscal 1984 on a National Income Accounts basis ($185 billion including off-budget spending) and, in the absence of significant policy changes, forecasts of the 1988 deficit range from $200 billion to $250 billion depending on assumptions about growth.

Extraordinary peacetime deficits are a recent phenomenon for the U.S.; nevertheless, the impact of government deficits and debt on key macroeconomic variables such as the interest rate and the growth rate has been of long-term theoretical and empirical interest to economists. (For an early survey of the theoretical literature, see Blinder and Solow (1); for a modern school of thought see Barro (2), for instance.) Despite the considerable theoretical work, however, there has been little convergence of views on the impact of federal deficits and debt. In another chapter in this book, Cao and Thai (3) examine these theoretical issues relating to the budget deficit.

In this chapter, we briefly review some of the recent empirical studies that have attempted to resolve the theoretical debate regarding the impact of the federal budget deficit. Then we simulate several scenarios in which the budget deficit is reduced. The simulation exercise, which uses an econometric forecasting model, provides another approach to analyzing how the government deficits affect interest

---

* This chapter is reprinted from an article of the same title in _International Journal of Public Administration_, Vol. 8, No. 1 (1986): 57 - 77.

rates and other important aggregate economic variables.

II. REVIEW OF EMPIRICAL ISSUES

One of the central propositions surrounding the discussion and analysis of the budget deficit issue is the relationship between the deficits and interest rates. The traditional theory argues that deficits absorb most private saving, and thus will result in higher interest rates. Higher interest rates will lead to a decline in private investment, which in turn will lead to a slowing down of economic growth and productivity in the long run. The net result is an intergenerational equity problem in which the current generation's welfare is increased at the cost of future generations. A more recent view, associated with Barro and Stiglitz, argues that under certain theoretical assumptions regarding perfect information and perfect capital markets, deficits will generate an increase in the current generation's saving, hence interest rates will not be affected by the federal budget deficits.

Although there is now a large body of empirical literature on the subject, it has not helped resolve the controversy on the impact of deficits. Both the Congressional Budget Office (4) and the U.S. Treasury Department (5) have surveyed recent empirical studies, paying special attention to the statistical relationships between the interest rate and the federal deficit or debt. The majority of the empirical studies they surveyed find the impact of federal deficits or debt on interest rates to be statistically insignificant, seemingly lending support to the Barro-Stiglitz camp.

However, there are serious statistical problems with most of these studies, which may account for the insignificant results. For one thing, virtually all these empirical works use single-equation specifications and therefore may be subject to simultaneous bias. Even within the single-equation approach, Barth, Iden and Russek (6) find that the empirical results of several studies regarding the interest rate impact of budget deficits are very sensitive to the way the debt variable is defined, the specification of the error term, and the estimation period. When they replicate some of these studies but remove serial correlation or change the measure of a variable or the estimation period, they sometimes get quite different results.

48

For example, in one of the papers they review, Hoelscher (7) considers a loanable funds model of interest rate determination and tests the resulting relationship between federal government borrowing and short-term interest rates using quarterly U.S. data for the period 1952:3 to 1976:2. The short-term interest rate used is the 3-month Treasury Bill rate and the federal deficit variable used is what Hoelscher calls U.S. Borrowing (the deficit on a National Income Account basis in constant dollars adjusted for non-credit market financial activities of the government and the credit market activities of off-budget federal enterprises). The estimated equations involve regressing interest rates on U.S. borrowing or the ratio of U.S. borrowing to GNP, changes in the monetary base, expected rates of inflation, and measures of overall economic activity. He finds that U.S. borrowing, whichever way measured, has a statistically insignificant effect on short-term interest rates. The same result holds when he uses instrumental variables to correct for possible simultaneous bias.

Since government deficits typically increase and interest rates fall during a recession, Barth et al. modify Hoelscher's study by decomposing the federal borrowing variable into structural and cyclical components and by removing unemployment. When they do so, they find the structural deficit has a significant positive impact on the interest rate and the cyclical deficit has a significant negative impact.

Another study Barth et al. review and replicate is that of de Leeuw and Holloway (8). Their dependent variable is the interest rate on Treasury bonds maturing in three years. They find the interest rate is significantly and positively related to the cyclically-adjusted federal debt (but not the deficit). It is also positively related to the expected inflation and negatively related to the monetary base. When Barth et al. replicate their study but adjust for serial correlation, they get similar results. In an interesting addition, they include government purchases of goods and services in the equation and find that it also has a positive significant coefficient while leaving the values of the other coefficients unchanged.

Carlson's study (9) finds the interest rate on corporate bond rates significantly related to privately held federal debt (excluding foreign holdings) as well as to expected inflation, GNP and the monetary base.

When Barth et al. attempt to replicate Carlson's
results but adjust for serial correlation, they do not
get significant results for the original estimation
periods (1953:2 - 1983:2); however, when they
reestimate the equation for the period 1955:1-1983:4,
the debt coefficient is positive at a higher level of
significance.

The potential impact of federal deficits/debt on
important macroeconomic variables other than the
interest rates has also been empirically examined.
Unlike the rather mixed empirical results regarding the
impact of federal debt on the interest rates, its
effects on GNP, demand for money, inflation, and
consumption have been found consistently significant.
(Among the more recent papers are Eisner and Pieper
(10), Hafer and Hein (11), Miller (12), and Kormendi
(13).)

The empirical studies we have cited are all
designed to determine whether federal budget deficits
matter. In a recent paper, however, Miller (14) argues
that the standard practice of regressing macroeconomic
variables such as interest rates, consumption, GNP, and
money demand on a number of explanatory variables
including the federal deficit or debt is simply not
capable of answering the issue of the impact of
deficits. Instead, he considers a highly aggregate
macro-model where the state of the economy is
characterized by a number of structural equations whose
specifications in turn depend on the two federal
government policies, namely, budget policy and monetary
policy. Budget policy is characterized by a path of
outside federal debt and monetary policy is
characterized by a path of outside money. It should
also be noted that the policy rule specifies that both
outside federal debt and outside money depend not only
their lagged values but also on the state variables
which describe the economic process. Federal deficits
are considered to matter if the economic process would
depend on a change in the government's deficit policy
rule. Operationally, the deficits matter proposition
is supported if changes in the deficit policy rule
would lead to structural changes in the equations
system which describes the state of the economy.

Results from Miller's empirical exercise indicate
that budget deficits do matter in the sense that higher
deficits lead to lower real growth, higher inflation,
higher nominal and real interest rates. This set of

results is particularly important not only because of its significant deviation from standard empirical works in which regression techniques are used to relate federal deficits/debt to other variables of interest but also because of its support of the conventional theory that deficits do matter. In our opinion, Miller's work may represent an important step toward correct assessment of the impact of deficits/debt on the national economy.

Although the theoretical and empirical controversy surrounding the deficit issue continues to exist, there seems to be a consensus that the huge budget deficit should be reduced. The Reagan administration wishes to do this through a cut in nonmilitary government outlays. A more balanced approach involving reductions in both domestic spending (including military spending) and an increase in tax revenue through tax reform was proposed by a group from the Brookings Institution (15). While some of these proposals are very comprehensive, none appears to have a careful study of how the deficit reduction proposal would affect other macroeconomic variables.

III. SIMULATION

In the remainder of this paper we use an existing econometric model, designed for forecasting, and run deficit reduction simulations on it to see if these simulations provide any insights on the impact of the deficit on interest rates, and to examine the effect of these exercises on the general state of the economy. We also test how sensitive the budget reduction results are to assumptions made about monetary policy and the foreign sector.

The model we use to run our simulations is the Fair Model, an econometric forecasting model developed by Ray C. Fair of Yale University. This is a 128 equation model of the U.S. economy which has been adapted for use on some microcomputers. By the standards of some of the commercial forecasting models it is small and cannot be used for detailed analysis of government spending changes or tax changes. However, for our purposes, it is quite useful in illustrating the magnitude of changes in policy required to reduce the federal deficit and their impact on the rest of the economy. It is beyond the scope of this paper to provide a detailed description of the Fair Model (see [16]); however, certain of its characteristics should be noted.

Rather than assuming an exogenous money supply
determined by the Federal Reserve, the model posits an
interest rate reaction function. That is, the Federal
Reserve has a target Treasury bill rate which depends
on the inflation rate, the level of real GNP, the
tightness in the labor market, and lagged values of
itself and the money supply. This target interest rate
is then achieved by the appropriate changes in the
monetary base. Because of this interest rate reaction
function, monetary policy reacts somewhat
countercyclically to events in the economy. For
example, an expansionary fiscal policy which raises
real GNP will lead to a higher target Treasury bill
rate and thus a tighter, but not completely offsetting,
monetary policy. It is possible to override the
interest rate reaction function and to assume whatever
rate of growth in the money supply or rate of interest
one wishes (within limits), an option we take in our
sensitivity analysis.

Another feature of the Fair Model is a base
forecast for the U.S. economy, developed for what Fair
considers reasonable assumptions about policy variables
and other exogenous variables. Our paper uses the
January 24, 1985 (see [17]) version of this forecast as
the starting point for our simulations, and therefore
it is necessary to provide a brief description of the
model's assumptions and the forecast.

Assumptions must be made about the future values
of the model's exogenous variables, which include a
number of fiscal variables for both federal and state
and local governments. Assumptions must also be made
regarding the exchange rate, exports, and a variety of
other less important variables. The base forecast
assumes mild expansion in government outlays over the
forecast period and no change in the tax equations.
The exchange rate is not expected to change much and
exports are expected to grow at 8 percent after 2
percent growth in the first half of 1985.

The forecast, which is for the period 1985 to
1987, predicts growth in real GNP of 4.6, 2.6, and 2.0
percent in 1985, 1986, and 1987 respectively. Thus the
model is predicting a slowdown in the economy after
1985, but not an actual recession. Inflation is
expected to be about 5 percent annually over the
period. Unemployment falls to 6.7 percent in 1987 and

interest rates rise; the forecast is for the bond rate to be 14.12 percent and the Treasury bill rate, 12.32 percent in 1987. The budget deficits, on a National Income Account basis (NIA), are predicted to be $185.3, $186.2, and $201.2 billion in each of the calendar years. Although many recent econometric forecasts have been quite far off the mark, the track record of the Fair Model has been better than most [18].

In our first set of deficit reduction simulations we use this January 24, 1985 forecast as the base for our simulations, including the forecasts for the deficits. We assume our target is to reduce the Federal Deficit on a NIA basis to $160 billion in calendar year 1985, $130 billion in 1986, and $100 billion in 1987. (Because of the many iterations required to reach a target, we accept a tolerance of plus or minus $2 billion in the deficit target.) We are limited to 1987 by the restrictions of the model and therefore, to have a reasonable time period for the simulation, we assume the steps taken to reduce the deficit begin in the first quarter of 1985.

Our first three simulations are somewhat extreme but allow a clear picture of the differential impacts of different policies on the economy. First, it is assumed that the budget deficit is met only by cutting various types of Federal government expenditures and transfer payments. With the tax structure untouched, the simulation requires substantial cuts in government purchases of goods, civilian government employment, military employment, transfer payments to households, and transfer payments to state and local governments. The model's assumptions about the relation of civilian and military wages to private sector wages are also adjusted downward. The result in this simulation is that federal government outlays are 3 percent lower than those of the base forecast in 1985, 7 percent lower in 1986, and 11 percent lower in 1987. Government outlays fall from 24.0 percent of GNP in 1984 to 21.8 percent of GNP in 1987. Reducing the deficit by just cutting nonmilitary government outlays is what President Reagan recommended to Congress in February 1985; however, our simulation does not attempt to replicate the specifics of his proposal and, in fact, it cuts expenditures on military employees.

The second simulation assumes only increases in business-related taxes. The corporate profits tax, the indirect business tax, and the employer Social Security

53

taxes are increased by large amounts. Our simulation shows that indirect business tax revenues are almost double the amount in the base forecast by 1987, total Social Security contributions are up about 10 percent, and corporate income tax revenues, after initially rising in 1985, are 17 percent lower in 1987, despite the higher rate because of the impact the first two higher taxes have on corporate profits. Although we know of no proposal to reduce the deficit strictly by raising business taxes, the Treasury's proposal for tax reform would probably raise business taxes and business groups have been concerned that the burden of reduction will fall unduly on business taxes. (See, for example, [19], [20]).

We are also not aware that anyone has seriously proposed reducing the deficit just by raising personal income taxes, and doing so would more than offset the cuts in recent years; nevertheless, our third simulation reduces the deficit by only increasing personal income taxes. Our personal income tax simulation raises the predicted marginal tax rate from the 1987 predicted personal income tax receipts of the government from $462.5 billion to $562.6 billion, an increase of 22 percent.

Finally, because we think reducing the deficit can only be accomplished politically by compromises with respect to spending and taxes, our fourth simulation takes a more balanced approach than the prior three in cutting government spending and raising personal and business taxes.

Table 1 shows the base forecast values as well as the simulated values of some important macroeconomic variables. (An extended version of this table and a table listing the specific assumptions in each simulation is available on request from the authors.)

Three of the four simulations (Simulations 1, 3, 4) support the traditional view that cuts in the budget deficit will lower interest rates, but the reductions in the nominal interest rates are quite small. The largest reduction in the nominal interest rates happens when government spending is cut; this finding tends to support the argument of Barth et al. that higher government spending also raises the interest rate independent of the size of the deficit. However, even in this case, the largest reduction in the nominal interest rates is only 78 basis points for the 1987

Table 1

Results of Deficit Reduction Simulations

Variable and Simulation	1984 (Actual)	1985	1986	1987
Budget Deficit, NIA, in billions of current dollars				
Base	176.5	185.3	186.2	201.1
Spending Cut (1)	-	161.0	130.5	101.0
Business Tax (2)	-	161.2	130.8	99.6
Personal Tax (3)	-	159.7	131.0	100.7
Balanced (4)	-	160.9	130.0	100.2
Treasury Bill Rate, in percentage points				
Base	9.57	10.16	11.54	12.32
(1)	-	10.02	11.11	11.54
(2)	-	10.23	11.62	12.37
(3)	-	10.12	11.34	11.84
(4)	-	10.12	11.31	11.84
Inflation Rate, as measured by GNP Deflator				
Base	3.52	4.54	5.36	5.35
(1)	-	4.36	5.05	4.86
(2)	-	4.93	5.79	6.06
(3)	-	4.53	5.19	5.01
(4)	-	4.59	5.20	5.13
Consumption Expenditures, in billions of 1972 dollars				
Base	1062.6	1111.1	1153.5	1188.2
(1)	-	1109.1	1148.7	1181.2
(2)	-	1109.6	1148.2	1176.5
(3)	-	1109.3	1146.8	1173.8
(4)	-	1109.1	1147.1	1175.9
Plant and Equipment Investment by Firms, in billions of 1972 dollars				
Base	148.2	162.1	166.7	162.7
(1)	-	161.4	163.6	156.8
(2)	-	161.8	165.0	158.7
(3)	-	161.6	164.2	156.9
(4)	-	161.0	163.3	156.7

Variable and Simulation	1984 (Actual)	1985	1986	1987
GNP, in billions of 1972 dollars				
Base	1639.0	1710.2	1767.4	1804.0
(1)	-	1703.3	1751.0	1776.6
(2)	-	1708.2	1759.6	1787.3
(3)	-	1707.5	1756.1	1786.1
(4)	-	1706.1	1753.7	1779.5
Bond Rate, in percentage points				
Base	12.71	12.64	13.33	14.12
(1)	-	12.58	13.11	13.64
(2)	-	12.67	13.39	14.18
(3)	-	12.62	13.24	13.86
(4)	-	12.62	13.23	13.85
Total Employment, Civilian and Military, in millions				
Base	107.2	110.2	113.2	115.7
(1)	-	109.9	112.4	114.2
(2)	-	110.1	113.0	115.1
(3)	-	110.1	112.9	114.8
(4)	-	110.1	112.7	114.6
Housing Investment by Households, in billions of 1972 dollars				
Base	58.2	64.3	71.1	74.2
(1)	-	64.2	70.9	74.3
(2)	-	64.1	70.4	73.0
(3)	-	64.1	69.8	71.7
(4)	-	64.1	70.3	72.8
Before Tax Profits of Firms, in billions of current dollars				
Base	207.2	206.3	198.8	174.1
(1)	-	198.1	181.0	143.1
(2)	-	194.2	159.2	95.8
(3)	-	203.0	183.4	139.0
(4)	-	200.6	179.1	137.2

Table 1 (continued)

Variable and Simulation	1984 (Actual)	1985	1986	1987
Balance on Current Account				
Base	94.5	118.8	133.9	138.5
(1)	-	118.5	132.8	136.8
(2)	-	118.5	132.3	134.7
(3)	-	119.0	134.5	139.6
(4)	-	118.6	133.3	137.2
Marginal Personal Income Tax Rate				
Base	.1595	.1674	.1768	.1860
(1)	-	.1670	.1754	.1832
(2)	-	.1674	.1766	.1855
(3)	-	.1760	.1940	.2144
(4)	-	.1712	.1837	.1970
Corporate Profit Tax Receipts, in billions of current dollars				
Base	69.7	67.3	65.4	59.1
(1)	-	65.2	60.9	51.2
(2)	-	70.2	65.5	48.9
(3)	-	66.4	61.4	50.2
(4)	-	68.4	64.9	54.9
Total Interest Payments, in billions of current dollars				
Base	116.8	145.2	182.9	229.5
(1)	-	144.5	177.9	213.6
(2)	-	144.9	180.2	219.8
(3)	-	144.6	178.8	215.9
(4)	-	144.7	178.8	215.9
Total Government Expenditures, in billions of current dollars				
Base	880.0	963.1	1047.5	1144.2
(1)	-	933.5	976.8	1013.1
(2)	-	962.8	1044.9	1134.2
(3)	-	962.5	1043.2	1129.5
(4)	-	953.8	1016.2	1082.8

	1984 (Actual)	1985	1986	1987
Government Expenditures as a percent of GNP				
Base	24.0	24.3	24.3	24.7
(1)	-	23.6	22.9	21.8
(2)	-	24.2	24.1	24.3
(3)	-	24.3	24.4	24.8
(4)	-	24.1	23.8	23.7
Personal Income Tax Receipts, in billions of current dollars				
Base	314.8	356.4	407.9	462.5
(1)	-	354.1	400.7	446.6
(2)	-	356.4	407.2	459.5
(3)	-	382.6	464.7	562.6
(4)	-	367.9	429.5	498.6
Indirect Business Tax Receipts in billions of dollars				
Base	55.7	59.9	65.2	70.6
(1)	-	59.8	64.8	69.9
(2)	-	73.1	97.6	139.9
(3)	-	59.8	64.8	69.6
(4)	-	62.9	71.2	83.5
Money Supply, in billions of current dollars				
Base	587.2	623.1	661.7	700.6
(1)	-	623.4	662.6	702.9
(2)	-	625.1	667.1	712.4
(3)	-	623.5	663.1	703.4
(4)	-	624.0	664.1	706.1
Unemployment Rate, in percentage points				
Base	7.51	6.90	6.56	6.67
(1)	-	7.08	7.22	7.95
(2)	-	6.90	6.65	6.92
(3)	-	6.80	6.38	6.45
(4)	-	6.91	6.77	7.13

Treasury bill rate. Also, another explanation for the drop in interest rates can be offered; interest rates and GNP tend to be positively related and the government spending cut simulation leads to the lowest level of real GNP of the four simulations.

The business tax simulation (Simulation 2) actually leads to higher nominal interest rates, though only by a few basis points. However, since higher business taxes also lead to more inflation, the real interest rate is not higher than in the base forecast. Thus despite the budget deficit cuts, the four simulations as well as the base forecast are all predicting rising nominal and real interest rates over the three year period.

With respect to other important macro variables, all four simulations lead in 1987 to a real GNP that is between 0.9 and 1.5 percent below the base forecast real GNP and employment, from 0.1 to 1.0 percent below. The unemployment rate behaves more erratically because households' supply of labor reacts differently to changes in taxes, earned income and transfer payments. As mentioned above, the business tax increase leads to slightly higher inflation, probably because higher Social Security taxes raise business costs and higher indirect business taxes raise prices to consumers. Cuts in government spending, on the other hand, lead to slightly lower inflation in all three years. Consumption and housing investment are little affected by the simulations. Plant and equipment investment falls from 2.5 to 3.7 percent by 1987, presumably because of lower GNP.

The Fair Model makes a number of assumptions in the base forecast about monetary policy, the foreign sector, and other exogenous variables, which we also use in our deficit reduction simulations. In order to see how sensitive our results are to these assumptions we next run three simulations in which the assumptions about monetary policy and the foreign sector are varied. For these simulations the base "forecast" is our fourth deficit reduction exercise, the one referred to as the "Balanced Approach."

In our first sensitivity simulation (Simulation 5) we assume the Federal Reserve allows the money to grow at 5.5 percent, the midpoint of its 1985 stated goal of 4 to 7 percent growth. Although in the base simulation the money supply is endogenous, it grows at about 6.4

Table 2

Sensitivity Analysis on Simulation Four (Balanced Approach)

Variable and Simulation	1984	1985	1986	1987		1984	1985	1986	1987
Budget Deficit, NIA, in billions of current dollars					GNP, in billions of 1972 dollars				
Base (4)	176.5	160.9	130.0	100.2	(4)	1639.0	1706.5	1753.7	1779.5
"Tight Money" (5)	-	167.4	146.8	126.2	(5)	-	700.5	1742.0	1767.4
"Easy Money" (6)	-	156.7	111.1	53.1	(6)	-	1709.4	1767.0	1805.6
Dollar Dawn (7)	-	155.2	118.6	83.6	(7)	-	1714.0	1762.3	1782.2
Treasury Bill Rate, in percentage points					Bond Rate, in percentage points				
(4)	9.57	10.12	11.31	11.84	(4)	12.71	12.62	13.23	13.85
(5)	-	11.11	12.16	12.94	(5)	-	13.07	13.87	14.73
(6)	-	9.23	9.86	9.16	(6)	-	12.27	12.36	12.06
(7)	-	10.50	12.19	12.99	(7)	-	12.76	13.71	14.65
Inflation Rate					Total employment, Civilian and Military in millions				
(4)	3.52	4.59	5.20	5.13	(4)	107.2	110.1	112.7	114.6
(5)	-	4.55	4.96	4.94	(5)	-	109.9	112.3	114.0
(6)	-	4.60	5.45	5.57	(6)	-	110.1	113.2	115.7
(7)	-	5.08	6.31	6.44	(7)	-	110.3	113.2	115.0

percent over the period, and thus Simulation 5 represents a tighter monetary policy.

The results for a small number of macro-variables from this as well as other sensitivity analyses are shown in Table 2. (More detailed information is available from the authors). The tight money simulation leads to the ususal results predicted for a tight money policy--higher interest rates, lower real GNP, lower inflation and a larger deficit. The interest rate change resulting from this somewhat tighter monetary policy is slightly larger in absolute value than that resulting from the substantial changes in the budget deficit, with interest rates about one percentage point higher in 1987.

All our deficit reduction simulations lead to slightly lower real GNP than that forecast in the base Fair model forecast. In our sixth simulation we seardh for an easy money policy which will keep real GNP at approximately the same level as in the original Fair forecast. We find that this requires 8 percent growth in the money supply in 1985 and 1986 and 9 percent in 1987. As one also expects, this simulation leads to higher employment, higher inflation, a much lower budget deficit and interest rates that are about two percentage points lower in 1987 than those in the "Balanced Approach" to budget reduction (Simulation 4).

Our first six simulations have used the same assumptions regarding the foreign sector as the basic Fair forecast. These are that exports grow at 2 percent for the first half of 1985 and 8 percent for the remainder of the period and the import price deflator grows at 5 percent. (The latter implies little change in the current exchange rate.) Given the current overvaluation of the dollar on a trade basis, we believe there is a significant chance that the dollar will depreciate. Thus, in our seventh and last simulation we reinstate the interest rate reaction function and assume the import deflator rises at ten percent a year, implying about a 5 percent depreciation of the dollar. We also assume that the cheaper dollar increases export growth to 12 percent a year.

Theory suggests that the lower exchange rate and higher exports will increase GNP, employment, and inflation, which our results in Table 2 show. The budget deficit is also lower and nominal interest rates are about one percent higher. Because of the higher

59

inflation, real interest rates are about the same as in the "Balanced Approach" (Simulatin 4).

These last three simulations show that the results of the deficit reduction exercises are quite sensitive to assumptions made about the foreign sector and even more sensitive to assumptions about monetary policy. Assumptions about monetary policy have a large impact on the forecasted government deficit because monetary policy has a large impact on real GNP and interest rates. If the Fair Model is to be believed, having a money supply that is $32.9 billion dollars or 4.7 percent higher in 1987 has a much more significant effect in reducing the interest rates. If the Fair Model is to be believed, having a money supply that is $32.9 billion dollars or 4.7 percent higher in 1987 has a much more significant effect in reducing the interest rate than a $100 billion reduction in the government deficit.

Although our findings tend to support the view that budget deficits do not have much impact on interest rates, particularly in comparison to monetary policy, our findings should be considered highly tentative as they are based on the use of one relatively small econometric forecasting model, and they may be the result of the peculiarities of that model. One particular characteristic of the Fair Model which is disturbing is that Fair's equation for investment in plant and equipment does not include an interest rate factor, any variable attempting to measure the impact of corporate tax policy, nor a measure of corporate profits. Traditional theory suggests that all these variables, which are influenced by monetary and fiscal policy, should affect investment. Another case in point is our simulation results which show that as government deficits are cut by 50 percent by the year 1987, the simulated levels of GNP and total employment are reduced by about 1 or 2 percent, regardless of which deficit reducing policy is adopted. Further, it appears that the model specifications suffer from a lack of interactive mechanisms in which important macro variables are interdependent. While the scope of this paper prevents us from a thorough and careful examination of econometric specifications, the simulation results indicate that each method of deficit reduction seems to have a sizable effect only on those variables which are directly related to it. Thus, business tax increases double the 1987 forecast indirect business tax receipts, and reduce base forecast before-tax profits of firms by about 45% in 1987; government spending cuts affect mainly total government expenditures and government expenditures as percentages of GNP; and personal tax increases significantly increase the personal income tax receipts (20 percent more than the base forecast value in 1987), and require a considerable increase in marginal personal income tax rate. It appears that these findings are direct consequences of the simplicity of the model specifications. Finally, we are also fully aware of the fact that the model is too aggregate to enable us to analyze the full impact of budget deficit reduction schemes on various sectors of our economy.

IV. CONCLUSIONS

Our review of the recent literature suggests that while the majority of empirical works find a statistically insignificant impact of budget deficits or debt on interest rates, there exist a number of important studies in which such an impact is found to be significant. Further, the federal deficits/debt have been found to have statistically significant effects on variables such as inflation, economic growth, consumption, and demand for money. These empirical findings reinforce the need for our policy makers to design policy schemes to bring down the budget deficits to more manageable levels. Our simulation exercises in this paper were done with this purpose in mind. The most striking finding from our simulation results is that the impact of various deficit reduction measures on general economic activities, with a few exceptions, is relatively small. In particular, the interest rates are not changed from the base line forecast levels in any significant way even when the current level of deficit is cut by one half in three years. We do not think this finding is sufficient to conclude that our exercise lends support to the Barro-Stiglitz theory because we also find that our hypothetical deficit reduction schemes do not have a sizable impact on other important macroeconomic variables either. These rather surprising results appear to stem from the structural specifications of the Fair econometric model. Despite the drawbacks associated with the Fair model, it is our hope that this work may initiate further detailed studies into this issue, in particular by using a more sophisticated and disaggregate econometric model.

REFERENCES

1. Blinder, Allan and Solow, Robert. "Analytical Foundations of Fiscal Policy" in The Economic of Public Finance, The Brookings Institution, Washington, D.C., 1972, 3-115.

2. Barro, Robert J. "Are Government Bonds Net Wealth?" Journal of Political Economy 82 (November/December 1974):1094-1118.

3. Cao, Le T. and Khi, Thai V. "Structural Budget Deficit in the Federal Government: A Theoretical Perspective," this book.

4. Congressional Budget Office. "Deficits and Interest Rates: Empirical Findings and Selected Bibliography." Appendix A in The Economic Outlook, February 1984.

5. U.S. Treasury. "The Effect of Deficits on Prices of Financial Assets: Theory and Evidence." Washington, D.C., March 1984.

6. Barth, James R., Iden, George, and Russek, Frank S. "Do Federal Deficits Really Matter." Contemporary Policy Issues, 3 (Fall 1984-85): 79-95.

7. Hoelscher, Gregory P., "Federal Borrowing and Short Term Interest Rates," Southern Economic Journal, 50 (October 1983): 219-333.

8. DeLeeuw, Frank and Holloway, Thomas M., "Cyclical Adjustment of the Federal Budget and Federal Debt," Survey of Current Business, 63 (December 1983): 25-40.

9. Carlson, Jack, "The Relationship Between Federal Deficits and Interest Rates," Statement Before the Joint Economics Committee, October 21, 1983.

10. Eisner, Robert and Pieper, Paul J. "A New View of the Federal Debt and Budget Deficits." American Economic Review 74 (March 1984): 11-29.

11. Hafer, R.W. and Hein, Scott E. "Financial Innovations and the Interest Elasticity of Money Demand: Some Historical Evidence." Journal of Money, Credit, and Banking 16 (May 1984): 247-252.

12. Miller, Preston. "Higher Deficit Policies Lead to Higher Inflation." Federal Reserve Bank of Minneapolis, Quarterly Review, 7 (Winter 1983): 8-19.

13. Kormendi, Roger C. "Government Debt, Government Spending, and Private Sector Behavior." *American Economic Review* 73 (December 1983): 994-1010.

14. Miller, Preston J., "Examining the Proposition That Federal Budget Deficits Matter," in Meyer, Laurence H. *The Economic Consequences of Government Deficits*, Kluwer-Nijhoff, Boston, 1983, pp. 3-24.

15. The Brookings Institution. *Economic Choices 1984*, edited by Alice M. Rivlin, Washington, D.C. 1984.

16. Fair, Ray. *Specification, Estimation, and Analysis of Macroeconomic Models*, Harvard University Press, Cambridge, 1984.

17. "The Fairmodel Forecast," Economica, Inc. *Fairmodel 1000 and 1230 User's Guide*, January, 1985, Appendix A.

18. Economica, Inc. "The Forecasting Record of Fairmodel," Mimeo, January 24, 1985.

19. Reilly, Ann, "Business will Bear the Brunt," *Fortune*, November 26, 1984, pp. 30-34.

20. "A Tax Bombshell for Business," *Business Week*, December 10, 1984, pp. 34-35.

PART II

BUDGET DEFICIT-REDUCING MEASURES:

AN EXPENDITURE PERSPECTIVE

CHAPTER 5

PROSPECTS FOR THE RESTRAINT OF FEDERAL EXPENDITURES*

Gregory B. Mills**

I. INTRODUCTION

Whether or not one feels that the federal
government spends too much, the prevailing consensus
for lower deficits - in the face of acknowledged limits
to revenue raising - implies a substantial degree of
spending restraint. This has become the uncomfortable
political reality of the federal budget debate,
especially since late 1981. President Reagan's belief
that tax cuts can force spending discipline seems to
have been borne out, though not to the extent that the
President envisioned and not without significant risks
to the economy through large intervening deficits.

Given the imperative of spending restraint, the
policy response over the last three years does not bode
well for the evolution of spending policies.
Increasingly, the President and Congress seem drawn
toward spending measures that appear undesirable as
continuing policies: e.g., the stretch-out of weapons
purchases, restraint in cost-of-living adjustments
(COLAs), limits to pay raises, across-the-board
spending freezes. Such actions may be legitimate as
interim measures. Indeed, they may be the only feasible
short-run solutions and may be preferable to no
spending restraint at all, if the latter exposes the
economy to the risks of mounting federal debt. However,
the long-term interests of substantive policy
development seem ill-served by the current syndrome of
repeated ad hoc restraint. Attention should begin to
focus now on how the next President and Congress can
best devote their energies to the longer run.

This chapter first reviews the context for the
debate over forthcoming cutbacks in federal spending.
The budget outcomes now projected for FY 1984 are taken
as the point of departure for policy decisions to
affect outlays in FY 1985-1989. As is the prevailing
budget practice, the impact of policy changes adopted

---

* This chapter is reprinted from National Tax Journal,
Vol. 37. No. 3 (1984): 361 - 375.

thus far under the Reagan administration is measured relative to a "pro-Reagan policy baseline" that assumes the policies of January 1981. The impact of possible forthcoming policy changes is measured here relative to a "current policy baseline" that assumes the policies of January 1984 (1).

At the outset, one should acknowledge that the question facing policymakers is not whether federal budget outlays should be restrained, but rather "by how much? and "by what means?" The prevailing judgment that spending must indeed be cut stems largely from the recognition that current policies will yield continuing deficits at unprecedented levels, even if revenues are restored to a peacetime high. To illustrate, the Congressional Budget Office (CBO) estimates that the federal policies of January 1984 would result in high-employment budget outlays equaling 24.5 percent of gross national product (GNP) by fiscal year (FY) 1989 (CBO, 1984d, p. 63). If high-employment revenues were restored from their projected FY 1989 baseline level of 19 percent of GNP to the FY 1981 peacetime high exceeding 21 percent of GNP, the FY 1989 high-employment deficit would still surpass any peacetime experience in the twenty-five years preceding the Reagan administration. Furthermore, federal debt would still exceed 35 percent of GNP in FY 1989, compared to 27 percent in FY 1979 (2).

Some policy analysts might consider ill-founded the incoming presumption that federal spending must be restrained. I will not seek to rebut this presumption; its pragmatic logic and ideological appeal has made it a fixture of the current policy debate. It nevertheless seems worth mention that the presumed need for restraint implies a desired aggregate level of outlays that is unambiguously below that associated with current policies. One would be hard-pressed to make this case convincingly on empirical grounds. One can certainly argue that our political system is inherently biased toward overspending for some activities or that some amount of excess spending results from poor program design or administration. By the same token, one might argue that other program activities are underfunded (or even that revenue needs can be met without any substantial increase in economic disincentives or distortions), and that these various considerations do not necessarily imply a net lowering of outlays.

At a minimum, it seems apparent that the focus of the spending debate on the restraint of budget outlays ignores the fact that much of federal program support comes in other forms, such as tax subsidies or off-budget credit assistance. Tabulations from the Office of Management and Budget (OMB) indicate that budget outlays comprise less than one-half of total program financing in such areas as energy, commerce and housing credit, training and employment, and social services (table 1). The scrutiny of tax expenditures and off-budget outlays, where much of the latter is associated with federal credit activity, should proceed as part-and-parcel of any attempt to limit budget outlays. For example, improved targeting of entitlements might be better implemented by greater taxation of transfer payments, rather than by altering the terms of eligibility and benefits.

II. THE POLICY CONTEXT FOR CURRENT BUDGET CHOICES (3)

President Reagan's budget proposals of early 1981 showed a balanced budget in FY 1984 of $770 billion, or 19.3 percent of projected GNP (table 2). This outcome assumed the administration's optimistic economic forecast and full adoption of its budget policies, including a substantial amount of unspecified "savings to be presented subsequently" (OMB, 1981b). At the same time CBO was projecting that, with no change in spending policies and with less optimistic economic assumptions, FY 1984 outlays would be 22.5 percent of GNP, or virtually the same as in FY 1980 (4). President Carter's outgoing budget, one that contained only modest policy changes and moderate economic assumptions, reflected outlay levels not far from the CBO baseline estimates.

Following three years of congressional policy action and economic developments - including of course the 1981 - 1982 recession that neither the Carter administration, the Reagan administration, nor CBO had anticipated - federal budget outlays for FY 1984 will be nearly 24 percent of GNP (CBO, 1984c, p.3). Without the changes in policy enacted during January 1981 - January 1984, outlays would have been even higher. The enacted restraint in nondefense program outlays will exceed the increase in defense and interest costs attributable to legislative action under President Reagan (table 3). With no further policy changes through the remainder of the 1980s, however, the continuing defense buildup would fully offset the

TABLE 1

FEDERAL BUDGET OUTLAYS, OFF-BUDGET OUTLAYS, AND TAX EXPENDITURES,
FY 1983 (actual)

	Budget outlays, $ billions	Off-budget outlays, $ billions	Tax expenditures (outlay equivalent), $ billions	Total, $ billions	Budget outlays as % of total
National defense	210.5	0.0	2.3	212.8	99
International affairs	9.0	2.9	4.4	16.3	55
General science, space, and technology	7.7	0.2	2.6	10.5	73
Energy	4.0	5.4	4.6	14.0	29
Natural resources and environment	12.7	0.0	3.0	15.7	81
Agriculture	22.2	0.7	1.2	24.1	92
Commerce and housing credit	4.4	2.3	170.6	177.3	2
Transportation	21.4	-0.1	0.2	21.5	100
Community and regional development	6.9	0.6	0.9	8.4	82
Education	14.6	0.0	3.1	17.7	82
Training and employment	5.9	0.0	10.4	16.3	36
Social services	6.1	0.0	9.6	15.7	39
Health (excluding Medicare)	28.7	0.0	27.7	56.4	51

Medicare	52.6	0.0	0.0	52.6	100
Income security (excluding Social Security)	106.2	0.4	97.1	203.7	52
Social Security	170.7	0.0	19.2	189.9	90
Veterans' benefits and services	24.8	0.0	2.6	27.4	91
Administration of justice	5.1	0.0	0.0	5.1	100
General government	4.8	0.0	0.3	5.1	94
General purpose fiscal assistance	6.5	0.0	32.0	38.5	17
Net interest	89.8	0.0	0.7	90.5	99
Undistributed offsetting receipts	-34.0	0.0	0.0	-34.0	100
Total	796.0	12.4	--[a]	--	--
Addendum: Portion of the above totals associated with federal credit activity	4.8	10.5	--	--	--

SOURCES: OMB, 1984a, table 7; OMB, 1984b, tables F-14 and G-1; and CBO, 1984b, table III-1.

a. The sum of the individually estimated outlay equivalents for tax expenditures would be a misleading statistic, as it would not reflect the interaction between the various tax provisions.

enacted nondefense program restraint. In addition, annual interest on the public debt is projected to be $100 billion higher in FY 1989 under current policies than under pre-Reagan policies. This is due most importantly to the faster accumulation of federal debt through lower revenues during FY 1982 - 1989 than would have resulted under pre-ERTA tax provisions (5). By the end of the decade, projected budget outlays climb to nearly 25 percent of GNP, despite assumed annual growth in real GNP of about 3.5 percent.

What degree of spending restraint should policymakers be seeking? The principal motivation for spending cuts is the concern that projected deficits may jeopardize sustained economic growth and moderate inflation. While spending policies should not be guided solely by such macroeconomic concerns, the terms of the current debate on program spending are now largely set by the consensus that lower deficits would improve long-term economic prospects. The matter of how much spending restraint is desirable depends most importantly on the society's collective views about: (a) the economic risks posed by the projected deficits; (b) how vital the existing programs really are; and (c) whether revenue increases can (or should) also be adopted.

There appears to be more consensus on the first issue than on the other two. The preponderance of expressed opinion, at least among mainstream economic analysts, suggests that the risks posed by deficits are significant enough to warrant policy measures that by FY 1989 would bring the annual deficit down from its baseline level by roughly $150 billion to $200 billion, if not more. Such action is implied by any number of prescriptive policy rules, as shown in table 4.

The matter of identifying the least defensible spending activities is plagued by the same free-rider problem that hinders the revelation of individual preferences as to the most desirable forms of spending. A lower deficit is a public capital good; if "purchased," it would presumably enhance the society's long-term consumption possibilites. However, everyone wishes to avoid the required sacrifice in short-term consumption that spending cuts (or tax increases) would impose. The clear incentive for voters and their representatives is neither to offer nor to accept any suggestion that "their" programs be cut, even if one honestly recognizes that such benefits or services have

TABLE 2

PROJECTIONS OF FEDERAL BUDGET OUTLAYS

	FY 1982	FY 1983	FY 1984
	Billions of Dollars		
Reagan budget (March 1981)	695	732	770
Carter budget (January 1981)	739	817	890
CBO baseline projection (February 1981)	740	819	906
CBO "current policy baseline" (February 1984)	728[a]	796[a]	853
	Billions of Constant (FY 1972) Dollars		
Reagan budget (March 1981)	288	283	281
Carter budget (January 1981)	300	307	311
CBO baseline projection (February 1981)	307	310	314
CBO "current policy baseline" (February 1984)	339[a]	355[a]	364[b]
	Percentage of GNP		
Reagan budget (March 1981)	21.8	20.3	19.3
Carter budget (January 1981)	23.0	22.6	22.0
CBO baseline projection (February 1981)	23.4	22.8	22.5
CBO "current policy baseline" (February 1984)	23.8[a]	24.7[a]	23.9

SOURCES: OMB, 1981a and 1984a; CBO, 1981b and 1984c. The four sets of projections are each internally consistent with respect to their policy policy, economic, and technical assumptions. However, the differences between the different projections for any given year and outcome variable differ because of noncomparability in the underlying economic and technical (as well as policy) assumptions.

a. Actual data. Constant-dollar estimates are based on OMB deflator method.

b. Based on OMB deflator method, applied to the CBO current-dollar magnitudes.

73

TABLE 3

IMPACT ON FEDERAL BUDGET OUTLAYS OF POLICY CHANGES
DURING JANUARY 1981–JANUARY 1984

	FY 1984	FY 1989
	Billions of Dollars (versus pre-Reagan baseline)	
National defense outlays	25	77
Nondefense program outlays		
Mandatory spending	−24	−36
Discretionary spending	−21	−38
Offsetting receipts (−)	−1	−3
Subtotal	−21	0
Net interest outlays		
Interest on the public debt	9	100
Interest collections (−)	−2	−1
Budget outlays	−14	98
Addendum:		
Revenues	−93	−239

SOURCE: CBO, 1984c, pp. 20, 116 and 117.

little rationale.

Prevailing judgments on the third issue posed above-the extent to which revenue increases can (or should) be adopted - appear to be tempered importantly by the recent historical experience. Unless federal revenues are to approach their peacetime record GNP share attained in FY 1981, the revenue increase for FY 1989 will be limited to about $100 billion. Even tax increases up to this full amount would still offset less than one-half of the net revenue reduction enacted between January 1981 and January 1984.

If $150 billion to $200 billion in policy action to reduce the FY 1989 deficit seems warranted, but if revenue increases of more than $100 billion seem unlikely, spending restraint must be in the range of $50 billion to $100 billion, if not more. What is the feasible range of action to reduce projected outlays for FY 1989, measured against CBO's current policy baseline? One can only speculate. For defense outlays, $75 billion is used here as the illustrative upper-bound. Such action would virtually offset the enacted defense buildup since 1981. (From table 3, the enacted buildup yields a $77 billion increase in projected FY 1989 outlays). Even to freeze annual defense budget authority at its FY 1984 real level throughout FY 1985-1989 would not be sufficient to achieve $75 billion in outlay savings for FY 1989.

For nondefense outlay restraint, $75 billion is also adopted as the illustrative upper bound. This would require forthcoming measures as large in their FY 1989 effect as those already taken under President Reagan (refer to table 3). It would be difficult for Congress to enact such restraint without presidential support. However, even the measures proposed by Ronald Reagan in his FY 1985 budget (February 1984) were only one-half this amount; those in his subsequent "Rose Garden" plan (March 1984) amounted to less than one-third (6). Moreover, both Walter Mondale and Gary Hart proposed budget plans in which projected FY 1989 nondefense savings (principally in health and agriculture programs) would be more than offset by increased spending for public infrastructure and human resource needs (7).

These observations only lend further support to the emerging conventional wisdom about the need for action on the federal budget. In order to

TABLE 4

ALTERNATIVE PERSPECTIVES ON DEFICIT REDUCTION

Prescriptive policy rule	Implied amount of FY 1989 reduction in program outlays and/or increase in revenues	Associated reduction in FY 1989 interest outlays
	Billions of Dollars	
To balance the "middle-expansion budget" by FY 1989[c] (allowing for balance in actual budgets over the business cycle)	293[d]	83
To balance the budget by Fy 1989 (as projected under the current policy baseline)	254	72
To balance the "high-employment budget" by FY 1989 (allowing only that amount of deficit due to the unemployment rate exceeding 6 percent)	233[d]	66
To reduce the high-employment budget deficit by FY 1989 to:		
1 percent of GNP	190[d]	54
2 percent of GNP	148[d]	42
To halt the rise in federal debt as a percentage of GNP:[e]		
By FY 1987[f]	185	53
By FY 1989[g]	139	40
To balance the "inflation-corrected budget" by FY 1989 (allowing only that amount of deficit necessary to offset the inflationary erosion of privately-held debt principal[h])	178	51

SOURCES: CBO, 1984c and 1984d; author's
           calculations.

a. Measured relative to the CBO current policy
baseline. Assumes that the budget impact of policy
action builds progressively throughout FY 1985- 1989
(with the FY 1985 impact equaling 20 percent of the
full FY 1989 magnitude, the FY 1986 impact equaling 40
percent, etc.).

b. Assumed the interest rates (and maturity
distribution of federal securities) of the CBO
economic forecast published in February 1984.

c. Based on methods developed at the Department of
Commerce. See DeLeeuw and Holloway, 1983.

d. Because of differences in the rates of unemployment
assumed under baseline, high-employment, and middle-
expansion estimates, this figure implies a slightly
different degree of policy action than would yield an
equivalent dollar reduction in the current policy
baseline deficit.

e. Assumes that, during FY 1987-1989, the annual growth
rate of nominal GNP equals the effective nominal
interest rate on federal debt.

f. Under this rule, federal debt would peak as a
percentage of GNP at 39 percent in FY 1986-1987.

g. Under this rule, federal debt would peak as a
percentage of GNP at 39 percent in FY 1988-1989.

h. This amount of deficit is considered not to be
stimulative, but necessary to prevent a presumed
increase in savings among bondholders in order to
restore the real value of their portfolios.

satisfactorily reduce the deficit, it will be necessary both to restrain spending and raise revenues. In addition, the limits of feasible action to restrain outlays for either defense or nondefense programs suggests that action will be required in both spending areas.

III. CONTROLLING OUTLAY GROWTH:
TECHNICAL AND POLITICAL DIMENSIONS

Restraint in budget outlays should be viewed as a lowering of the outlay growth that would occur if policies remained unchanged. What is this baseline pattern of growth? As shown in table 5, national defense comprises one-half of the $378 billion of projected nominal growth from FY 1984 to FY 1989 in annual program budget outlays (including offsetting receipts, but excluding net interest and off-budget outlays). Defense, Social Security, and Medicare together account for more than 80 percent of such growth.

The extent to which future program outlays can be controlled by forthcoming policy action depends on whether one seeks to control the outlays projected for next year or for several years hence. The longer interval over which policy changes might occur, the greater the extent of policy control. Year-to-year budget controllability is indeed limited in that more than one-half of program outlays in each future year consists of entitlements and other mandatory spending. Changes in basic authorizing legislation is necessary to limit such outlays. In addition, short run restraint is hindered by prior spending contracts and obligations in annually funded, discretionary activities. In the projected FY 1985 defense budget, more than one-third (36 percent) of outlays result from budget authority already enacted. Much of this defense spending momentum comes in military procurement, where more than four-fifths (81 percent) of projected FY 1985 outlays stems from prior contracts and obligations. In nondefense discretionary spending, nearly one-half (46 percent) of projected FY 1985 outlays is linked to prior commitments (8).

If one's budget outlook is extended as far as FY 1989, however, the amount of discretionary outlays attributable to budget authority enacted prior to FY 1985 becomes relatively small. This is true even for military procurement, where less than $5 billion of the

TABLE 5

PROJECTED GROWTH IN FEDERAL BUDGET OUTLAYS
UNDER CURRENT POLICY BASELINE

	FY 1984	FY 1989	Growth
	Billions of Dollars		
National defense [a]			
Military personnel [b]	65	93	28
Operation and maintenance	69	119	50
Research, development, test, and evaluation	24	45	21
Military procurement	64	134	70
Other [c]	13	28	15
	235	419	184
Entitlements and other mandatory spending			
Social Security	173	243	70
Medicare	64	120	56
Other non-means-tested benefits [d]	80	94	14
Medicaid	21	32	11
Other means-tested benefits [e]	40	48	8
Farm price supports	7	18	11
Other [f]	15	16	1
	400	570	170
Nondefense discretionary spending			
Employee pay raises	1	9	8
Other [g]	155	189	34
	156	198	42
Offsetting receipts			
Medicare premiums	-5	-8	-3
Other [h]	-41	-56	-15
	-46	-64	-18
Subtotal	745	1,123	378
Net interest	108	219	111
Total	853	1,342	489

Sources: CBO, 1984c.

a. FY 1989 allocation among defense categories is based on CBO's reestimate of the administration's FY 1985 budget.

b. Includes benefit accruals for military retirement and allowances for employee pay raises.

c. Includes military construction, family housing, atomic energy defense activities, and other defense-related outlays.

d. Includes unemployment compensation, railroad retirement, federal employee retirement and disability, and veterans' benefits.

e. Includes Food Stamps, Aid to Families with Dependent Children, Supplemental Security Income, veterans' pensions, guaranteed student loans, child nutrition, and other smaller programs.

f. Includes general revenue sharing, social services, and other smaller programs.

g. Includes all programs considered to be subject to annual congressional appropriations. CBO divides such programs into the following categories (in declining order of outlay amount): benefits and services to individuals, infrastructure, federal government operations, research and development, aid to foreign governments and international organizations, and assistance to business and commerce.

h. Includes agency contributions for federal employee retirement, proceeds from the sale or lease of natural resources, and other proprietary receipts.

projected $134 billion in FY 1989 outlays is associated with action prior to FY 1985 (CBO, 1984a, p. 116). For nondefense programs, only in such areas as housing finance and other capital construction would one find projected FY 1989 outlays to be importantly attributable to budget authority enacted for years prior to FY 1985.

In a technical sense, policy action can thus affect virtually the entire amount of program outlays to occur five years hence. Nevertheless, one obvious consequence of policy delay is a shortening of the time interval during which action can be taken to affect the outlays projected for a fixed future date. This shrinking interval would increase the uncontrollable portion of projected outlays. The example of military procurement is once again instructive. As implied above, only 3 percent of outlays five years hence is not subject to control through the intervening enactment of budget authority. However, if one waits until FY 1987 before enacting restraint, the uncontrollable portion of FY 1989 outlays will have risen to nearly 20 percent. Any fixed amount of budget savings would thus become more difficult to achieve. For example, if one reduced the annual real growth rate of procurement budget authority by 2 percentage points during FY 1985-1989, the savings in FY 1989 outlays would be $7 billion. By delaying action two years, one must then reduce annual real growth by 4 percentage points during FY 1987-1989, in order to achieve the same amount of savings.

It is one thing to say that virtually all federal program outlays now projected for FY 1989 are subject to policy control; it is quite another to suggest feasible policy measures that would yield appreciable savings. The business of proposing policies to reduce spending (and to increase taxes) has become almost a cottage industry in Washington. Yet, at least on the nondefense side, precious little in genuine spending restraint has been enacted since passage of the 1983 Social Security compromise (9). Some domestic programs that survived the early rounds of budget cutting under President Reagan seem to have acquired a strengthened resistance. Many of those that were targeted for cuts have now been so reduced in size or now contribute so little to projected spending growth as not to warrant further assault. Alternatively, some programs remain large and growing, but are felt to have already contributed more than enough to the cause of deficit reduction. Any hope that the President's Private Sector Survey on Cost Control (the Grace Commission) could identify readily attainable savings through improved program management seems fleeting. Many of the commission's proposed initiatives pertain to basic policy changes that offer little chance of enactment, even though they address program areas where the need for reform is well documented and widely recognized - e.g., the purchase of military spare parts, federal employee retirement benefits, and farm subsidies. CBO and the General Accounting Office (GAO) have rendered the judgment that the savings associated with many of the management initiatives are also questionable (CBO and GAO, 1984).

Attempts at restraint in domestic programs have been frustrated by the natural reluctance in the administration and Congress to tamper with benefits flowing to the middle class and elderly populations. Yet it is these programs, especially Social Security and Medicare, that are the largest and fastest growing components of domestic spending. To the extent that the bulk of such spending is financed through trust funds, policy action must also counter the prevailing notion that these programs should not be restrained in the interests of a lower budget deficit. The hard-fought 1983 Social Security legislation was necessary (and, under most assumptions, sufficient) to insure the solvency of that program's trust fund into the twenty-first century. Social Security has thus been effectively removed from the legislative agenda. While the Medicare trust fund shows declining year-end balances in the latter 1980s, the fund will not be depleted until the early 1990s under current assumptions. This prospect may be too distant to provoke any action soon enough to have appreciable impact by FY 1989.

On the defense budget, Congress has been more willing to enact restraint, perhaps reflecting the public mood that military spending growth has been excessive. Here, the administration and Congress seem to have settled into a pattern that each finds politically comfortable. The President poses his defense budgets as spending cuts, when viewed relative to his prior requests (even though they are not cuts, when viewed relative to enacted policy); the Congress criticizes the administration's extravagance, sets a limit on the growth of budget authority (below the baseline projection), and claims credit for the corresponding deficit reduction; the President expresses his dissatisfaction, but acquiesces. The enacted defense restraint has typically involved no sacrifice of major weapon systems, but primarily a slower rate of weapons acquisition, with some squeeze on personnel costs and operation and maintenance expenses. Many experts view this trend as one that may jeopardize the readiness of our armed forces (see Committee for National Security, 1984).

IV. PROSPECTS FOR CONGRESSIONAL ACTION: THE BIAS TOWARD AD HOC FORMS OF RESTRAINT

The recent action on the defense budget is symptomatic of the prevailing tendency in Congress to adopt ad hoc forms of spending restraint, in lieu of more basic structural program changes. Thus, rather than eliminate low-priority weapon systems, Congress has been more inclined to defer purchases in a range of defense programs. Similar examples abound in the nondefense area. Rather than alter the basic eligibility conditions and benefit levels for entitlements, Congress has opted more frequently to restrain COLAs. Rather than seek a better match between the funding of discretionary programs and public priorities, Congress has tended to adopt across-the-board freezes. Such enacted policies make little sense except as a short-term last resort; their principal virtue is political expedience. However, to repeatedly take such action can only serve to pervert the long-run evolution of spending policies.

Several factors have contributed to this recent bias toward ad hoc restraint. One is President Reagan's increasing reluctance since late 1981 to initiate structural spending reforms. Much to the President's credit, the spending cuts enacted in the summer of 1981 came through altering the basic features of entitlement programs or through substantial reductions in funding for discretionary programs. Whether or not one viewed these policy changes as desirable, they could hardly have been characterized as incremental or ad hoc. However, the administration's subsequent budget-cutting initiatives were increasingly modest and relied less on targeted structural changes. A host of circumstances were responsible for this. The administration had largely depleted OMB's "shelf inventory" of feasible cost-cutting proposals. The politically vulnerable programs had fallen victim early; resistance to further cuts in these low-income assistance programs made the

83

administration sensitive to the "fairness" issue. Proposed cuts in the non-means-tested entitlements also provoked stiff opposition, as the administration found in its ill-fated 1981 Social Security package. The administration also lost its working coalition in the House in the 1982 elections and sought to avoid alienating program constituencies as the 1984 elections loomed ahead. The President opted to "take the heat" on the deficit and interest rates, anticipating that either the economy would remain strong or that blame could be shifted to the Congress or the Federal Reserve.

Through 1982, 1983, and into 1984, Congress was thus left with the task of forging legislative compromises without the benefit of a credible budget blueprint from the executive branch, without the required resources or consensus to fully craft a budget itself, and without the political protection that the President's active involvement in budget negotiations would have provided. Under such circumstances, the difficulty of reaching congressional agreement on anything but ad hoc measures to restrain spending has reflected more the sheer magnitude of the task thrust upon the Congress, rather than either a failure of the established budget procedures or a lack of congressional will. To restore order promptly to a federal budget thrown out of balance by $200 billion to $300 billion was hardly the kind of challenge that the 1974 budget act was designed to meet.

The requirement to enact an annual budget resolution has without question forced the Congress to explicitly address its program funding decisions in the context of fiscal policy. In doing so, however, it has also elevated the substantive debate on program policies in each house above the level of the authorizing and appropriations committees to the budget committee and, by extension, to the "committee of the whole." This has encouraged free-wheeling floor consideration of alternative budget plans, whereby the programmatic issues tend to get aggregated under simple rules of thumb: limits to the annual rate of real growth of defense budget authority, across-the-board restraint in entitlement COLAs, uniform restrictions to discretionary inflation adjustments in appropriated program funding, etc. The authorizing and appropriations committees, the logical source of programmatic initiatives, are relegated to the perfunctory task of executing the committee-specific

"reconciliation instructions" or appropriations limits
that accompany the enacted budget resolution. It is
true that these committees are provided the opportunity
at an early stage of the annual budget process (by
March 15 in each house) to submit their "views and
estimates" for forthcoming action to the budget
committees. However, the incentive has been for each
committee to use this preliminary statement to
establish a defensive posture in protection of its
program interests.

What would improve the prospects for structural
program reforms as a means of spending restraint?
Ideally, the incoming president in 1985 would initiate
such proposals in his FY 1986 budget request. If not,
the agenda for congressional budget action should be
set to accommodate a more deliberative policy review,
especially among the authorizing and appropriations
committees, than now seems possible. While this
committee review would best proceed under agreed-upon
targets for spending, the time required to establish
such targets and then allow for committee action would
contribute to a further unrestrained rise of federal
debt. This implies a two-phased approach whereby
interim, time-limited policy measures are adopted to
keep spending below some aggregate target level, and
whereby the debate over long-term policies can proceed
without exposing the economy to further risks. The
following scheme is suggestive of the decision-making
approach that the next Congress might adopt.

The 99th Congress that takes office in January
1985 is scheduled to enact a FY 1986 budget resolution
(for FY 1986-1988) in its first year, and a FY 1987
budget resolution (for FY 1987-1989) in its second
year. FY 1989 is thus the end-year of its effective
budget horizon (and the last year for which the
incoming president will submit a budget). The first of
these resolutions could be adopted as usual by mid-
1985, but with the inclusion of aggregate budget
targets to be reached by FY 1989 (10). In the course of
enacting this resolution, Congress would agree upon
interim policies consistent with the aggregate targets.
Because such measures would have an explicit time limit
of perhaps two years, the members of Congress would
presumably be more inclined to reach agreement than if
the policies were viewed as permanent. The remainder of
1985 and early 1986 could then be devoted to committee
review of spending policies, with the intention of
substituting the interim measures with longer-term

TABLE 6

POLICY INSTRUMENTS FOR SPENDING RESTRAINT

Suggestive policy instrument	Suggestive limit of restraint for FY 1985-1989	Associated reduction in FY 1989 outlays, $ billions [a]

National defense
(General restraint)
Real growth in
  budget authority
	Reduce (from 5 percent)
	  to 0 percent
		64

(Selective restraint)
Real growth in
  budget authority for
  military procurement
	Reduce (from 7 percent)
	  to 2 percent
		26

Civilian empoloyee pay levels	Eliminate pay raises	6
Military employee pay levels	Eliminate pay raises	18
Entitlements and other mandatory spending		

Program eligibility
  provisions (all
  benefit entitlements)
	Tighten enough to
	offset expected growth
	in recipients
		27

Cost-of-living
  adjustments (all
  indexed entitlements)
	Eliminate all COLAs	61

Provider reimbursement
  rates for medical care
  (Medicare and Medicaid)
	Tighten enough to
	offset expected growth in
	medical costs
		36

Coverage of medical
  services (Medicare
  and Medicaid)
	Tighten enough to offset
	expected growth in medical
	care utilization[b]
		23

Target prices for farm price supports	Freeze at 1984 crop-year levels	6

Nondefense discretionary spending

Program budget authority (excluding employee pay)	Freeze at FY 1984 nominal levels	26
Civilian employee pay levels	Eliminate pay raises	8

Offsetting receipts

Monthly premium for Supplementary Medical Insurance (part B of Medicare)	Raise premium to cover 50 percent of program costs FY 1989 (versus 18 percent as in baseline)	11

Sources: Adapted from CBO, 1984a and 1984 c.

a. Relative to CBO current policy baseline.

b. As an example, for every percentage point by which one restrains the growth of hospital reimbursement schedules in Medicare throughout FY 1985-1989, the outlay savings in FY 1989 would be $3 billion.

reforms, but still within the agreed-upon aggregate targets for spending. The committees would be required to propose these longer-term reforms in their "views and estimates" submitted to the budget committees in March 1986, for consideration in adopting the budget resolution for FY 1987. If a program reform could not be accommodated within the relevant spending target, it would be incumbent upon the sponsors of the reform to find sufficient additional revenue (or spending restraint elsewhere) (11).

What kind of policy measures might be adopted in 1985 on an interim basis? One principal concern should be to impose austerity without so disrupting programs as to preclude possible long-term options. For example, the imposition of restrictive physician fee schedules in Medicare, even on an interim basis, might drive many doctors away from the program and greatly complicate the consideration of structural reforms.

Table 6 identifies some suggestive policy instruments that could be manipulated in setting interim measures. The indicated amount of savings is an illustrative upper bound; lesser degrees of restraint (and thus lesser savings) are more likely for each. The required extent of total savings would depend on the prescribed outlay targets. These general forms of restraint are indeed largely those characterized earlier as ad hoc and less desirable. The point is that such interim measures stand a better chance of timely adoption so as to allow more extended consideration of subsequent structural reforms.

V. CONCLUDING THOUGHTS

The last three years have witnessed mounting congressional resistance to spending restraint. The programs surviving each successive round of budget-cutting have become increasingly resistant to further cuts. As with a crucible in which metals have different melting points, more heat is needed to liquify the remaining material; someone must turn up the heat.

In this context, it may not be surprising that Congress tends to exercise spending restraint through ad hoc rules-of-thumb. Political consensus is more easily reached when austerity comes in an indiscriminate, across-the-board fashion. The policies are thus more easily explained and rationalized to voters; sacrifices are broadly shared. This is perhaps all that one can expect, given the divisiveness that would result from more selective measures. It may be that policy analysts, like beggars, should not be choosers.

However, one should not lose sight of the substantive content of spending policies, as they emerge from the process of repeated restraint. One should at least question whether the separate policy changes, motivated principally by the need to lower the deficit, have such adverse allocative or distributional consequences as to negate the expected gain to marcoeconomic performance.

FOOTNOTES

** Any views expressed herein are those of the author and should not be ascribed to The Urban Institute or its officers or trustees.

1. Both such baselines, as projected by the Congressional Budget Office (CBO) and used in this paper, are described in CBO, 1984c. The current policy baseline published in the above report was later revised slightly by CBO to reflect updated technical assumptions. See CBO, 1984b. The downward revision to projected budget outlays (and the deficit) amounted to $18 billion (0.3 percent of GNP) by FY 1989. The reader is assumed here to have some familiarity with federal budget concepts and the types of data published by CBO and the Office of Management and Budget.

2. Throughout this paper, such calculations assume that the impact of deficit-reducing measures would build progressively throughout FY 1985-1989. The magnitude of the FY 1985 policy impact, measured against the CBO baseline projection, is assumed to be 20 percent of the FY 1989 magnitude, with the FY 1986 magnitude equaling 40 percent of the FY 1989 figure, etc. The associated reduction in FY 1989 interest outlays is computed on the basis of CBO's baseline projection of interest rates and the maturity distribution of federal securities. As is the conventional practice, the projections of the deficit and public debt are all made under the same set of economic assumptions and thus embody no interaction between budget policy, fiscal stimulus, and macroeconomic performance. In particular, policy measures to reduce the deficit are not assumed to lower interest rates below their projected baseline levels.

High-employment estimates are based on a 6 percent unemployment rate.

3. Further discussion of recent budget developments and the projected budget outlook is contained in Mills, 1984; Mills and Palmer, 1983 and 1984; and Palmer and Mills, 1982.

4. See CBO, 1981, pp.3-5; and CBO, 1981b, p.1. In deriving its economic assumptions, CBO did assume a 10 percent personal income tax cut (effective in July 1981), accelerated depreciation as then proposed by the Senate Finance Committee (retroactive to January 1981), and other unspecified tax cuts amounting to $50 billion in FY 1984. In sum, these tax cuts would leave FY 1984 revenues at 20 percent of GNP. Such fiscal stimulus was deemed necessary (and sufficient) to prevent any slowdown in economic activity.

5. These observations are not meant to suggest that the tax provisions preceding the Economic Recovery Tax Cut of 1981 (ERTA) could have been sustained throughout the 1980s. Under CBO's current economic assumptions, the pre-ERTA tax law would have yielded revenues exceeding 23 percent of GNP in FY 1989. A different counterfactual is to assume tax cuts equivalent to an indexing of the personal income tax beginning in October 1981. Under current economic assumptions, this policy scenario would have yielded FY 1989 revenues equalling 20.7 percent of GNP, rather than the currently projected 18.9 percent. With such an alternative tax policy benchmark against which to measure the enacted policy changes, the FY 1989 increase in interest on the public debt would be somewhat less than $50 billion, not $100 billion.

6. CBO estimates that the President's FY 1985 budget would yield savings of $38 billion in FY 1989 nondefense program outlays (CBO, 1984a, p.5). The Rose Garden compromise plan offered by the President and the Senate Republican leadership was estimated by CBO to yield $24 billion in savings. Both estimates are relative to the CBO current policy baseline.

7. It is of course possible that an incoming president in 1985 might opt to support a much more ambitious set of nondefense spending cuts than he had endorsed in 1984. Even allowing for this possibility, however, $75 billion seems a plausible upper bound for reductions in nondefense spending.

8. These estimates are derived from the pattern of spending in President Reagan's budget request for FY 1985. See CBO, 1984a and OMB, 1984a.

9. Congressional action during calendar year 1983 was estimated by CBO to result in FY 1988 outlay savings of only $4 billion in national defense and $1 billion in nondefense discretionary spending (CBO, 1984c, .p.50). Of the estimated FY 1988 savings of $11 billion for entitlements and other mandatory spending, one-half resulted from the six-month COLA delay included in the 1983 Social Security amendments (for OASDI, SSI, and veterans' pensions).

10. As a general proposition, I would prefer to see these targets expressed in high-employment terms, according to some standard methodology, perhaps coordinated between CBO and the Commerce Department's Bureau of Economic Analysis. A target level for revenues (and thus net interest and the deficit) would of course also be specified.

11. This notion is similar to the "pay-as-you-go" concept introduced in the House-passed first concurrent budget resolution for FY 1985.

References

Committee for National Security, pending for a Sound Defense: Alternatives to the Reagan Military Budget (Washington, D.C.: Committee for National Security, 1984).

Congressional Budget Office, An Analysis of President Reagan's Budget Revisions for Fiscal Year 1982 (Washington, D.C.: Government Printing Office, 1981a).

Congressional Budget Office, An Analysis of the President's Budgetary Proposals for Fiscal Year 1985 (Washington, D.C.: Government Printing Office, 1984a).

Congressional Budget Office, An Analysis of the President's Credit Budget for Fiscal Year 1985 (Washington, D.C.: Government Printing Office, 1984b).

Congressional Budget Office, Baseline Budget

Projections for Fiscal Years 1985-1989 (Washington, D.C.: Government Printing Office, 1984c).

Congressional Budget Office, _Reducing the Federal Budget: Strategies and Examples, Fiscal Years 1982-1986_ (Washington, D.C.: Government Printing Office, 1981b).

Congressional Budget Office, _The Economic Outlook_ (Washington, D.C.: Government Printing Office, 1984d).

Congressional Budget Office, _Analysis of the Grace Commission's Major Proposals for Cost Control_ (Washington, D.C.: Government Printing Office, 1984).

De Leeuw, Frank and Thomas M. Holloway, "Cyclical Adjustment of the Federal Budget and Federal Debt," _Survey of Current Business_, vol. 63, no. 12 (December 1983), pp.25-46.

Mills, Gregory B., "The Budget: A Failure of Discipline," in John L. Palmer and Isabel V. Sawhill, eds., _The Reagan Record: An Assessment of America's Changing Domestic Priorities_ (Cambridge, Mass.: Ballinger Press, 1984).

Mills, Gregory B. and John L. Palmer, _The Deficit Dilemma: Budget Policy in the Reagan Era_ (Washington, D.C.: The Urban Institute Press, 1983).

Mills, Gregory B. and John L. Palmer, eds., _Federal Budget Policy in the 1980s_ (Washington, D.C.: The Urban Institute Press, 1984).

Office of Management and Budget, _Federal Government Finances_, (Washington, D.C.: Government Printing Office, 1981a and 1984a).

Office of Management and Budget, _Fiscal Year 1982 Budget Revisions_ (Washington, D.C.: Government Printing Office, 1981b).

Office of Management and Budget, _Special Analyses, Budget of the United States Government, FY 1985_ (Washington, D.C.: Government Printing Office, 1984b).

Palmer, John L. and Gregory B. Mills, "Budget Policy" in John L. Palmer and Isabel V. Sawhill, eds., _The_

Reagan Experiment: An Examination of Economic and Social Policies under the Reagan Administration (Washington, D.C.: The Urban Institute Press, 1982).

CHAPTER 6

MANAGING THE SOCIAL SECURITY SYSTEM*

I. INTRODUCTION [1982]

The Social Security system faces both a long-term and a short-term financing problem. The long-term problem stems primarily from changes in the age structure of the population that are expected to occur after the year 2000. The short-term problem reflects the current economic situation, which has caused Social Security outlays to rise faster than receipts. Although some action will be necessary within the next year to allow the continued payment of benefits, as the economy recovers payroll tax receipts should provide enough income to cover outlays for retirement, survivors, and disability benefits until the ratio of workers to beneficiaries begins to decline rapidly after 2010.

The long-term problem for Social Security is primarily demographic rather than economic in nature. A decline is expected in the number of workers contributing to Social Security, relative to the number of people receiving Social Security benefits. In 1980, there were about five people of working age for every person age 65 or over. By 2030, when the "baby boom" generation has retired, that ratio is expected to be cut in half, to about two and one-half working-age persons to each person 65 or over. If Social Security benefits were maintained at the same levels as under current law, therefore, and if no other major changes were made in the program, workers would have to contribute a larger proportion of their earnings to Social Security than is now required.

The ratio of workers to beneficiaries at any point in time is important for Social Security, because the system is funded on a pay-as-you-go basis. In other words, current tax receipts are used to pay current benefits, rather than being held in reserve to pay benefits for today's workers when they retire. The system does build up reserve funds when tax receipts

---

* Reprinted from U.S. Congressional Budget Office, Financing Social Security: Issues and Options for the long Run (Washington, D.C.: U.S. Government Printing Office, 1982).

exceed benefit payments, which it draws against in periods when benefit outlays exceed income. In the last 20 years, however, these funds have never held more than the equivalent of two years' total benefit payments (1).

The projected decline in the ration of workers to beneficiaries over the next 75 years is such that -- under current -- the income received by the Social Security system is expected to average about 13 percent less than the annual outlays needed to pay benefits (2). This gap, although large, is not as large as might be anticipated, given the increase in the relative size of the beneficiary population. There two major reasons for this. First, payroll tax rates are already scheduled to rise under current law, in 1985 and 1990. Tax rates for employers and employees and the self-employed will go up about 15 percent between 1982 and 1990. Second, and even more important, these projections assume that real wages -- that is, wages adjusted for inflation -- will grow by about one and a half percent a year, on average, over the next 75 years. This rate of growth, which is expected to result in a similar growth in payroll tax receipts, is high compared with the experience of the last 5 years, when real wages have declined by an average of 1.7 percent per year. It is quite comparable to the rate of growth in average annual wages over the 15 years before that, however.

Social Security balances are expected to fall in the 21st century even if the economy performs better over the next few decades than it has in the recent past. The magnitude of the problem will depend to some extent on factors such as productivity increases, birth rates, and mortality rates over the next three or four decades. While these variables are difficult to predict accurately, a long-run deficit for the trust funds is projected under all but the most optimistic economic and demographic assumptions (3).

Thus, it may be desirable to enact legislation now to strengthen the financial position of the system over the long run. In a program like Social Security, around which people make long-term plans and decisions, sudden changes can prove very disruptive. Further, frequent changes and projections of long-run insolvency undermine public confidence in the system.

Long-run balances can be improved in only two

major ways: revenues can be increased, or benefits can be reduced relative to the levels they will reach under current law. This paper focuses on these options, and analyzes several specific proposals of each type. In addition, it examines some recent proposals to stabilize trust fund balances in order to prevent recurring fluctuations resulting from cyclical economic performance.

Two important caveats need to be mentioned before the plan of the paper is presented. First, this paper deals only with the two Social Security trust funds that provide cash benefits--the Old Age and Survivors Insurance (OASI) fund, which provides benefits for retirees and their families and for the survivors of deceased workers, and the Disability Insurance (DI) fund, which provides benefits for disabled workers and their families. The third Social Security trust fund financed through payroll taxes, the Hospital Insurance (HI) trust fund, provides hospitalization benefits under Medicare, and is projected to have much more severe long-run financing problems than the OASI and DI funds (4). Both the causes and the timing of these problems, however, are different from those facing OASI and DI. Consequently, options for change in HI also differ substantially and therefore are not addressed in this paper (5).

Second, this paper considers only incremental changes in the Social Security system. It assumes, for example, that Social Security benefits will continue to be linked to lifetime earnings through a benefit computation process similar to that now employed. Similarly, it assumes that financing for Social Security will continue, at least primarily, to be provided through specially earmarked tax revenues. Further, only options aimed primarily at ameliorating the financial problems of the system are discussed here. In the recent past, a number of plans for a more complete restructuring of the Social Security system have been proposed, but these are beyond the scope of this paper. Options of this type include, for example, plans to divide benefits into two parts, one means-tested and the other linked to earnings;(6) earnings-sharing between spouses; and the elimination of benefits for spouses and dependents (7).

Instead, this paper focuses on options to improve the financial position of the trust funds without changing the basic structure of the system, by reducing

97

benefit levels or by increasing revenues [.... Sections
II and III] analyze two major ways in which outlays for
benefits could be reduced relative to current law over
the long run: lowering the levels of initial retirement
and   disability   benefits through changes in   the
computation formula, and raising the retirement age.
[Section IV] considers changes in benefit indexation
procedures aimed at stabilizing trust fund balances
over the long run [...]*

II. CHANGES IN THE COMPUTATION OF INITIAL SOCIAL SECURITY BENEFITS

The long-run financial outlook for Social Security
could be improved by reducing the relative level of
benefits for all new beneficiaries [...].

Such a change would have several advantages as a
means of restraining growth in the long-run costs of
the system.   It would affect the majority of new
beneficiaries similarly, rather than concentrating its
effects on particular subgroups within the beneficiary
population as do other savings proposals (8). Changes
in the benefit computation formula could be phased in
gradually, if desired, in order to reduce disparities
among different age groups.   Moreover, if wages
increased faster than prices in the future, as is
expected, gradual phase-in might allow real benefit
levels to continue to rise--although more slowly than
under current law--even with the gradual decline in
replacement rates.   And if total resources available
for benefit payments were found to be greater than
expected, most of the proposed formula changes could
also be phased out relatively easily (although
recipients whose basic benefit levels had been lowered
as a result of the formula change would, in general,
continue to have relatively lower benefits, unless ad
hoc benefit increases were provided).

Proposals to change benefit computation methods
also have some drawbacks.   In general, they would
affect only new beneficiaries, who even under current
law will receive lower benefits relative to
contributions than those now on the rolls.   In
addition, for some of these proposals the total impact

---

* This editor uses the term "section" instead of
"chapter" in the original text and deletes some words
or sentences. Deletions are indicated by [...].

would depend heavily on the rate of growth in wages and the rate of inflation, both of which are difficult to predict accurately. Further, some of the proposed changes would lower replacement rates most for those with higher benefits, whose benefits are already a relatively small proportion of wages. This could be seen as undesirable, since it would increase the already existing disparity between rates of return on contributions for high earners and those for lower earners. Finally, some of the proposals are fairly complex, and both their intent and their probable effects may be difficult to explain or to understand.

A. Options for Changing the Calculation of the Primary Insurance Amount

Computations of the primary insurance (PIAs) are calculated by applying a progressive formula to each worker's average indexed monthly earnings (AIME). This formula has three brackets, and a declining percentage of earnings is included in the PIA from each successive bracket. For example, for those turning 62, dying, or becoming disabled in 1982, PIAs equal 90 percent of each worker's AIME up to $230, 32 percent of the AIME between $230 and $1,388, and 15 percent of the AIME over $1,388. The two dollar amounts in this formula, $230 and $1,388, known as bend points, are adjusted each year to reflect changes in average annual wages, so a new formula is created each year for each new group of workers becoming eligible for benefits.

1. Reductions in Bend Points

Recently, the discussion of ways to restructure the benefit formula has focused on reductions in the formula bend points relative to AIMEs. If the bend points were indexed by 75 percent (rather than the current 100 percent) of the increase in average wages, for example, over a period of 12 years beginning in 1984, they would decline gradually relative to AIMEs (9).

Thus, a larger proportion of each worker's AIME would fall into the upper brackets of the formula, where the percentage of earnings replaced by benefits is lower. As a result, replacement rates (annualized PIAs as a proportion of the final year's earnings) would fall for almost all workers over the 12-year

99

period, but would stabilize at those lower rates when full wage indexation of the bend points resumed in 1996.

Under this proposal, PIAs would decline most for those with relatively high AIMEs, as Figure 2 shows (10). In general, those with AIMEs at or above the higher bend point under the current law formula (point D in Figure 2) would have the largest relative decline in their benefits under the proposal, since a larger proportion of their AIMEs would be shifted into the top bracket of the formula where replacement rates are the lowest. Because of the shift in the bend points, however, workers with AIMEs near the lower bend point (point B in Figure 1) would also experience relatively large reductions. Only a small proportion of recipients--those with AIMEs below point A in Figure 2--would be completely unaffected by the reduction in bend points.

Reducing bend points in this way would produce substantial long-run savings -- about 0.9 percent of payroll over the next 75 years (see Table 4) (11). If the reductions were phased in over a period of 12 years, major differences in benefits received by those born a few years apart could be avoided, and projected benefits would be changed very little for those retiring in the very near future. After the proposal was fully phased in, benefits would be reduced by about 8 percent on average, although those who were retired before the phase-in started would be unaffected. Because those with the highest earnings--who are also those most likely to have incomes from private pensions and investments--would experience the greatest decline in benefits, it could be argued that this proposal would focus cuts on those best able to afford them.

On the other hand, rates of return on Social Security taxes paid are already lower for high earners than for those with low earnings, and by the end of this century contributions will exceed expected benefits for some high earners, even under current law (12). Any change in the benefit formula that further reduced benefits for those with high earnings would exacerbate this situation.

In addition, if the increase in bend points did not exceed the increase in benefits resulting from the cost-of-living adjustment (COLA) in any given year, this proposal could result in lower real benefits for

100

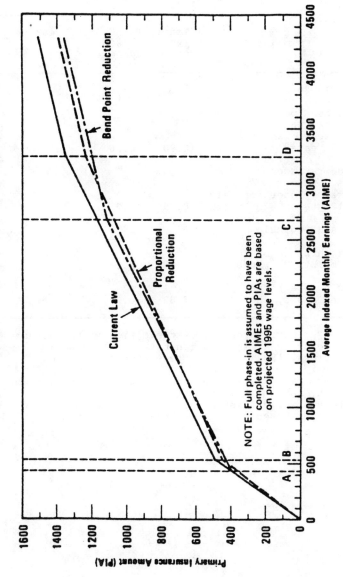

Figure 2

Primary Insurance Amounts in Relation to Average Indexed
Monthly Earnings Under Current Law and Two Options, 1995.

101

TABLE 4. LONG-RUN SAVINGS OF SEVERAL FORMULA CHANGE
OPTIONS, RELATIVE TO CURRENT LAW
(As a percentage of taxable payroll)[a]

Option	Total, 1982–2056	Twenty-five-year Periods		
		1982–2006	2007–2031	2032–2056
Change PIA Formula				
Index bend points by 75 percent of increase in wages, for 12 years[b]	0.90	0.26	1.09	1.36
Reduce replacement rates within brackets proportionately, for 12 years[b]	0.89	0.25	1.08	1.35
Change AIME Formula				
Index earnings by the CPI, bend points by wages[c]	1.06	0.14	1.20	1.85
Index both earnings and bend points by the CPI[c]	2.83	0.27	2.76	5.45

SOURCE: Estimates provided by the Office of the Actuary, Social
Security Administration based on Alternative II-B assumptions, 1982 OASDI Trustees' Report.

a. Taxable payroll is the total of all wages on which Social
Security taxes are paid.
b. Proposals would first affect the benefit formula in 1984.
c. Estimates based on indexing changes beginning in 1983.

those retiring in that year than for those retiring earlier. This situation already occurs in some years when wage growth is less than price growth, but this option could exacerbate it. In order to avoid this problem, reductions could be limited to the higher of 75 percent of wages or the previous year's COLA (13).

2. Changes in Replacement Rates Within Brackets

An alternative to changing the formula bend points would be to change the percentage replacement rates within each bracket of the formula. For example, these rates could be reduced proportionately over a period of 12 years, so as to provide long-run savings comparable to those achieved under the proposal to reduce bend points. This option would result in a somewhat flatter replacement curve overall than under present law, but all workers' PIAs would be reduced by the same proportion. Thus, for any given worker, the PIA under this option would be the same proportion of current law PIA, regardless of the level of the worker's AIME.

If replacement rates were reduced proportionately in all three brackets, rates of 82.7 percent in the first bracket, 29.4 percent in the second bracket, and 13.8 percent in the highest bracket would be needed to achieve the same long-run savings as under the bend-point option. The current law rates are 90 percent, 32 percent, and 15 percent.

Under this proposal, PIAs for those with very high earnings would be reduced less than under the bend-point proposal, while those for workers with AIMEs near the average would be reduced somewhat more (see Figure 2). Benefits for those with very low AIMEs--below the lowest bend point--would also be lower than under the bend-point option, although they would still be a larger proportion of earnings for these workers than for those with higher earnings.

Since this option would maintain the present relative distribution of benefits, its advantages and drawbacks would be similar to those of the current law formula. For example, under this option retirees with high AIMEs would have their rates of return on contributions reduced by the same proportions as all other retirees, rather than by a larger percentage than the average as under the bend-point option. Since their rates of return are already lower than those of other workers, this may be seen as an advantage. On the other hand, these beneficiaries are more likely than other Social Security recipients to have other sources of income such as private pensions and investments, and may therefore be better able to adjust to lower benefit levels. Further, such recipients may also benefit more from the tax-exempt status of Social Security benefits.

Additionally, this formula would result in lower benefits for those with very low AIMEs than either current law or the bend-point proposal (14). Those with low AIMEs who would lose under the reduced replacement-rate option would, for the most part, be those with limited work histories, since it is difficult to have an AIME below $200 (approximately the point at which the proposed formula would become more favorable than the reduced bend-point formula) if a person has worked steadily in covered employment (15). A worker with lifetime earnings at the minimum wage who became 62 in 1982, for example, would have an AIME of $563. Many workers with AIMEs lower than $200, therefore, will have had some other source of income during their working lives, and may continue to do so after retirement. Further, the current benefit structure provides a very high rate of return on contributions for workers with very low AIMEs.

On the other hand, many of those with irregular work histories, and thus low AIMEs, are women who have spent some time out of the labor force because of home responsibilities. Many of them will also be entitled to benefits as spouses or widows, but such benefits may be inadequate for divorced women whose former husbands are still alive. Other workers with discontinuous work histories include those with periods of illness or unemployment, who are also unlikely to have significant incomes in addition to their benefits. Under either the reduced replacement-rate option or the reduced bend-point option, additional protection could be provided to low-income recipients by strengthening means-tested benefit programs for the elderly and disabled, such as Supplemental Security Income (SSI). This would mitigate the effects of this proposal for low-income beneficiaries, but would also reduce its long-run budget savings.

Thus, the long-run savings generated by these proposed formula changes would be similar, but their effects would differ for different types of beneficiaries. Table 5 summarizes their impact on

replacement rates for three types of workers: a minimum
wage earner, someone with earnings at the average of
earned wages, and someone with earnings at the taxable
maximum. Each of these proposals would reduce benefits
relative to current law for all three types of workers,
but under the bend-point option the impact would be
greatest for a maximum wage earner, while under the
proportional reduction option, the relative reductions
in replacement rates would be the same for all workers.

B. Options for Changing the Computation of Average Indexed Monthly Earnings

Savings could also be generated by changing the
method used to calculate AIMEs. Currently, the AIME
consists of a worker's average monthly earnings,
corrected for the growth in wages over time. These
corrections are based on an index of average annual
wages.

Because average wages are projected to grow faster
than prices over the long run, one option for reducing
AIMEs and hence benefits is to index earnings by the
CPI or some other price index, rather than by average
wages. (16). The savings to be gained in the immediate
future from the implementation of this proposal would
probably be limited, since real wage growth is not
expected to increase dramatically within the next few
years. In the long run, however, the savings from
using a price index rather than a wage index to
calculate AIMEs could be substantial if wages again
start to rise more rapidly than prices, as is expected.
If the PIA formula remained as under current law,
savings from this proposal would be about 1.06 percent
of long-run payroll (see Table 4).

Under this proposal, bend points would continue to
be wage indexed, and they would rise relative to the
price-indexed AIMEs if real wage growth took place.
This would mean that a higher proportion of all
earnings would be shifted back into the bottom brackets
where the proportion of AIME replaced is highest. This
would result in a flatter overall distribution of
benefits that would to some extent offset the savings
generated by the shift to price indexation of earnings.

Alternatively, both bend points and earnings could
be price indexed. This would maintain the current
relationship between AIMEs and PIAs, but would shift
more earners into the higher brackets as real wage

TABLE 5. REPLACEMENT RATES FOR THREE WORKERS AGE 62 IN
1995:   CURRENT LAW AND FOUR OPTIONS

Option	Replacement Rate in 1995 (annualized PIA as percentage of last year's earnings)		
	Minimum Wage Earner[a]	Earner with Average Wages[b]	Earner with Wages at Maximum[c]
Current Law	58.0	42.5	25.3
Change PIA Formula			
Index bend points by 75 percent of increase in wages, for 12 years	53.7	40.4	22.8
Reduce replacement rates within brackets proportionately, for 12 years	53.3	39.1	23.3
Change AIME Formula			
Index earnings by the CPI, bend points by wages[d]	56.4	41.0	24.8
Index both earnings and bend points by the CPI[d]	52.8	39.3	22.7

SOURCE: Congressional Budget Office, based upon the Alternative
II-B assumptions of the 1982 Trustees' Report.
a. Calculations are based upon the earnings of a worker who
always was employed full-time (2,080 hours per year) at the
federal minimum. The minimum wage after 1982 is assumed to
increase at the same rate as the average earnings in the
economy.
b. Calculations are based upon the earnings of a worker who
always earned the average wages in the economy.
c. Calculations are based upon the earnings of a worker who
always earned the Social Security maximum taxable earnings.
d. Replacement rates would continue to decline for all workers
under these proposals, if wage increases exceeded price
increases as projected. Replacement rates are calculated
assuming that indexing changes begin in 1984.

TABLE 6. EFFECTS (RELATIVE TO CURRENT LAW)
OF DIFFERENT METHODS FOR EARNINGS AND BEND POINTS

Bend Points Indexed by:	Earnings Indexed by:	
	Wage Index	CPI
Wage Index	Current law	Benefits reduced because, although the bend points would be the same as under current law, AIMEs would be lower. Savings= 1.06 percent of long-run payroll.
CPI	Benefits reduced because more of AIMEs would be shifted to high-er brackets, which have lower replacement rates. Savings = 2.03 percent of long-run payroll.	Benefits reduced because both indexed earnings and bend points would be lower in the future than under cur-rent law. Savings = 2.83 percent of long-run payroll.

NOTE: This assumes that wages will rise faster than prices. If -- contrary to projections -- prices were to increase faster than wages over the long run, effects of these indexing alternatives would differ from those shown. Under those circumstances, price-indexing proposals would increase benefits.

growth took place, thus reducing replacement rates (see Table 5). Savings from this proposal would be very large--about 2.83 percent of long-run payroll. The effects of the various combinations of wage and price indexing of the formula's bend points and of earnings are summarized in Table 6.

The effects of these proposals on beneficiaries would also depend on the relative behavior of wages and prices. The differential in rates of change between wages and prices has not been constant over time, however. Before 1974, wages generally rose faster than prices, often by a fairly large margin. Since then, prices have often risen faster especially in the last few years. Thus, for any given worker, the difference between wage and price indexing of earnings would depend heavily on which years were included in the earnings history, and on total earnings in each of those years.

Under either of the proposals affecting AIMEs, benefits for successive generations of retirees would rise with price increases and would maintain their real purchasing power over time. Any savings from these proposals would occur as a result of increases in real wages. On the other hand, if real wages grew over the long run, replacement rates would decline, and the standard of living of retirees would fall relative to that of workers. Conversely, in periods like the recent past when price increases exceeded wage increases, benefit levels would rise relative to wage levels, and total outlays under these proposals would be greater than under current law. If the relative behavior of wages and prices continues to be as volatile in the future as in the recent past, and the income of the system is still tied to wages, price indexing of earnings or bend points could lessen the stability of the system and lead to future short-run financing problems.

III. CHANGING THE AGE OF RETIREMENT

One frequently recommended solution for the long-term problem of financing rapid increases in the ratio of beneficiaries to workers during the early 21st century is to raise the retirement age (17). This would expand the pool of workers and decrease the number of beneficiaries. Proponents argue that because life expectancies are increasing, total lifetime benefits per worker will rise considerably under

108

current law. An increase in the retirement age could
simply require workers to spend at least some of this
increased life expectancy in employment rather than in
retirement. On the other hand, a higher retirement age
could impose hardships on certain groups of aged
workers who might be relatively less able to adjust to
such an increase--those in poor health who do not
qualify for disability benefits, for example, or the
chronically unemployed.

       This [section] focuses on options for increasing
the age of retirement. The first section describes
current retirement practices, both with regard to
Social Security policy and with reference to the actual
behavior of workers. The next section analyzes several
specific options for change.   The last section details
some of the major factors that affect the age of
retirement, and outlines the advanatages and drawbacks
of proposals for later retirement as they relate to
each of these factors.

A. Current Retirement Practices

       Sixty-five has been the age at which a worker
becomes eligible for unreduced retirement benefits
since the passage of the original Social Security Act
in 1935.   It was not selected after scientific or
gerontological analysis, but rather because it was
deemed to be the most acceptable age(18).   An element
of flexibility was later introduced by permitting early
retirement at ages 62-64, but with lower benefits. In
addition, workers who delay retirement beyond age 65
receive increased benefits (19).

       The actual pattern of retirement behavior
indicates that no single age may be accurately
described as "normal." Roughly two out of every three
Social Security retired worker beneficiaries begin
receiving benefits before age 65.   In addition,
approximately 20 percent of the age 65-69 population
are employed, although some also receive retirement
benefits.

B. Policy Options

       Social Security could be redesigned in two basic
ways to delay retirement. One would be to increase the
relative benefits from delaying retirement.   The other
would be to raise the retirement age.   In either case,
changes in other programs such as Disability Insurance

109

(DI) and Supplememtal Security Income (SSI) could also be made in order to mitigate the adverse impacts of retirement age changes.

1. Increasing the Relative Benefits for Delayed Retirement

Incentives for later retirement could be increased either by providing greater rewards for those who continue to work or by further reducing the benefits for those who retire early.

Increasing the delayed retirement credit to the same level as the factor used to reduce benefits for those who retire early would probably result in workers remaining employed longer after turning 65, but would not result in long-term outlay savings (20). If the delayed retirement credit was increased to roughly 9 percent per year, (21) workers who now retire at ages 65 to 70 could be expected to work on average about two to three months longer than under current law. Most of the increase in benefits would go to higher-earning beneficiaries, who are more likely to remain employed than are those with lower earnings.

In contrast, reductions in pre-age 65 benefits could result in major cost savings. For example, if benefits at age 62 were reduced to 55 percent of full benefits rather than the current 80 percent, as proposed by the Administration in May 1981, the estimated savings over 75 years could be as much as 0.7 percent of payroll (see Table 7). These savings would result primarily from reduced benefits received by those continuing to retire early, however, rather than from increases in the average age of retirement. If almost all retirees delayed their retirement until 65 as a result of this proposal, there would be no savings (22).

Other more limited benefit reductions could also be instituted to encourage some persons to work longer. For example, benefits for children of early retirees could be eliminated, since they may provide an added incentive for some workers to apply for benefits before reaching age 65, while their children are still young enough to be eligible. Since only a relatively small portion of early retirees have young children, however, elimination of such benefits would probably have only a small effect on early retirements. Long-run cost savings resulting from this proposal would also be small--only about 0.02 percent of payroll.

2. Increasing the Eligibility Age

Raising the age of eligibility for full retirement benefits from 65 to 68 is one of the most commonly mentioned options for reducing Social Security costs, and would result in substantial savings. For example, under the Alternative II-B assumptions of the 1982 Trustees' Report, increasing the retirement age to 68 (and from 62 to 65 for early retirement benefits) over a 12-year period ending in 2012, as proposed by the 1981 National Commission on Social Security, would reduce the 75-year deficit by an estimated 1.0 percent of payroll (23). The Commission's proposal would also involve indexing earnings for the computation of AIMEs up to age 63, rather than to age 60 as under current law. If the retirement age was increased as under that proposal, but earnings were indexed only to age 60, the 75-year cost savings would be larger by about 0.3 percent of payroll.

If the age of eligibility for full benefits was raised to 68, but early retirement benefits were sitll available at 62, benefits received by those retiring before age 65 would have to be reduced in order to maintain the cost savings. Under H.R. 3207, for example, which was introduced by Congressman Pickle, benefits at age 62 would be reduced to 64 percent of the full benefits, rather than 80 percent as under current law. Long-run savings under H.R. 3207 would actually be slightly larger than under the commission's proposal, since earnings would be indexed only to age 60 as under current law, rather than to age 63 as under the proposal.

The arguments for and the potentially adverse consequences of an increase in the age of eligibility for retirement benefits for some older workers are discussed below. To some extent, adverse consequences could be mitigated either through adjustments in existing programs or through the creation of new public programs. For example, the definition of disability under DI and SSI could be liberalized for older workers, to give greater weight to vocational factors. This would allow older workers with health problems sufficiently serious to affect their ability to work in their accustomed occupations to receive some disability benefits, which would to some extent offset the reductions in retirement benefits. Such a proposal

111

TABLE 7. LONG-RUN SAVINGS RELATIVE TO CURRENT LAW OF
SEVERAL OPTIONS TO DELAY RETIREMENT (As a
percentage of taxable payroll)

| Option | Total, 1982–2056 | Twenty-five-year Period | | |
		1982–2006	2007–2031	2032–2056
Increased Delayed Retirement Credit[a]	-0.15	-0.05	-0.16	-0.23
Reduce Benefits for Early Retirees[b]	0.71	c	c	c
Raise Age of Eligibility for Full Benefits to 68 and Reduced Benefits to 65[d]	1.03	0.12	1.41	1.55
Raise Age of Eligibility for Full Benefits to 68 Without Increase in Eligibility Age for Reduced Benefits[e]	1.17	0.21	1.40	1.89

SOURCE: Estimates provided by the Office of the Actuary, Social
Security Administration. Negative numbers indicate costs.

a. Increase in Delayed Retirement Credit to actuarially fair
    equivalent.
b. The Administration's May 1981 proposal to reduce benefits at
    age 62 to 55 percent of full benefits.
c. Twenty-five-year estimates of savings not available.
d. Based on the proposal of the 1981 National Commission on
    Social Security, which would allow early retirement benefits
    at age 65 of 80 percent of the age 68 benefit. Proposal would
    also index earnings to age 63 rather than to age 60 as under
    current law. Savings would be larger by about 0.3 percent of
    long-run payroll if earnings were indexed only to age 60.

e. Based on H.R. 3207 introduced by Congressman Pickle, which
    raises age for full benefits to 68 and increases the
    reduction for age 62 benefits to 36 percent from 20 percent.

would reduce long run cost savings from this option, however.

Retention of age 62 as the early retirement age, but with a greater reduction factor, would also lessen the impact on such workers of an increase in the age of eligibility for full retirement benefits. This option would not necessarily reduce long-run savings resulting from delaying the age of eligibility for full retirement benefits, since total savings would depend upon how much early retirement benefits were reduced. If a reduction factor was chosen that would make age 62 benefits actuarially equivalent to those received at age 68, however, benefits for those retiring at 62 would be reduced to 64 percent of the full retirement benefit.

C. Pros and Cons of Increasing the Retirement Age

To assess the merits of increasing the age of retirement, different factors must be taken into account. These include health, employment opportunities, and available retirement income.

1. Health Factors

Some view an increase in the retirement age as a logical response to the major health improvements that have occurred since the beginning of the Social Security program and that are expected to continue. They argue that it is unrealistic to continue a policy that encourages workers to spend all of their increase in expected lifetime in retirement. In this view health improvements, as measured by life expectancy, result in older persons who are healthier than those in earlier generations, and therefore more able to continue active work.

Increases in life expectancy affect the retired worker population for Social Security by increasing both the proportion of successive generations that attain age 65 and the average number of years over which benefits are received. Since the program first paid benefits in 1940, expected lifetimes of individuals have lengthened considerably. For men aged 65, the increase in expected lifetime since 1940 has been 2.2 years or about 18 percent. Increases for women have been even larger--5.1 years or about 38 percent (24).

These improvements in life expectancies are projected to continue. The average life expectancy of men aged 65 is projected to increase an additional 10.5 percent by the year 2000, and that of women almost 13 percent over the same period. On the basis of these figures, an increase in the retirement age to 68 in the year 2000 would leave male workers with 0.7 more years of retirement benefits than their 1940 counterparts and 1.5 fewer years than those retiring at age 65 in 1980. For women the figures would be 4.5 and 0.6, respectively (25).

These figures obscure substantial differences in life expectancies between different population subgroups. There is evidence that workers in different occupations have systematically different life expectancies, for example, and that those engaged in less arduous employment live longer than those in more strenuous jobs (26). Moreover, a recent study of Social Security retirees found that men accepting benefits before age 65 had significantly higher mortality rates than those who postponed retirement to age 65 or later (27). Consequently, an increase in the retirement age could reduce the proportion of workers that live long enough to receive benefits, and therefore could have more of an impact on some groups of workers than on others.

Further, measures of health status other than life expectancies indicate that the ability of older Americans to work may not have improved, or may even have declined slightly over the last decade. Indeed, improvements in life expectancies may partly reflect longer survival periods for those with serious or chronic health problems. A comparison of Health Interview Survey data indicates that in 1980 higher proportions of men in the 60-64 and 65-69 age groups reported being unable to work due to chronic health conditions than 1970 (28). While these data may reflect many factors other than actual health status, such as changing health expectations, changing life styles, and other problems associated with self-reporting, they lead one to question the assertion that, on average, the health of older workers has improved.

On the other hand, a recent study by the General Accounting Office (GAO) indicates that the proportion of early retirees reporting ill health as their principal reason for retirement has declined considerably over the last decade. According to the GAO study, about 19 percent of early retirees reported that they retired because of poor health, as compared with 54 percent in a Social Security Administration study of workers retiring in 1968 through 1970 (29). This decline may be partially attributable to the expansion of the Disability Insurance program during the 1970s since a larger proportion of those aged 62-64 who are in poor health may now be receiving DI benefits. Since 1977, however, awards for DI benefits have been declining, which may lead to future increases in early retirements because of poor health. In addition, the proportion of workers retiring early increased substantially over this decade, so even if workers' health status has not improved, the proportion retiring early because of ill health would have declined as early retirement for other reasons increased.

If an increase in the age of eligibility for retirement benefits was legislated, presumably some of those who suffered from ill health would become eligible for disability benefits, thereby offsetting some of the reduction in outlays for retirement benefits. The availability of disability benefits for at least some older workers in poor health would also help to mitigate the adverse affects of an increase in the retirement age for this group.

2. Employment Factors

Arguments for an increased retirement age also assume changes in certain characteristics of future retirees, such as educational attainment. The proportion of the population attending college has grown steadily in recent years, suggesting that this may delay entry into the labor force and shorten working lives. In conjunction with the trend toward less physically demanding jobs, this has led some to argue that a higher proportion of later generations will be able to continue working past age 65.

The trend to college education has not included all workers, however. Almost one-quarter of the work force still lacks high school diplomas, and even among younger workers (those 25-29), about 15 percent have not graduated from high school (30). Employment opportunities for workers with little education or low skill levels tend to be in relatively more arduous occupations than for those with higher educational

115

attainment. Many of these workers could have difficulty continuing to work past 65, therefore, especially if the changes in the occupational mix and skill requirements of the labor force reduce the relative number of unskilled and semiskilled jobs over time. In addition, even though the average number of years of schooling has increased for the labor force as a whole, there is no evidence that this has decreased labor force participation rates for young people (31).

On the other hand, demographic factors may facilitate the absorption of increased numbers of older workers into the labor force in the future. The population aged 20 to 64 is projected to decline as a proportion of the total population after 2010. This demographic shift may cause the demand for older workers to increase as employers find younger workers increasingly scarce. This could cause wage rates for older workers to rise, which would also encourage many of them to continue working to a later age (32).

3. Retirement Income Factors

For many, income is a critical factor in determining whether to continue working. An increase in the age of eligibility for Social Security retirement benefits or a substantial reduction in early retirement benefits would cause such persons to delay retirement. It would also reduce lifetime Social Security benefits, which some economists believe would induce people to work and save more in order to offset the decline in their expected retirement incomes (33).

The impact of Social Security changes designed to encourage later retirement would also depend in part on the responses of private pension plans. Many private pension plans now allow workers to receive benefits at earlier ages than does Social Security, and the trend has been toward even lower eligibility ages (34). Since eligibility for pension benefits is expected to increase considerably in the future, the trend toward lower eligibility ages might work against changes in Social Security rewarding later retirement. If it did, however, it could require major increases in funding for pension benefits. The reason is that many plans have benefit formulas that pay one level of benefits before a worker is eligible for Social Security and a lower level after eligibility, so that an increase in the Social Security retirement age would increase the liabilities for this type of pension fund. The

116

prospect of these increased costs might cause pension plans to reverse the recent trend and delay eligibility ages in a way corresponding to the modifications made in Social Security. If this occurred, the increasing availability of pension benefits would be less likely to offset the effects of an increase in the retirement age.

Workers nearing retirement age in the future may increasingly have access to other sources of retirement income. Recent tax law changes provide substantial incentives for people to save through Individual Retirement Accounts (IRAs) and Keogh plans. While it is still too early to access the impact of these new incentives, some increase in retirement savings through IRAs and Keoghs is likely. Expanded access to this type of investment income in the next century could partially offset the effects of changes in Social Security intended to encourage later retirement.

IV. ADJUSTING BENEFITS FOR COST-OF-LIVING CHANGES

As recent experience has shown, Social Security balances can fall rapidly in periods when wages rise more slowly than prices. To some extent, this problem results from the fact that trust fund revenues are based on wages, while benefit levels rise with prices because they are adjusted each year to reflect changes in the cost of living. One way to decrease the sensitivity of trust fund balances to economic performance would be to modify the procedure used to adjust benefit levels, so that benefits would not rise faster than wages even in periods of slow wage growth. This section outlines several such proposals to change cost-of-living adjustments (COLAs) to provide more stable trust fund balances.

Reductions in cost-of-living adjustments have also been suggested as a partial solution to the short-run financing problem, and they could indeed produce substantial short-run savings. If benefits were increased by much less than the increase in prices over a long period of time, however, their purchasing power could decline substantially. Further, reductions in COLAs would have a cumulative effect over time, and if maintained over an extended period would cause the purchasing power of benefits to decline further in each year of retirement. Thus, COLA reductions implemented over extended periods could substantially increase poverty rates for older recipients. In addition, both

117

health status and employment opportunities tend to decline with age, making it more difficult for very old recipients to adjust to large declines in their real incomes.

For these reasons, COLA reductions, as distinct from indexing changes designed to promote the financial stability of the trust funds, are not generally proposed as a means of generating long-run cost savings. This section concentrates instead on options primarily aimed at decreasing the volatility of trust fund balances. The next section provides some background information on benefit indexation and its effects on the trust funds, and the final section examines options to stabilize trust fund balances over the long run.

A. Automatic Benefit Adjustments: History and Effects on Trust Fund Stability

Automatic indexing of Social Security benefits was legislated as part of the 1972 Social Security amendments, although various indexing schemes had been proposed before that (35). Somewhat ironically, a major impetus for the plan was that it was expected to help restrain the growth of benefits. In the seven years preceding the passage of the amendments, benefits had been raised three times--by 13 percent, 15 percent, and 10 percent--resulting in a cumulative increase of 43 percent between February 1965 and January 1971, over the same period the Consumer Price Index had risen only 27 percent. For this reason many legislators believed that linking benefit increases to the CPI would help keep down Social Security costs. Under the 1972 amendments, the first automatic cost-of-living adjustments became payable with the June 1975 benefits, although an additional benefit increase of 20 percent was also given in September 1972.

The methodology for computing Social Security benefits has not changed since 1975. Under current law, Social Security benefits are indexed to increases in the Consumer Price Index for urban wage earners and clerical workers (CPI-W). The COLA is determined by dividing the average CPI in the first calendar quarter of one year by the corresponding CPI for the previous year. If the increase is more than 3 percent, benefits are adjusted, starting with the payment received in July, to reflect the rise in the CPI (36).

The purpose of this method of adjusting benefits is to maintain the purchasing power of benefits over time. If benefits were not adjusted as prices rose, their purchasing power would erode and the adequacy of retirement benefits would decline as beneficiaries got older. Because of these adjustments, however, outlays rise as prices go up. Revenues will not necessarily increase by the same amount, since most trust fund income comes from the payroll tax, which is a proportional tax on wages. Prices may rise even in periods of slow wage growth. In periods of slow wage growth, prices may rise faster than wages, causing increases in outlays to exceed increases in revenues, as in 1979-81. If price increases exceed wage growth over an extended period, total outlays may exceed total revenues, causing trust fund reserves to deteriorate.

Extended periods of slow wage growth can threaten the solvency of the trust funds even in periods when the ratio of wage earners to beneficiaries is relatively high. If no major benefit reductions or tax increases are enacted, for example, and another period comparable to the recent past occurs in the late 1980s or early 1990s, the trust funds could face another financing crisis in spite of the relatively favorable demographic conditions projected for that period.

The estimates presented in this paper assume that the economy will reach long-term trend levels of growth in key variables within the next ten years, and maintain those levels indefinitely. In practice, however, while the economy may on average achieve the assumed rates of growth, its actual year-to-year behavior is likely to continue to vary in a cyclical manner. Such cycles are not built into the assumptions because their occurrence is very difficult to predict, and over the long run the average rate of growth is a more important determinant of trust fund solvency than the variation around that average. Under current law, however, until the trust funds accumulate large reserves, they will continue to be vulnerable to serious financing problems in periods when prices grow rapidly relative to wages.

B. Policy Options

Options intended to increase trust fund stability generally involve linking benefit increases to a measure that will not rise faster than wages, so outlays cannot increase more rapidly than revenues

(37). This section examines three options that would
link benefit levels to revenue levels through some form
of wage-indexing.

1. Substitution of a Wage Index

The simplest way to prevent benefit increases from
exceeding wage increases would be to base adjustments
on a wage index rather than on the CPI.   Use of a wage
index would maintain the relationship between the
incomes received by workers and the level of benefits
regardless of changes in prices.   Since revenues and
benefits would both be linked to wages, such an index
would also prevent benefits from rising faster than
revenues during periods of poor economic performance.

Over the long run, however, productivity increases
have made it possible for wage growth to exceed growth
in prices, and such a pattern is expected to hold again
in the future.   In that case, the long-run costs of
wage-indexing benefits would exceed the costs of price-
indexing.   Under the Alternative II-B assumptions,
long-run real wage growth is assumed to be 1.5 percent
per year, which would result in additional outlays over
the next 75 years of about 2.3 percent of long-run
payroll if benefits were wage-indexed rather than
price-indexed (see Table 8).   In addition, the
purchasing power of benefits would fluctuate more than
under the present system and, in periods of poor
economic performance, the value of benefits could
decrease substantially.

2. Indexing by a Reduced Wage Index

In order to provide the stable trust fund balances
that would result from linking both income and outlays
to wage growth, without the long-run cost increases
that could be expected if benefits were simply indexed
by wages, some analysts have proposed using a wage
index that has been adjusted downward by the expected
long-run differential between wages and prices--1.5
percent, under the Alternative II-B assumptions (38).
Under this proposal, growth in benefits would equal
growth in prices over the long run if the real wage
increases projected by the Social Security
Administration were achieved.

In addition to stabilizing balances, this proposal
would keep benefit increases proportional to increases
in wages. Periods of low and negative real wage growth

TABLE 8. LONG-RUN SAVINGS OF SEVERAL INDEXING OPTIONS,
RELATIVE TO CURRENT LAW (As a percentage of
taxable payroll)

Option	Total 1982–2056	Twenty-five-year Periods		
		1982–2006	2007–2031	2032–2056
Substitution of an Alternative Price Index for the CPI	0	0	0	0
Substitution of a Wage Index for the CPI[a]	-2.3	b	b	b
Indexing by Wage Inreases Minus 1.5 Percent				
If implemented immediately	0.09	0.24	0.01	0
If implemented after 1990	0	0	0	0
Indexing by the Lower of Wage or Price Increases[c]	0.43	0.16	0.48	0.65

SOURCE: Estimates provided by the Office of the Actuary, Social
Security Administration, based on the Alternative II-B
assumptions of the 1982 OASDI Trustees Report.

a. Minus signs denote cost.
b. Estimates not available on a 25-year basis.
c. This assumes no "catch-up" provision. A catch-up provision
could be enacted to allow benefit increases to exceed price
increases during periods of economic recovery, until benefit
levels were as high as they would have been under current
law. See text for discussion.

121

impose hardships on workers, and some have argued that those burdens should be shared by retirees. Cost-of-living adjustments for Social Security recipients would be limited in periods of low wage growth, without the increases in Social Security costs that would result from simple wage-indexing.

On the other hand, more stable trust fund balances would be achieved at the cost of greater fluctuations in benefit levels relative to the cost of living. If wage increases did not exceed price increases by at least 1.5 percent, real benefits would fall. Periods of low or negative real wage growth, like the recent past, would result in substantial real benefit declines. If this proposal had been in effect since 1975, for example, benefit levels would now be about 13 percent lower than under current law. Thus, under this proposal, the risks of poor economic performance would be shifted from the trust funds to beneficiaries.

3. Indexing by the Lower of Wage or Price Increases

Another alternative to stabilize trust fund balances would be indexing by the lower of wage or price increases. This option would restrict the growth of benefits in periods when prices are growing faster than wages, but would not cause long-run Social Security costs to rise. On the other hand, benefits could decline substantially under this option, both in real terms and in relation to earnings. If periods of real wage growth alternated with periods when increases in prices exceeded those in wages, as in the recent past, benefit increases would not keep up with either prices or wages.

In addition, an index based on the lower of wage or price increases would affect the degree to which Social Security benefits would replace wages lost as a result of an insured worker's retirement, disability, or death. Stabilizing these replacement rates was the guiding principle behind the indexing procedures enacted with the 1977 amendments. For workers retiring at age 65, indexing by the lower of wages or prices would result in lower replacement rates for some retirement cohorts than for others. This difference would depend upon the relationship between wage and price growth between the retiree's sixty-second and sixty-fifth birthdays. Since benefits are initially computed based upon eligibility at age 62 and price indexed thereafter, an experience similar to 1978-1981 would lower replacement rates as compared to current law by 8 percent for certain retirees.

A "catch-up" provision could be enacted, allowing, for example, benefit increases that exceeded price increases when the economy was coming out of a recession, until benefit levels were as high as they would have been under price-indexing. Such a provision would avoid large long-term declines in benefit levels, although temporary fluctuations in the purchasing power of benefits would still occur.

There would be little long-run savings if a catch-up was provided, however, and it could have very different effects on those retiring in different years. For example, some proportion of those whose benefits were reduced during an economic downturn would die before their losses were caught up. In addition, retirees coming into the system at the beginning of a catch-up period would receive windfall gains, since they would get catch-up increases but would never have experienced any benefit reductions. In order to avoid these overpayments, it would be necessary to compute separate adjustments for those who retired in each different year, which could prove to be an administratively difficult task.

FOOTNOTES

1. While this statement is true of the combined reserves of the three Social Security trust funds, individual funds have accumulated larger reserves in relation to their particular benefit outlays. Unless special enabling legislation is passed, reserves in one trust fund cannot be used to pay benefits from another.

2. This includes taxes and outlays for the OASI and DI programs only. Unless otherwise stated, all long-run projections given in this paper are based on the Alternative II-B economic and demographic assumptions of the 1982 Annual Report of the Board of Trustees, Federal Old Age and Survivors Insurance and Disability Insurance Trust Funds. The CBO does not develop long-run economic projections.[...]

3. In this context, the term "optimistic" means favorable to the trust funds. Thus, an optimistic path is one that combines strong economic performance with high mortality and fertility rates.[...]

4. Medicare benefits other than hospitalization benefits are provided through the Supplementary Medical Insurance (SMI) fund. Although SMI is technically part of the Social Security system, it is funded through general revenues and premiums paid by beneficiaries rather than through the payroll tax, and is not discussed in this [chapter].

5. For more information on problems facing the Medicare program and on options for that program, see the forthcoming CBO paper on the benefit structure of Medicare.

6. See Michael Boskin, ed., The Crisis in Social Security: Problems and Prospects (Institute for Contemporary Studies, 1977).

7. See U.S. Department of Health, Education, and Welfare, Social Security and the Changing Roles of Men and Women (February 1979); Rita Ricardo Campbell, Supplementary Statement to the Report of the Quadrennial Advisory Council on Social Security (May 1975); and Virginia Reno and Melinda Upp, "Social Security and the Family," American Enterprise Institute Conference on Taxation and the Family, October 1981.

8. Changes in the reduction factors for early retirement would also lower initial benefits for some, although not all, beneficiaries. Such reductions do not relate to the computation of the basic benefit or PIA, however; instead, they are imposed after the PIA is computed. Therefore, they are not discussed here.

9. The Administration included a somewhat more rapid decline in bend points as part of its May 1981 package of Social Security proposals. The formula change proposed there would have involved indexing bend points by 50 percent of wage increases over a period six years. A faster implementation of such a proposal would result in greater savings, but would increase disparities between different retirement cohorts. The 12-year restriction on the increase in bend points is an option proposed by the staff of the National Commission on Social Security Reform.

10. Since this proposal would affect bend points prospectively, Figure 2 shows PIAs and AIMEs under current law and under the proposal as they would be after 12 years. Bend points inflated to 1995 levels would be $537 and $3,234 under current law (using the

Alternative II-B projections of average growth in wages) and $445 and $2,684 under the proposal. The AIMEs of full-time workers--minimum wage earner, average earner, and maximum wage earner--who would be age 62 in 1995 are projected to be $1,264, $2,432, and $4,303, respectively.

11. This compares to an estimated long-run deficit in OASDI of 1.8 percent of long-run payroll. Total savings would of course depend upon the level of wage growth during the phase-in years.

12. See Robert J. Myers, "Money's Worth Comparison for Social Security Benefits," National Commission on Social Security Reform, Memorandum 45 (August 12, 1982).

13. Alternatively, bend-point increases could be linked to the same index as the COLA. Indexing bend points by the CPI would save 2.03 percent of payroll over the next 75 years. If bend points continued to be indexed by the CPI over the long run, however, declines in benefits relative to current law, and in replacement rates, would be continuing and very substantial. See further discussion below.

14. PIAs for those with AIMEs just above the first bend point under the reduced bend-point option (point A in figure 2) would actually be slightly higher under a proportional reduction than if bend points were reduced, however.[...]

15. The $200 figure is in 1982 dollars. Figure 2 is in 1995 terms. In 1995, the AIME at which the proportional formula would become more favorable would be about $500.

16. See Congressional Budget Office, Financing Social Security: Issues for the Short and Long Term (July 1977), for a discussion of the various indexing options, including indexing earnings by prices, that were considered at the time of the 1977 amendments.

17. The 1975 and 1979 Quadrennial Advisory Councils on Social Security, the 1981 National Commision on Social Security, and the President's Commission on Pension Policy, for example, all discussed versions of this option.

18. See Wilbur J. Cohen, Retirement Policies Under

Social Security (University of California Press, 1957) for discussion of this point.

19. Benefits are reduced by 5/9ths of 1 percent for every month of benefits received prior to age 65, with the maximum reduction being 20 percent for those retiring at age 62. This rate of reduction was chosen in order to make expected total lifetime benefits for all retirees with a given PIA approximately the same, regardless of when they actually retire. For each month retirement is delayed (up to age 72), benefits are increased by one-quarter of 1 percent, or 3 percent per year.

20. In fact, because of the benefit recomputation provision, additional earnings might result in increased outlays.[...]

21. The specific proposal is to increase the credit so that it would be "actuarially fair." That is, the expected lifetime benefits for a given worker would be the same regardless of the age at which benefits were first received.

22. For further discussion of this and other options to increase retirement ages, see Congressional Budget Office, *Work and Retirement: Options for Continued Employment of Older Workers* (1982).

23. For further details on this specific proposal, see National Commission on Social Security, *Social Security in America's Future*, the final report (March 1981), chap. 5

24. In 1940, average life expectancies at age 65 were 12.1 years for men and 13.6 years for women. U.S. Department of Health and Human Services, Social Security Administration, Office of the Actuary, *Social Security Area Population Projections, 1981*, Actuarial Study no. 85 (July 1981).

25. These calculations assume that the same proportion of future retirees will retire early as now do. Under the intermediate mortality assumptions of the 1982 Social Security Trustees' Report, men would not regain their 1980 position until 2050, whereas women could expect the same number of retirement years beginning between 2010 and 2020.

26. Robert M. Butler, Statement before the National

Commission on Social Security Reform, June 21, 1982.

27. John R. Wolfe, "Perceived Longevity and Early Retirement," Econometrics Workshop Paper no. 8105, Michigan State University (May 1982).

28. Jacob Feldman, "Work Ability of the Aged Under Conditions of Improving Mortality," Statement before the National Commission on Social Security Reform, June 21, 1982, p.17

29. General Accounting Office, Demographic and Economic Characteristics of Social Security Retiree Families, HRD-82-131 (September 28, 1982). Social Security Administration, Reaching Retirement Age, Research Report no.47 (1976).

30. A proposal that would mitigate the effects of an increase in the retirement age for those who start work at an early age would be to base eligibility for benefits on either a minimum number of years worked or the attainment of a minimum age.

31. Labor force participation rates have in fact increased slightly for men 16-19 years old over the last 20 years, and are about the same level as they were 20 years ago for men 20-24 years old. For women, labor force participation rates have increased significantly in both age categories. See Bureau of Labor Statistics, Handbook of Labor Statistics (December 1980), Table 4, p. 13.

32. Younger workers could also be affected by an increase in the retirement age. The retention by employers of older workers would diminish the opportunities for promotion of younger employees.

33. See Martin Feldstein, "Social Security, Induced Retirement, and Aggregate Capital Accumulation," Journal of Political Economy, vol. 82, no. 5 (September/October 1974), pp. 905-26.

34. For a survey of the plans for 240 large corporations, see Bankers Trust Company, Corporate Pension Plan Survey (1980).

35. For a discussion of efforts to index benefits, see Indexation of Federal Programs, prepared by the Congressional Research Service for the Senate Committee

127

on the Budget, 97 Cong. 1 sess. (May 1981).

36. If the CPI increase is less than 3 percent, then
the next year's COLA is based on the price increase
over the two-year period.

37. An alternative would be to stop indexing benefits
and return to a system of discretionary benefit
adjustments, or a system that required an annual vote
on benefit increases, which would allow greater
flexibility. Before benefit indexing began, however,
such discretionary adjustments generally exceeded price
increases.

38. This is one of the options proposed by the staff of
the National Commission on Social Security Reform. The
technical aspects of the proposal are still being being
developed, and the specific percentage by which wages
would be reduced to determine annual benefit increases
would depend upon the choice of the wage measure.
Under the Alternative II-B assumptions, if an hourly
earnings index was chosen, the growth rate that would
produce no long-run effect on the trust funds would be
1.8 percent rather than 1.5 percent because such an
index would rise more rapidly than an annual wage
index.

CHAPTER 7

MANAGING DEFENSE EXPENDITURES*

Fred Thompson

Most of the attention given to the Grace Commission report (1) has focused on the numbers - on the meaning, validity, and accuracy of its savings estimates (2). So far as the Department of Defense (DOD) is concerned, this focus is regrettable. In the first place, total defense outlays appear to be fairly insensitive to program content. No matter what happens to the Grace Commission's proposals, defense outlays will increase in real terms for the next several years. Even if all of the proposals were adopted and successfully implemented, the savings would amount to less than 5 percent of annual defense outlays. Of course, several of the commission's proposals could lead to increased military effectiveness - more efficient investment in weapons and support systems, increased readiness and sustainability, and perhaps even a better match between the military-force structure and logistical-support capabilities, on the one hand, and foreign-policy objectives and overseas commitments, on the other. Given the current gap between the United State's defense strategy - i.e., raising, equipping, organizing, and using the military forces in support of political objectives-and its foreign-policy commitments, such an outcome would be reassuring indeed. Unfortunately, this happy outcome is largely hostage to the way DOD and Congress do business.

In the second place, because there are no numbers to be found there, most commentators have simply skipped over the sections of the report concerned with the management role of the Office of the Secretary of Defense (OSD) and the DOD management climate. Yet these are likely to be the most valuable portions of the report. On reflection, the reasons for their value are apparent. In many respects the DOD is unique:

1. It is by far the United State's largest and most

---

* Reprinted from Control of Federal Spending, Proceedings, Vol 35, NO. 4 (New York, the Academy of Political Science, 1985): 72 - 84.

complex organization. It employs more than 3 million people, over 60 percent of all Federal personnel. It spends about $200 billion a year (in 1984 dollars), over 25 percent of total Federal outlays. And it operates over 5,600 installations around the world.

2. Military leadership and tradition are critical to the capacity of the DOD to protect and defend the United States. Military leadership is not entirely or even primarily a managerial role (one does not "manage" men into combat, they must be led). Military tradition constrains reorganization and personnel options to a considerable degree.

3. Because of its size and distinctive mission, the DOD is the sole customer of many of its private-sector suppliers. Monopsony implies the elaboration of idiosyncratic transactional arrangements. Because the DOD is unique, lessons learned by managing and operating other organizations do not apply to it. Hence, the Grace Commission's proposals generally make the most sense when they deal with problems common to all organizations (e.g., asset management) and the least when they deal with problems specific to the DOD (e.g., management of uniformed personnel or research and development acquisitions). All organizations must make policy, align their structure with their strategy, design and implement managerial controls, and allocate responsibility and authority. Consequently, the Grace Commission report addresses these issues with special insight, eloquence, and urgency.

I. THE 6RACE COMMISSION DIAGNOSIS

The commisssion's criticism of the DOD in general and OSD in particular is quite straightforward: the DOD has not confronted these issues. Because top managers in the OSD have failed to perform the functions of top management - planning, organizing, staffing, and organizational development - they have by default been forced to assume lower-level management functions-operating, controlling, and budgeting. Thus overwhelmed by administrative detail, top managers in the OSD have no time to perform their proper functions. As a result, the DOD has become turgid, sluggish, and burdened with offices, departments, and installations that are no longer vital, and managers have no clear idea of their responsibilities and constantly bicker over who should do what. According to the Grace Commission report:

> Government, and DOD in particular, does not delegate authority well. The impact of holding authority at the top of the organization...is to weaken the entire organization. The lower levels do not create or innovate. They respond to the hierarchy rather than propose and initiate; they...avoid risks...The upper levels of the organization become overloaded. They respond quite naturally by adding deputies and assistants...[and] layers to the organization, and this diffuses authority and responsibility even further.

> This is in direct contrast to private sector experience which has clearly demonstrated that the effectiveness of a large, complex organization improves when authority is delegated down into the organization along with responsibility. Decisions then are made by those with either the most pertinent knowledge of the situation or with the highest stake in the outcome of the decisions (3).

The Grace Commission is also critical of certain excuses given for the failure of OSD's top managers to perform top-management functions:

> If the top managers do not have time to plan ahead, and to set goals and manage by objectives, how can they possibly expect their subordinate managers to do so? We were told repeatedly that goal setting was more difficult in government because the profit motive was absent. Our conclusion is that, because there is no profit motive and because there is such a high turnover in top management, there is far greater need for long-term goal setting in government than in the private sector (4).

Nevertheless, while the commission criticized the OSD's excuses for its inattention to strategic planning and organizational structure and its consequent failure to delegate authority, it blamed neither the secretary or defense nor his predecessors for this state of affairs. It is clear that each incumbent and his subordinates have been constrained by equally shortsighted, often externally imposed, piecemeal solutions to earlier organizational problems. Those solutions define current problems and limit the available solutions. The cumulative consequences of these earlier decisions were probably never contemplated and were certainly never sought. As P.D. Larkey observed, no one acquires cirrhosis of the liver by choice; it is acquired one sip at a time over an extended period.

The fact is that responsibility cannot be delegated by fiat. Decentralization requires prior clarification of the purpose, function, or product of each organizational unit, procedures for setting goals and incentives, and an information system that links each of these centers of responsibility to the goals of the organization as a whole. When an organization lacks direction and discipline, decentralization provides an ideal environment for the pursuit of parochial self-interest to the detriment of the organization as a whole. In DOD this propensity is most visible in the behavior of the uniformed services, but parochialism permeates the organization.

Unfortunately, OSD has no authority to redesign DOD into an efficient and effective operation. As the Grace Commission pointed out, where the secretary of defense had the authority to act, he has acted. In both the Defense Logistics Agency and the Defense Mapping Agency, the two largest operating units under the direct authority of the OSD, the commission observed experienced senior managers, clear objectives, effective decentralization, and high performance levels.

Although OSD cannot redesign DOD, it can decide where certain decisions will be made. When subordinates cannot be trusted to make sound decisions or to understand the implications of their decisions, the locus of decision making shifts upward, as it has in OSD. Indeed, this shifting of responsibility is a recurring problem in most organizations. Superiors are more capable of recognizing their own advantages than they are of recognizing their subordinates' advantages. One of the major aims of managerial training is learning how to overcome this bias. In the DOD, structural problems make it almost overwhelming.

132

II. ITS PRESCRIPTIONS

The Grace Commission report proposed a radical redesign of OSD/DOD. Its key recommendations included:

1. Reorganization of the civilian management functions of the OSD, perhaps along the lines of the DOD program budget categories, with separate deputy secretaries for production and R & D acquisitions.

2. Careful delineation of organizational units performing line and staff functions.

3. Further pruning of decision making and review committees.

4. Elimination of the civilian military departments: air force, army, and navy.

5. Reorganization and redefinition of the role of Joint Chiefs of Staff (JCS).

6. OSD assumption of responsibility for the delivery of civilian support services: base support operations, wholesale warehousing, traffic management, contract administration, audit, direct health care, and overseas military sales.

This last recommendation would consolidate many of the functions currently performed by the services under the direct authority of OSD. Consolidation, however, is not inconsistent with the commission's endorsement of decentralization. Rather, the report concludes that, so far as civilian support services are concerned, decentralization along service lines makes no sense - that it would be better to organize them on regional or geographic lines.

This conclusion may also be read as an implicit criticism of the procurement decentralization program adopted by Secretary of Defense Caspar Weinberger as part of the so-called Carlucci Initiatives. This program has trimmed the power of central planning units in the OSD and increased the role of the individual service secretaries in the systems acquisition process. The commission did not challenge the thrust of the program, though it observed that "after more than a year, the Initiatives are still mostly top-level talk and grass roots inaction. What has been said by the Pentagon policy makers is not being done. This is sad...Most Managers in industry and government alike believe that [many of] the changes...proposed by these initiatives...will be helpful in reducing the cost...of major weapons systems" (5).

The report also hints at a similar dissatisfaction with military organization by noting that a dominant theme of Eisenhower reorganization (Defense Reorganization Act of 1958) was the reorganization of combat command along regional lines. In theory, the area commands created during the Eisenhower administration were to be the principal instruments of United States defense policy, each using forces supplied by all four services. The services were to recruit, train, and equip forces for combat. Einsenhower believed that area commanders were best situated and motivated to plan operations, to carry out assigned combat missions, and to make trade-offs between force size and elements, readiness, sustainability, and investment levels. Furthermore, under this concept, to the extent that they were free to choose between forces offered by competing services, area commanders would have been able to exploit fully the potential benefits of interservice rivalry. However, these benefits would have been realized only if financial or budgetary resources had been provided to the services through the area commands, and the act did not establish this system. Consequently, area commanders are forced to take whatever forces the services choose to supply, and the services retain full administrative control over those forces. Indeed, most area commands are now identified with a single service even where forces from other services are assigned to them.

The Grace Commission report did not explicity endorse the logic of the Eisenhower reorganization, but it did stress that externally imposed organizational constraints severely burden OSD's efforts to use interservice rivalry to advantage (the Grace Commission recognized the benefits that can be gained from intraorganizational rivalry) and to exacerbate its counterproductive aspects.

Some might conclude that the commission overemphasized these constraints, that the report gives too much importance to organizational issues. Eliminating these constraints will not automatically produce a better alignment between military purpose and organizational structure; nor will a good organization guarantee a sound, effectively implemented defense policy. But DOD labors under bad organization, and bad organization makes both wise policy and effective implementation impossible. S.E. Huntington correctly observed that: "Criticism has been directed at many aspects of Defense department organization, including, for instance, procedures for weapons procurement. Varied as the criticisms have been, however, they have tended to focus on the strategic side of the defense establishment-i.e., how decisions are made on overall policy, on the development of military forces, programs, and weapons, and on the use of military force. Those criticisms tend to articulate in a variety of ways a single underlying theme: that there is a gap between defense organization and strategic purpose. This gap is the result of the failure to achieve the purpose of organizational reforms instituted 25 years ago" (6).

III. RIGHT DISEASE, WRONG PATIENTS

The problem with the Grace Commission's diagnosis is not that it is wrong but that it may be irrelevant. To carry out the prescribed reforms, Congress would have to delegate OSD enough authority to manage its operations and to allocate and deploy its resources. Congress has shown no predisposition to do that. On the contrary, Congress has increasingly used its legislative and fiscal powers to deny operational authority to executive branch managers. Indeed, to say that government does not delegate authority well is largely to say that Congress does not delegate authority at all.

Centralized authority is not principally characterized by policy direction from the top, hierarchically established goals, or even central control procedures - all of these may be characteristics of effectively decentralized organizations. Rather, centralized authority is characterized by ex ante controls (i.e., rules and regulations that specify what must be done, where, how, and by whom, and what must not be done) as opposed to ex post controls (i.e., incentives). Congress has always been predisposed to rely on ex ante controls: the organization of OSD, the structure and functions of the JCS, and the missions of the uniformed services are all written into law, as are policies governing

135

staffing, promotion, termination, and compensation of DOD personnel. Recently, however, Congress has increased the rigor and specificity of these controls, especially concerning the military budget and procurement regulations.

Budgets in the private sector are generally used to decentralize authority and responsibility. While most large firms produce comprehensive operating reports describing most aspects of the performance of responsibility centers and programs, their budgets seldom contain many details. Nor should they. In this context, the purpose of a budget is to establish performance targets that are high enough to elicit the best efforts from an organization's operating managers. Conceivably, such budgets could contain a single number for each responsibility center (e.g., a sales quota, a unit cost standard, or a profit or return on investment target).

In contrast, the legislative budget tends to centralize authority. For the most part, operating managers in DOD can do only what the Defense Appropriations Act says they can do; they cannot do what they are not authorized to do. Furthermore, the legislative budget focuses exclusively on resources to be acquired by individual organizational units and how they are to be used-on objects-of-expenditure or line items, rather than performance targets. Congress could delegate the authority to manage resources to OSD by reducing the individual line items to a handful and by delegating substantial reprogramming authority (i.e., the authority to transfer funds between programs/line items and time periods) to OSD. Instead, it has done the reverse. In fiscal year 1960, the Defense Appropriations Act contained about 200 individual line items; in 1983 there were more than 1,200. Moreover, about two-thirds of these line-items are now placed in the "special interest" category. In these cases, DOD is denied even the minuscule reprogramming authority ($2 million on R & D programs and $5 million on procurement) elsewhere delegated to it. Furthermore, when Congress fails to pass an appropriations act before the beginning of the fiscal year - as is usually the case - DOD remains locked into the previous year's spending schedule on each line item.

The legislative budget now leaves the DOD little flexibility to manage its resources in a cost-effective fashion. What DOD can do is sacrifice performance, stretch out acquisitions programs, and play games with Congress - which is, of course, what it does. While these behaviors are perhaps evidence of managerial initiative within DOD/OSD, they are not perceived that way by Congress. Consequently, congressional dissatisfaction with what it views as failures, on the part of DOD in particular and the executive branch in general, has led to still greater congressional involvement in the details of administration and the elaboration of ever-stricter and more detailed ex ante controls.

Not only does Congress decide what DOD will buy, but it also tells DOD how to buy. More than 60 percent of DOD outlays are for the procurement of goods and services supplied by the private sector. These acquisitions are directly or indirectly governed by at least thirty public laws; the regulations that have been elaborated to implement these laws comprise over 8,000 pages of the **Federal Register**. Moreover, the relevant portions of the **Code of Federal Regulations** increased by one-third during the 1970s, while the sections of the **Federal Register** relevant to defense acquisitions more than doubled.

These regulations are supposed to protect the Treasury and also to ensure other outcomes deemed worthwhile by Congress-that most constituencies are recipients of defense spending, that small and minority businesses get their "fair share" of contracts and subcontracts, that contractors maintain proper security and comply with the standards of Occupational Safety and Health Administration, Environmental Protection Agency, Federal Employees Pay Council, and other agencies. However, the Grace Commission correctly observed that these regulations frequently prevent the DOD from making timely and efficient acquisitions, deny suppliers prompt payment, and result in substantial compliance costs. The commission also provided an implicit estimate of these costs. Most large firms and other governments and jurisdictions realize savings of 3 to 15 percent by purchasing petroleum products on long-term contracts awarded by competitive bid. However, because of the costs of complying with cumbersome, legislatively mandated procurement regulations, many petroleum-product suppliers refuse to offer discounts to DOD. Consequently, DOD pays market prices for about 80 percent of its petroleum products. This implies that the cost of complying with procurement regulations represents 5 to 10 percent of

137

the cost of supplying services to the DOD, or $8 billion to $15 billion annually. Of course, these regulations frequently make sense, and the costs of complying with them must often be borne to avoid even worse outcomes. The point is not that complex procurement regulations are unnecessary but that Congress denies DOD the discretion to determine where to exercise judgment and where to exercise specific rules.

Finally, Congress has long reserved the right to review all DOD proposals to close domestic military bases or installations. However, during the mid-1970s it increased the burden of proof that DOD must bear if it is to justify closure. The Grace Commission report concludes: "The legislation of the mid-1970s has had the effect of making it extremely difficult to close or realign bases. Little has been done for almost four years, even though previous secretaries and top OSD officials...believe the current base structure is underutilized" (7).

If centralization within OSD is regrettable (though bad organization is probably better than disorganization), centralization of managerial authority in the hands of Congress is a disaster. In the first place, Congress's distinctive competence is not management. Its proper function is the aggregation and articulation of interests and values, a function it performs best when it deals with broad national issues that demand the attention and scrutiny of the majority of its members. In the second place, the task is overwhelming. Despite the 600 percent increase in budget line items and in witnesses called to testify in committee hearings on the defense budget between 1960 and 1983, Congress still holds only one hour of hearings for each $100 million it spends on defense.

To cope with this increased workload, Congress has increased its internal division of labor and jurisdiction - in 1960, twenty committees and subcommittees in both houses heard testimony on the military budget; in 1983, defense witnesses testified in hearings before ninety-six committees and subcommittees. Unfortunately, undisciplined decentralization is just as conducive to narrow self-seeking in Congress as it is in any other organization. One of the well-recognized consequences of the progressive devolution of authority in Congress - from the party leadership to committee chairmen, then

138

to subcommittee chairmen, and finally to the individual members-has been an increased responsiveness to special constituency interests and the rise of pork barrel politics. As Congress has immersed itself in ever-greater administrative detail, it has also given less attention to what public money buys for the citizenry at large and more attention to how and where it is spent and who gets it.

IV. MILITARY R & D AND PROCUREMENT PROGRAMS

The effect of the shift in the locus of operational authority - first to OSD, then to Congress, and finally to the subcommittee level of Congress or lower - is perhaps most evident in military R & D and procurement programs, as are the consequences of constituency politics. Decisions to initiate, expand, or terminate programs are now routinely made by Congress rather than by OSD. Most students of the procurement process believe that an optimal R & D/acquisition strategy would feature a high degree of experimentation at the concept exploration and testing phase of the systems-development process, carry at least two competitive systems prototype development, and ruthlessly select systems for procurement from those available for production, producing a relatively small number of new systems at optimal production rates. This process is called the "acquisition funnel." What Congress chooses to do is almost the complete opposite. It is critical of experimentation at each phase of the R & D process; apparently Congress would prefer each systems-development program to contemplate a distinct military mission. Congress also tends to buy every system available for production, even those OSD has tried to kill. Since it cannot afford to produce every system at optimal volumes or rates, almost all of its purchases involve inefficient production rates and therefore excessive unit costs.

This pattern may be wasteful, but it is perfectly rational from the standpoint of constituency interests. R & D projects generate relatively few jobs in a small number of congressional districts; systems procurement produces a large number of jobs in many districts. Production stretch-outs affect unit costs and annual outlays, but they have minimal effects on direct employment levels. Of course, the same level of procurement spending at efficient rates would generate roughly the same number of jobs in about the same number of districts. But the logic of special interest

139

politics tends to be blind to this fact. People are far more likely to participate in the political process to protect what they have than on behalf of a potential opportunity.

Before 1980, OSD responded to congressional propensities with heroic efforts to defend the acquisition funnel and achieved some notable successes (e.g., the lightweight fighter program or the army's multiple launch rocket systems program). However, OSD's efforts were not generally successful. Typically, OSD would propose a responsible R & D and acquisiton budget that featured many experiments and few systems for procurement; Congress would then modify the budget by pruning the number of experiments (particularly those involving the greatest technological risk), by increasing the number of systems procured, and by reducing the procurement rates on most of the systems proposed for acquisition by DOD. Over the long run this pattern of interaction between OSD and Congress substantially eroded the United States's military-capital stock.

Top officials of the Reagan administration have apparently abandoned the largely futile defense of the funnel - although it retains a prominent place in the Carlucci Initiatives. Rather, they appear to be trying to exploit Congress's propensities to rebuild the depleted defense capital stock. Having observed that congressional appropriations are a function of DOD requests (Congress influences what DOD will buy but exercises little control over total outlay levels), OSD has in recent years simply asked for everything, including a substantial number of systems that previous administrations had opposed (e.g., AV-8 Harrier) and several systems that are still in the preproduction phase of development.

The payoff to this strategy is illustrated by the cruise missile program. Previous administrations would have likely tried to develop two systems and recommended procurement of one of them. Congress would then have supported the production of a smaller number of both. OSD actually supported the development of five distinct systems performing five distinct missions and requested funds to deploy all five systems, and that is what Congress approved. While none of these systems is currently being produced at an optimal rate, DOD may get twice as many cruise missiles under its current legislative strategy as it would have under its earlier, more prudent approach.

The payoff to DOD's current strategy is also evident when it operates under the authority of continuing resolution (i.e., when Congress fails to pass a defense appropriation act before the beginning of the fiscal year - something it has failed to do in thirty of the past thirty -three years). Efficient production rates imply a moderately high rate of production startups and shutdowns. Under continuing resolution, existing programs must shut down on schedule, but new procurement programs cannot start up until they have been approved. However, under the current OSD strategy, nearly everything that can be produced is already in production and almost no program is scheduled for termination. Consequently, procurement rates are not substantially affected by Congress's inability to enact a budget on schedule.

Furthermore, DOD has resurrected some of the budget ploys it abandoned during the McNamara era, when they were used primarily by the services against OSD (e.g., the "Washington Monument" game, in which DOD claims that failure to provide the desired budget will mean the sacrifice of its highest priority activities; "foot-in-the-door," often combined with the negotiation of high project termination penalties; "coercive deficiency," in which DOD exhausts outlay authority on high-priority projects early enough in the fiscal year to demand a supplemental appropriation, and "take-or-leave-it," in which DOD presents Congress with a single price-quantity production acquisition option). Not surprisingly, the Grace Commission was appalled by the incoherence and waste that have resulted from OSD's attempts to exploit congressional propensities and primly criticized DOD for paying more attention to what Congress will buy than to the cost-effectiveness of its proposals (8).

The commission concluded that since Congress has refused to kill production programs, DOD should:

- Install self-disciplinary limits on the number of new weapons programs started each year (9).

- Subject every new program to in-depth affordability review over the projected life cycle of the program.

- Review new-start affordability in relation to all

141

other new starts being proposed and programs already in the system.

- Base affordability on [realistic] estimates of DOD total budget resources and price escalation for the ten-year planning period (10).

Undoubtedly, OSD would prefer to execute its rebuilding program in a cost-effective fashion; taken as a whole, perhaps Congress would, too. But given actual circumstances, OSD will continue to take what Congress appropriates. DOD could act unilaterally, but it will not; neither will Congress.

V. PROSPECTS FOR COOPERATION

If one assumes that Congress is as much a victim of its own earlier decisions as OSD and that it never contemplated the indirect or longer-term consequences of its reliance on **ex ante** controls, there may be some hope for improvement. Such an assumption is consistent with claims made by most members of Congress that they would gladly relinquish their involvement with the details of administration, if only DOD would demonstrate the competence and the motivation to manage its own affairs. Furthermore, most legislators (unlike their staffers) appear to have a profound respect for their own limited capabilities to manage DOD and to be fully cognizant of their inability to resist special-interest demands when they are forced to do so by OSD failures.

In any case, if this assumption is valid, the situation is a classic prisoner's dilemma. That is, both OSD and Congress would be better off if they cooperated - if Congress were to delegate to OSD the authority as well as the responsibility it needs to manage its own affairs and if the DOD did not use that flexibility to extract higher appropriations from Congress. Unfortunately, cooperation requires trust and, based on recent experience, Congress has no reason to trust the DOD. Nor, if history is any guide, will DOD trust Congress. DOD has chosen to defend its activities piecemeal, because of the fear that, if Congress did not have to face the tough realities of cutting specific programs, it would make across-the-board budget cuts, rationalizing its action by the claim that DOD could easily be 5 or 10 percent more efficient. Given this choice on the part of DOD, detailed congressional involvement in the management of

142

DOD resources is hardly surprising.

However, in this case the past may not be the best predictor of the future. Historical analogy overlooks two considerations. First, Congress seems nearly as committed to rebuilding United States defenses as the administration. In the near term, the prospect of an across-the-board cut is an unlikely one. Second, OSD is no longer playing the game to lose. What was a winning game for Congress during the 1970s and a losing game for DOD has become a losing game for both, given Congress' commitment to rebuilding United States defenses. Game theorists say it is easier to convert lose-lose situations to win-win than it is to convert lose-win situations to win-win. This conversion, however, requires a contract or treaty that would address the legitimate concerns of both Congress and OSD. Not coincidentally, within a few months of the publication of the Grace Commission report on DOD, the Committee for Economic Development (CED) presented its recommendations on reform of the Federal budget process, which included the outline of just such a treaty (11). The CED's key proposal is a multi-year legislative budget oriented primarily to total obligation authority (initially providing real increases of, perhaps, 3 to 4 percent a year) and containing guidelines to the allocation of resources between major programs and budget categories. Under multi-year budgeting, Congress would still engage in an annual review of defense spending. For example, given the three-year legislative budget suggested by the CED, Congress would annually add a fourth year to replace the year expiring. However, as J.S. Gansler observed, "this overlap, unlike the current overlap, would force both the executive and the legislative branch to plan for the longer term - something that neither is able to do today " (12). Furthermore, if Congress denied itself the opportunity to tinker with individual line items (perhaps by requiring a two-thirds majority in both houses to reopen the budget issue for either the current fiscal year or the first out-year and by collapsing the number of individual line items to a manageable number), it would provide itself with the opportunity to do what it was designed to do, to "analyze the correlation between national policy objectives and the budget-something else that is not done today (13). By typing its own hands, Congress would also pre-empt strategic gaming on the part of DOD. Additional proposals might include:

1. Full authority to execute the multi-year budget should be delegated to OSD and not to the uniformed services. OSD must have both greater authority and flexibility if it is to manage efficient and effective programs.

2. Congress should require OSD to provide it with far better operational reports-including information on the performance of each major program and program element: capabilities, readiness, and sustainability status of each of the regional commands; and comparative data on the cost-effectiveness with which each of the uniformed services have performed their missions as force suppliers.

Flexibility is a necessary but not a sufficient condition for improved management of DOD. Congress must demand evidence that delegation of authority has resulted in higher military performance. DOD must supply that evidence-otherwise, Congress may reassert the panoply of ex ante controls under which OSD currently labors. (Indeed, given the conditions outlined here, the threat that ex ante controls will be reasserted if DOD performance is unsatisfactory is very probably Congress's most powerful ex post control.

The multi-year budget provides a framework for the implementation of the Grace Commission's proposals on OSD/DOD management climate and organization. Such a contract would address the legitimate concerns of both Congress and DOD. The real problem is negotiating it. The OMB director might effectively manage the executive branch's side of the issue. However, the military appropriations subcommittee chairs would be the obvious spokespersons for Congress-they would also be almost the only members of Congress who would stand to lose from such a contract. This would not appear to augur well for the prospects of negotiating such a contract, but even subcommittee chairs can act contrary to their own narrow self-interest where matters of national importance are concerned (e.g., former Senator Howard Cannon and trucking deregulation).

VI. CONCLUSIONS

Defense spending is both overcontrolled and out of control. It is governed by too many rules and not enough (or the wrong kinds of) policy direction. Obviously, this situation cannot be corrected by the imposition of more rules: further congressional attempts to manage DOD will merely exacerbate an already bad situation. Carried to its logical conclusion, the Grace Commission report may be read as a plea to Congress to base its relationship with DOD on far-sighted, self-denying ordinances that would exempt DOD operations from detailed prior scrutiny or control. It is also a plea to OSD to accept the responsibility that goes with the authority to manage its own affairs. These are timely pleas. Cost-effectiveness is the consequence of, not the cause of, effective management. The world in which we live is dangerous, our treasure is finite, and we can ill-afford less than the best from our defense efforts, let alone the instability, waste, and incoherence that we now have.

FOOTNOTES

1. President's Private Sector Survey on Cost Control (Grace Commission), Task Force Report on the Office of the Secretary of Defense (13 July 1983).

2. See, e.g., General Accounting Office - Congressional Budget Office, Analysis of the Grace Commission's Recommendations on Cost Control (March 1984).

3. Grace Commission report, 47-48.

4. Ibid., 49.

5. Ibid., 58.

6. S.E. Huntington, "Defense Organization and Military Strategy," Public Interest, No. 75 (Spring 1984): 21.

7. Grace Commission report, 107.

8. Ibid., 182.

9. Ibid., 178.

10. Ibid., 85.

11. Committee for Economic Development, Strengthening the Federal Budget Process: A Requirement for Effective Fiscal Control (June 1983).

12. Jacques S. Gansler, "Reforming the Defense Budget Process," Public Interest, No. 75 (Spring 1984): 68.

13. Ibid., 69.

PART III

BUDGET DEFICIT-REDUCING MEASURES:

A REVENUE PERSPECTIVE

CHAPTER 8

REFORMING THE FEDERAL TAX SYSTEM: A THEORETICAL PERSPECTIVE*

Subcommittee on Goal
and Intergovernmental Policy

I. INTRODUCTION

In recent years, the Federal income tax has come under increasing attack from taxpayers, businessmen, and professional economists who believe its problems have grown so serious they can no longer be solved simply by tinkering with individual provisions in the tax code. Complete and comprehensive reform of the income tax, with all the problems cleaned up at the same time, has become the only reasonable way of improving the system. Tax reform will be one of the most important issues facing the 99th Congress.

On Monday, November 26, the Treasury Department submitted a tax simplification plan to President Reagan, as he requested during his January 1984 State of the Union Message. This plan may form the core of any tax reform legislation submitted to Congress by President Reagan. In addition, during the 98th Congress, almost two dozen comprehensive tax reform bills were introduced. Academics and trade associations have also fielded tax reform plans. Each of these plans entails a different approach to tax reform, but all promise a complete overhaul of the existing system.

This increased interest in comprehensive tax reform has occurred because, by virtually every criterion, our tax system falls short. It fails to raise enough revenues to fund the government. It is riddled with unjustifiable deductions, exclusions, credits, and other preferences that erode the tax base while making the tax code incomprehensible to the vast majority of taxpayers. It distorts investment decisions, causing billions of dollars to be wasted in unproductive tax shelters while pressing capital needs go unmet. It violates all the principles of tax fairness. It has become a source of economic

---

* U.S. Congress Joint Economic Committee on Goal and Intergovernmental Policy, Tax REform: A Staff Study (Washington, D.C., GPO, 1985).

instability and an impediment to intelligent personal
and business planning.

In addition to broad agreement that the income tax
should be thoroughly revised, a consensus is developing
on the right kind of tax reform. Virtually all of the
major tax reform proposals would broaden the tax base
by eliminating most of the existing deductions,
exclusions, and credits while at the same time reducing
marginal tax rates. Most aim at revenue neutrality,
though some taxpayers would pay more and some less.
The differences fall into four main areas:

- The choice of the tax base, with some
  proponents of reform advocating that the base
  should be consumption rather than income;

- The degree of rate progressivity, with proposals
  ranging from a straight flat tax to progressive
  tax;

- The treatment of details, with proposals
  differing over the list of deductions to retain
  and eliminate, how to treat capital gains and
  losses, whether to retain indexation of the
  zero-bracket amount and the tax brackets,
  whether to permit indexation of capital basis
  and interest rates, how to treat depreciation of
  capital, and whether to change deductions into
  credits; and

- Taxation of corporate income, with some reform
  advocates suggesting that the corporate income
  tax be eliminated by integrating it with the
  personal income tax.

This study will address these issues in two steps.

First, it will develop the reasons why we should
replace our present complex and inequitable tax system
with a simplified progressive income tax that would
broaden the tax base and reduce tax rates. Second, it
will present recommendations for handling some of the
detailed problems that will be encountered in designing
an appropriate simplified progressive income tax.

Although there are a number of tax reform proposals, three have merited the most serious attention:

- The Fair tax (H.R. 3271, S. 1421), introduced by

150

Senator Bill Bradley and Congressman Richard Gephardt. This is a broad-based income tax with a progressive rate structure and a top marginal tax rate of 30 percent. It would retain and reform the corporate income tax.

- The Fair And Simple (FAST) tax (H.R. 6165, S. 2948), introduced by Congressman Jack Kemp and Senator Bob Kasten. This is also a broad-based income tax, but with a single 25 percent flat tax rate. It is a mildly progressive tax, however, because it increases the standard deduction and the personal exemption and exempts 20 percent of earned income up to about $40,000. It would also retain a separate tax on corporate income.

- The Treasury Department's tax simplification proposal. This would resemble the Fair tax in that it would broaden the base and incorporate a simplified progressive rate structure, but with a top marginal tax rate of 35 percent. It differs from the Fair and FAST tax proposals mainly in the list of tax preferences that would be replaced or limited and in the treatment of indexing. The corporate profits tax would be retained and revised, but would be partially integrated with the personal income tax.

All three of these proposals are simplified progressive income taxes that differ primarily in degree of progressivity and the details of how taxable income would be computed. The Fair tax and the FAST tax have been widely analyzed and, with selected changes, either could constitute a significant improvement over the present Federal income tax. The Treasury proposal follows the same broad outlines as the Fair and FAST tax proposals, but certain specific provisions in the proposal could pose serious problems.

II. THE PRINCIPLES OF TAX REFORM

The present income tax is held in such disrepute because it violates virtually every principle of taxation. Although it would be naive to suggest that tax reform legislation could escape the pressures that have pummeled the present tax system, any new tax system that disregards basic tax principles would likely be as bad as the current one. The following principles should form an adequate basis for judging among the different approaches to tax reform:

1. **Revenues.** The main purpose of the tax system is to
generate the revenues needed to finance the legitimate
activities of the Federal Government.

Our current tax system falls far short of meeting
this goal. According to the most recent figures from
the Office of Management and Budget (OMB), we will have
deficits in the range of $190 billion to $210 billion
per year into the indefinite future, even with
continued strong growth (1). This is a disturbing
break with the past. Until recently, the tax system
successfully funded the Federal Government. As Chart I
shows, tax revenues came to 97.5 percent of Federal
spending during the 1950's and 95.6 percent during the
1960's. In the 1970's, the overall revenue/spending
ration fell to 90.7 percent--a significant decline but
one largely attributable to the major recessions during
the Nixon and Ford Administrations.

Even though the revenue-raising goal of taxation
was gradually eroded by other goals following World War
II, the view was still widely accepted through the
1970's that, at least in years of relatively full
employment, the government should be funded primarily
by tax revenues. All previous postwar Administrations
have accepted the fact that the Federal Government must
run a deficit during recessions, with the revenue gap
filled by Treasury borrowing the needed funds in the
private credit market. These deficits, however, have
always been considered temporary, to be reduced and
eliminated as the economy recovered and resumed its
normal growth.

With the proposal and enactment of the Economic
Recovery Tax Act of 1981 (ERTA), however, this
Administration officially abandoned the goal of funding
the government through tax revenues in favor of the
view that the incentive effects of taxation should
take precedence over revenue needs. As a result, even
after accounting for the revenues raised by enactment
of the Tax Reform Act of 1984, taxes will fund only 80
percent of spending from Fiscal 1985 onward, as Chart I
shows. This represents a permanent 20 percent revenue
shortfall. Despite the hope expressed by President
Reagan during the fall election campaign that growth
would eliminate the deficit, even OMB now admits that
huge deficits will persist year after year unless we
make fundamental changes in tax and spending policies.

CHART 1

Federal Receipts As A Percent of Outlays
1950 to 1989

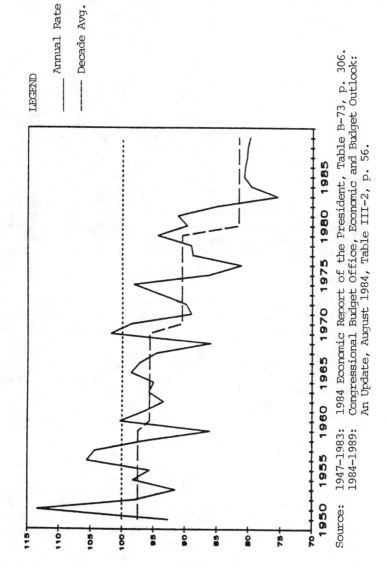

LEGEND

——— Annual Rate

------- Decade Avg.

Source: 1947-1983: 1984 Economic Report of the President, Table B-73, p. 306.
         1984-1989: Congressional Budget Office, Economic and Budget Outlook:
                     An Update, August 1984, Table III-2, p. 56.

153

Some fraction of the deficit can be erased by cutting spending. But, as OMB Director David Stockman has said, spending has been cut to the bone (2). A major part of any serious attempt to reduce the revenue shortfall will require an increase in taxes.

Unfortunately, the three major tax reform proposals were all designed to be revenue neutral, generating no more revenues in 1985 than the present tax system. Although all three plans could yield more revenue growth in the future, since they would repeal a long list of deductions and exclusions that have been growing at a more rapid rate in recent years than has the tax base, none of the proposals would make a substantial improvement in the revenue shortfall. Generating adequate revenues should be an integral goal of tax reform, not a separate issue. All three major reform proposals thus need to be altered, either by further broadening the tax base or by incorporating slightly higher or more progressive tax rates.

2. **Stabilization.** The Federal tax system should contribute to economic stability over the business cycle by cushioning cycle-related swings in consumer and business incomes.

Discretionary changes in fiscal and monetary policy can be powerful tools for improving economic performance during recessions or periods of high inflation, but discretionary policy measures take time to enact and implement -- a lag that can be filled by automatic stabilizers which act without the need for new legislation.

Until recently, the Federal income tax has acted as an automatic stabilizer because the rate structure is progressive. Tax revenues have usually declined more rapidly than incomes during recessions and have risen more rapidly during expansions, thus cushioning swings in disposable income. ERTA reduced the ability of the income tax to act as an automatic stabilizer by incorporating the proposal to index tax brackets for inflation. During upswings, the tax system will no longer act as a brake on inflation. In fact, the income tax may become a destabilizing influence, since the annual tax rate reduction will be larger with higher inflation.

The major tax reform proposals will be nominally less progressive than the present income tax, and so they will contribute less to economic stabilization over the business cycle. The FAST tax, with a single flat tax rate and indexing of exemptions, would be least stabilizing. The Fair tax, which eliminates indexing and has a progressive rate structure, would be most stabilizing.

3. **Fairness.** The tax system should be a progressive one, with taxes levied on the basis of ability to pay. Taxpayers with equal incomes, regardless of source, should pay roughly equal taxes, while taxpayers with higher incomes should pay more tax than those with lower incomes.

More than 2,000 years ago, Plato wrote in Book 1 of The Republic: "When there is an income tax, the just man will pay more and the unjust less on the same amount of income." Recent polls indicate that Americans consider the Federal income tax to be the most unjust of all taxes (3). This reflects the fact that many taxpayers, particularly the wealthy, pay less than their fair share of taxes because of their ability to use, and abuse, loopholes in the tax code that are not available to the average taxpayer. To be judged as fair, a tax system must meet two requirements. One is horizontal fairness -- taxpayers with the same ability to pay taxes should pay roughly the same amount of tax. The other is vertical fairness -- taxpayers with a greater ability to pay taxes should pay more tax.

Just over 70 years ago, we made the income tax the core of our tax system, reflecting the widely held belief that income is the best measure of ability to pay taxes. It is not ideal, since people with the same income may have different financial obligations and thus may differ in their ability to pay taxes. But the income tax recognizes this by permitting certain deductions -- such as the zero-bracket amount and the personal exemptions, the deductions for catastrophic medical and casualty expenses, and the deduction for costs incurred in earning an income -- to assure that the tax burden is not distributed unfairly. With these allowances, tax fairness requires that those with equal incomes, regardless of the source, pay approximately the same amount of tax.

For the past 70 years, we as a Nation have also been solidly committed to progressive taxation, holding that wealthier taxpayers should pay a higher fraction of their income in taxes than their less fortunate counterparts down the income scale.

Although one argument for the progressive income tax is to reduce the inequality of income distribution, the most powerful reason for progressive taxation is that those with the highest incomes receive the greatest benefits from our system of stable government and free enterprise and thus should contribute the most to its support and preservation. Individual incomes are based primarily on ability to produce. But no one would be able to fully exercise his or her ability to earn income if the Federal Government did not fulfill its responsibilities to preserve free enterprise, keep us safe from foreign enemies, enforce contracts, prevent crime, develop a nationwide system of transportation and communications, encourage education, stabilize the economy, and regulate trade both within the United States and with foreign countries. By permitting those with special abilities to earn as much as they can, the government confers a blessing that must be paid for. As William Jennings Bryan said to the Democratic National Convention in 1896:

> The income tax is just. It simply intends to put the burdens of government on the backs of the people. I am in favor of an income tax. When I find a man who is not willing to bear his share of the burdens of the government which protects him, I find a man who is unworthy to enjoy the blessings of a government like ours.

The degree of progressivity is a matter of personal preference. Few, however, would disagree with the principle of progressive taxation.

Our present income tax, for all its other faults, is progressive. As Table I shows, the average tax burden rises with income. For example, in 1982, the average tax paid by those with adjusted gross incomes (AGI's) of less than $5,000 came to 2.8 percent of income, while those with AGI's of $1,000,000 or more paid an average of 39.3 percent. Taxpayers in between paid intermediate but rising amounts.

In other ways, however, the Federal income tax does not measure up to the basic principles of tax fairness. Because of the many deductions, credits, and exclusions in the tax code, it is quite possible for taxpayers with the same incomes to pay widely varying

TABLE I
AVERAGE TAX RATES BY INCOME CLASS
1981-1982

| Size Of Adjusted Gross Income | Filers With Income Tax Liability | | | | Percent Of Filers With No Income Tax Liability |
| | Average Tax (Whole Dollars) | | Tax As Percent Of Adjusted Gross Income | | |
	1981 (1)	1982 (2)	1981 (3)	1982 (4)	1982 (5)
Total	$ 3,703	$ 3,604	16.5	15.4%	19.2%
Less than $1,000	8,626*	9,298*	--	--	99.6
$ 1,000 under $ 3,000	123	92	6.0	5.0	95.0
$ 3,000 under $ 5,000	120	117	2.9	2.8	41.9
$ 5,000 under $ 7,000	357	321	5.9	5.4	31.4
$ 7,000 under $ 9,000	571	521	7.1	6.5	20.7
$ 9,000 UNDER $ 11,000	834	746	8.3	7.4	6.8
$ 11,000 under $ 13,000	1,160	1,026	9.7	8.6	4.0
$ 13,000 under $ 15,000	1,498	1,324	10.7	9.5	2.3
$ 15,000 under $ 17,000	1,830	1,665	11.5	10.4	1.5
$ 17,000 under $ 19,000	2,179	2,001	12.1	11.1	1.8
$ 19,000 under $ 22,000 M	2,645	2,399	12.9	11.7	1.2
$ 22,000 under $ 25,000	3,209	2,956	13.7	12.6	1.3
$ 25,000 under $ 30,000	3,976	3,676	14.5	13.4	0.6
$ 30,000 under $ 35,000	5,103	4,605	15.7	14.2	0.5
$ 35,000 under $ 40,000	6,370	5,743	17.1	15.4	0.5
$ 40,000 under $ 50,000	8,379	7,468	18.9	16.9	0.5
$ 50,000 under $ 75,000	13,050	11,803	22.2	20.1	0.5
$ 75,000 under $ 100,000	22,867	20,865	26.8	24.5	0.4
$ 100,000 under $ 150,000	36,323	33,321	30.9	27.9	0.2
$ 150,000 under $ 200,000	58,439	54,447	34.2	31.8	0.5
$ 200,000 under $ 300,000	88,930	82,400	37.2	34.3	0.2
$ 300,000 under $ 500,000	149,990	135,233	40.1	36.2	0.1
$ 500,000 under $1,000,000	278,182	252,751	41.8	37.8	0.1
$1,000,000 or more	925,655	877,132	44.0	39.3	0.1

* For many taxpayers at this level, includes amounts of additional tax for tax preferences.
M = Median taxpayer.
Source: U.S. Department of the Treasury, Internal Revenue Service. Statistics of Income Bulletin, Fall 1984. p.73.

157

amounts of tax. Furthermore, tax preferences let some taxpayers with high AGI's face lower tax rates than other taxpayers further down the income scale (4). In fact, in every income group -- even among those with AGI's in excess of $1,000,000 -- there were some taxpayers in 1982 who paid no tax, as Table I shows.

The main source of tax inequity is the long list of preferences that are not available to all taxpayers on even terms. The Joint Committee on Taxation lists 108 deductions, credits, exemptions, and other preferences in the tax code, including those affecting corporations, that can be used to shelter income from taxes (5). This is double the number -- 53 -- listed in 1970 (6). Many tax preferences, particularly those which reduce the rate of tax on capital income, primarily benefit those at the top of the income scale. In addition, according to the Joint Committee on Taxation, the benefits of even the most widely used itemized deductions are concentrated among those earning $30,000 or more (7).

Prior to 1981, tax reduction bills sought to concentrate the benefits among lower-income and middle-income taxpayers. The Revenue Act of 1971 did this by increasing the standard deduction and the personal exemption. The Tax Reduction Act of 1975 raised the low-income allowance and established a 10 percent earned income credit for low-income families (8). By contrast, ERTA sought to give the largest tax cut to upper-income taxpayers. Although all tax rates were reduced 23 percent over three years, the largest dollar benefit went to those at the top, as Table I shows. In 1982, median taxpayers, with an AGI between $17,000 and $19,000, received an average tax cut of $178. By contrast, the 8,408 wealthiest taxpayers, with AGI's of $1,000,000 or more, received an average $48,523 tax cut -- an amount in excess of the AGI of 95 percent of all taxpayers. Between 1980 and 1982, the average tax liability of those with incomes over $1,000,000 fell by more than $122,000 (9).

The major tax reform proposals are all less progressive in nominal terms than the present income tax. The FAST tax incorporates a single 25 percent tax rate that would apply to all taxable income, while the Fair tax has three rate brackets and a top marginal rate of 30 percent. The Treasury tax simplification plan would also have three rate brackets, but a top marginal tax rate of 35 percent. Although the Treasury plan is nominally more progressive than the Fair tax, with a top rate of 35 percent versus 30 percent for the Fair tax, the overall distribution of the tax burden for both plans will probably be similar since the Fair tax does a more thorough job of closing loopholes and broadening the tax base than does the Treasury plan. Both would retain the Nation's commitment to a progressive income tax while still reducing tax rates.

The FAST tax, despite a flat tax rate, would still be progressive although not as progressive as the Fair tax. First, the proposal would increase the personal exemption and zero-bracket amount. Second, it would exempt 20 percent of wage income up to $40,000, yielding an effective marginal tax rate of only 20 percent on the first $40,000 of earned income. Thus, over the low-income and middle income ranges, the tax burden would gradually rise from zero to 25 percent. The wage exemption would be gradually phased out for those making more than $40,000, so the marginal tax rate would actually rise to about 28 percent for those making up to about $100,000 where it levels off at a flat 25 percent.

The vast majority of middle-income taxpayers would pay no more tax under the Fair tax than they do at present, according to the Joint Committee on Taxation. Unlike most flat tax proposals, there would be no redistribution of the tax burden from upper-income taxpayers onto those in the middle. Almost 70 percent of all taxpayers, most of whom take the standard deduction rather than itemize, would be taxed at the basic 14 percent tax rate and would actually receive a small tax cut. Those dependent on tax preferences would experience an increase but there would be no major shift of the tax burden among income classes under the Fair tax.

The Treasury plan has not been in circulation long enough to have undergone the kind of scrutiny applied to the Fair tax and so its effect on the middle class is unknown. According to the Treasury Department, the plan was designed so as not to alter the tax burden among income classes, although it would provide some relief to those below the official poverty level. Eighty percent of taxpayers should experience no increase in their tax burden and many may receive tax cuts. If the Treasury's proposal does shift the burden onto the middle class, the rate structure and various specific provisions would have to be altered to prevent this.

The FAST tax, unfortunately, would shift some of the tax burden onto middle-class taxpayers. According to the Joint Committee on Taxation, those making over $100,000 would on average pay less tax under the FAST tax than at present. Those at the bottom would also pay less than at present because the higher personal exemption and the wage exemption would permit families making under $14,000 to pay no Federal income tax. More of the tax burden would thus have to be borne by middle-income taxpayers. Following the massive tax cuts enjoyed by the wealthy under the Economic Recovery Tax Act in 1981, it is not likely that middle-class taxpayers would look favorably on another measure that put even more of the tax burden on their shoulders. The progressive rate structure of the Fair tax and possibly the Treasury plan would thus result in a more equitable distribution of the tax burden than the flat rate of the FAST tax.

There is, however, nothing sacred about the existing tax distribution. The need to raise revenues will require that at least some taxpayers pay more tax than at present. Keeping the current distribution means all taxpayers will face a higher tax burden. There is no reason why the added revenues should not come primarily from those at the top, since they have received the largest tax decreases since 1981. Under all three plans, this could be accomplished by adding another marginal rate bracket which would be higher than currently proposed but still significantly lower than the present top rate of 50 percent. The progressivity of the income tax would be improved while preserving the benefits of lower tax rates.

4. **Efficiency.** The Federal tax system should interfere as little as possible in the allocation of resources. Tax preference should be eliminated unless they serve an important national goal.

Most of the problems with our tax code can be traced to the fact that it has been decimated by a panoply of deductions, exclusions, and credits designed to alter economic behavior. These can be traced to two broad motives. One is to stimulate savings and investment in order to enhance economic growth and productivity, leading to such tax preferences as the investment tax credit, the long-term capital gains exclusion, and the individual retirement account (IRA).

160

The second is to channel resources into particular economic activities, giving rise to such preferences as the credit for energy-saving home improvements, the exclusion of interest on general obligation bonds, and the deduction for charitable contributions.

According to numerous studies, tax preferences can result in a waste of the Nation's resources, particularly by those which only serve the interests of specific industries rather than broad national interests. Ill-advised tax preferences also result in business and investment decisions being based on tax rather than economic consequences. The major tax reform proposals would make a significant improvement because they eliminate all but a handful of the preferences in the present income tax. No tax reform, however, can eliminate the influence of taxes on decision-making. The best we can do is adopt a system which minimizes such interference except through those few preferences which serve important national goals.

5. Simplicity. The personal income tax should be understandable by the individual taxpayer.

For a growing number of Americans, the income tax has become incomprehensible. In 1983, according to the Internal Revenue Service (IRS), professional tax preparers signed the returns of 37.2 million taxpayers -- all influenced by the fear they would miss deductions or pay too much tax if they did not consult a tax professional -- at a cost of more than $3 billion (10). Tax preparation is also time-consuming. One recent study found that the average American taxpayer needs about 21.7 hours to prepare state and Federal income taxes and to maintain necessary records, with actual preparation of the tax forms taking up about one-fifth of the total. With 97 million taxpayers, the total amount of time devoted to tax compliance comes to more than two billion hours per year.

The main culprit is the long list of deductions, exclusions, and credits that make it virtually impossible for the taxpayer to know whether or not he is paying the minimum legal tax or being treated fairly. This has become an increasingly important problem for two reasons. First, as incomes, mortgage interest, and state taxes have gone up in recent years, more people have been itemizing deductions. Second, each new tax bill has added new deductions or exclusions or closed up old loopholes with new rules

161

that must be taken into account by taxpayers in computing their tax liabilities. Recently, IRA's were made available to all taxpayers with earned income, a deduction was enacted for married couples when both work, and a portion of social security benefits was made taxable for upper-income taxpayers. Each change requires additional computations that further increases the complexity of the tax code.

In recent testimony before the Joint Economic Committee, Congressman Richard Gephardt spelled out the implications of a tax system that has grown too complex (11):

> People sense that the law that we are living with today is unfair. And I think the worst part of it is that the American people feel their neighbors and their relatives and their friends are cheating at their expense. They're often right.
> I think they resent having to spend extra hard-earned dollars to hire a tax expert to guide them through what they think is the maze of our tax laws, and I think, as Senator Bradley said, we pay a heavy price for their mistrust.
> It creates compliance problems that we are all aware of . People increasingly believe that it's permissible, in fact necessary, to cheat to some extent and that everybody else is doing it and getting away with it.
> Not only does it make it more difficult for the government to raise the revenues required, but it makes it also harder for the government to accomplish anything in any area. And it's my belief that suspicions about the Tax Code translate into a general distrust and distaste for government.

The major tax reform proposals would reduce the complexity of the tax code for individuals by eliminating many of the special tax preferences. Nonetheless, simplifications should not be carried to the point where it conflicts with other important goals of the tax system. Complex tax preferences that are available to only a limited number of taxpayers and serve only marginally useful purposes should be eliminated. But deductions and exclusions that are widely available and useful should be retained, including the deduction for interest on home mortgages,

the charitable contribution deduction, the deduction
for state and local income and real property taxes, the
exclusion of interest on general obligation bonds, and
a selected list of others that serve a useful social
purpose or contribute to the fairness of the personal
income tax. In his testimony before the Joint Economic
Committee, Professor Musgrave explained the limits to
tax simplification (12):

> The gains in simplification should not be
> exaggerated. The point is that even if
> deductions and exclusions were abolished, it
> would still be necessary to properly
> determine the taxpayer's _net_ income, i.e., to
> determine which items should be included as
> cost of doing business, how costs such as
> depreciation should be measured, and how
> capital gains are to be determined.
> Broadening of the income tax base, while
> greatly desirable in terms of tax equity,
> should not be confused, as it might be in the
> public mind, with the substitution of a tax
> on _gross_ income. In all, simplification
> makes an important contribution but the
> primary gain from base broadening is in
> horizontal equity and the efficiency of the
> income tax.

6.Compliance. The tax system should minimize the
incentive and opportunity for taxpayers to evade
taxation by underreporting income or overstating
deductions and exemptions.

The growing frustration with the Federal tax
system in recent years has lead to a disturbing
increase in tax evasion. The Federal Government
depends heavily on voluntary compliance to enforce the
tax laws. Taxpayers -- both individuals and
corporations -- report their own incomes and compute
their own tax liabilities. If some taxpayers fail to
report all their income or overstate deductions and
exemptions, the result is a reduction in revenues and
higher taxes for law-abiding taxpayers. It also means
that some government resources have to be devoted to
tax-law enforcement that could be put to better use
elsewhere.

The revenue loss from tax evasion is significant
and growing. In 1981, taxpayers failed to report
$249.7 billion in legally earned income (13). This

163

TABLE II

VOLUNTARY REPORTING PERCENTAGES FOR INDIVIDUAL FILERS AND NONFILERS, BY SOURCE OF INCOME, 1973-1981

Category	Percent of Income Reported			
	1973	1976	1979	1981
Wages and salaries	95.4	94.9	94.4	93.9
Dividends	90.7	87.1	85.7	83.7
Interest	87.6	88.1	86.3	86.3
Capital gains	75.7	64.3	63.4	59.4
Nonfarm proprietor income and partnership and small business corporation income	84.0	82.2	80.7	78.7
Farm proprietor income	88.6	92.6	89.5	88.3
Informal supplier income	20.7	20.7	20.7	20.7
Pensions and annuities	81.5	85.3	85.0	85.2
Rents	94.7	94.0	95.4	95.6
Royalties	74.3	65.6	64.2	61.2
Estate and trust income	82.0	79.2	75.7	76.2
State income tax refunds, alimony, and other income	66.0	55.2	62.3	62.0
Total income	91.2	90.4	89.8	89.3

Source: Internal Revenue Service, Income Tax Compliance Research: Estimates for 1973-1981. Washington, D.C.: Internal Revenue Service, July 1983. p.10.

cost the Federal Government $81.5 billion in lost revenues, according to the most recent study of taxpayer compliance by the IRS. Both figures are about triple the unreported income and revenue loss calculated by the IRS for 1973. Unreported income from illegal sources, including drugs, gambling, and prostitution, cost an additional $9 billion in lost tax revenues in 1981.

The IRS calculates that the amount of income reported by individual and corporate taxpayers declined from 91.2 percent in 1973 to 89.3 percent in 1981 (14). As Table II shows, the worst compliance record belongs to taxpayers with income from capital such as dividends, interest, and capital gains, where the IRS has lacked a reliable means of verification. All three tax reform proposals could improve compliance in two ways -- by eliminating preferences that taxpayers can misuse to shelter income and by reducing tax rates to reduce the incentive to cheat. Should this fail to make a significant improvement in compliance, tax reform will have to be supplemented by increased enforcement.

7. **Federalism.** The Federal income tax should not impede the ability of state and local governments to raise the revenues needed to fulfill their responsibilities within our Federal system of government.

The federal income tax currently permits taxpayers to deduct income, property, and sales taxes paid to other levels of government. The interest on bonds issued by state and local governments is also exempt from federal income taxes. These provisions ease the burden of state and local finance on the individual taxpayer and help state and local governments serve public needs. As Table III shows, the exclusion of interest on state and local bonds and the deduction for state and local taxes reduced federal taxes for individuals and corporations by more than $50 billion in 1984. Under current policies, Federal tax support for state and local government finances will rise to $80 billion by 1988. Wholesale repeal of these tax provisions would create intense taxpayer pressure on state and local governments to cut spending and services or to seek more aid from the Federal Government. While the state and local tax deductions and interest exclusion make the tax code more complex and permit some taxpayers to pay less Federal tax than others, they serve an important national interest as

TABLE III

FEDERAL TAX SUBSIDIES
FOR STATE AND LOCAL GOVERNMENTS1/
($ Millions)

Tax Provision	Revenue Loss				
	1984	1985	1986	1987	1988
Deductibility of nonbusiness state and local government taxes other than on owner-occupied homes	$19,840	$21,635	$25,510	$28,690	$32,030
Exclusion of interest on general purpose state and local government debt	11,510	12,995	14,560	16,160	17,800
Deductibility of property tax on owner-occupied homes	8,775	9,640	10,770	12,180	13,720
Exclusion of interest on state and local government industrial development bonds	3,400	3,865	4,470	5,000	5,130
Exclusion of interest on state and local government housing bonds for owner-occupied homes	1,785	1,820	1,775	1,755	1,750
Exclusion of interest on state and local government bonds for pollution control and sewage and waste disposal facilities	1,755	1,920	2,115	2,330	2,585

166

Exclusion of interest on state and local government bonds for hospital facilities	1,215	1,515	1,820	2,135	2,455
Exclusion of interest on state and local government housing bonds for rental housing	1,095	1,365	1,685	2,010	2,370
Exclusion of interest on state and local government student loan bonds	380	525	700	865	1,030
Exclusion of interest on state and local government bonds for private educational facilities	375	465	560	660	760
Exclusion of interest on state and local government industrial development bonds for energy production facilities	150	180	205	235	270
Exclusion of interest on state and local government mass transit bonds	110	125	120	110	125
Total	$50,390	$56,050	$64,290	$72,130	$80,025

1/ Includes tax savings for individuals and corporations.

Source: Joint Committee on Taxation. "Estimates of Federal Tax Expenditures for Fiscal Years 1984-1989." Washington, D.C.: U.S. Government Printing Office, November 9, 1984. Table 1, pp. 9-17.

167

long as we want strong state and local government.

The Fair tax would retain the present deductions for state and local income and real property taxes, while repealing the deduction for sales taxes. In addition, it would retain the exclusion for interest on general obligation bonds. Interest on bonds issued for other purposes would be taxable. The FAST tax would make the same changes as the Fair tax with one exception -- under the FAST tax, state and local income taxes would not be deductible. Both would thus continue limited use of the tax code to ease the revenue burdens on state and local governments.

The Treasury Department's tax simplification proposal would eliminate the current deductions for state and local income taxes, sales taxes, and property taxes. While this would simplify the process of computing Federal taxes, it would weaken our Federal system of government. A strong case can be made for retaining at least some of the current tax preferences designed to support state and local governments.

8. Predictability. Changes in the tax code should be made infrequently in order to minimize disruption of decision-making by businesses and investors.

Since 1975, seven major tax bills have been enacted, each making significant changes in the tax code for both individuals and corporations. Congress also passed dozens of minor tax bills that made smaller changes in the code (15). In the last decade, according to Professor Richard Cooper of Harvard University, we have added "nearly 1,800 pages of new legislation to the basic 1954 tax code (which itself took 929 pages), plus more than 4,000 pages of accompanying legislative history issued by Congress (16).

Frequent tax changes are disruptive because they divert attention from the economic consequences of business decisions to the tax consequences. As Professor Cooper points out:

We have "reformed" the tax code on average every 15 months since 1976...The problem is that constant changes in the tax rules greatly complicate decision-making by individuals and businesses. No one makes a financial decision without thinking about the tax code, and almost annual changes in the code greatly disrupt the way people make these decisions. Instead of thinking about how to make their companies more efficient, high-level business people devote their attention to manipulating the next round of "tax reform" to their corporate advantage.... It takes considerably longer than a year for people to adjust to a new tax law --and it takes the government longer than that to understand how the public is responding and decide whether or not the new law is furthering its stated purpose...Clearly, there is something to be said for the adage: "Any old tax is a good tax (17).

Although ERTA included a three-year tax cut aimed at improving predictability, the resulting deficits required that additional major tax legislation be enacted in 1982 and again in 1984. Although President Reagan still clings to the hope that economic growth will solve the deficit problem, the truth is that only a fiscal policy change -- including a tax increase -- can cut the deficit. This threat of another major tax bill in 1985 -- the fourth in five years -- hangs like a dark cloud over investors. This problem of uncertainty will only be solved if tax reform addresses the deficit as well as the structural issues in the tax code. Going only part way will inevitably result in the need for further tax legislation and more uncertainty.

III. SHOULD WE ADOPT A CONSUMPTION TAX?

The growing recognition that the present Federal income tax is permeated with faults has led in recent years to proposals to replace the income tax with a consumption tax. It seems unlikely that Congress will consider a consumption tax during the 99th Congress, since the major tax reform proposals are simplified progressive income taxes. Many industry associations, however, have been lobbying for adoption of a consumption tax since it would reduce the tax burden on saving and investment. One option listed in the Treasury study is a value-added tax. If opposition from special interests skuttles the tax reform effort in the 99th Congress, some form of consumption tax may be revived as a way of raising revenues even without reform of the income tax.

In its purest form, a consumption tax system would compute the tax base by adding up all spendable cash received during the tax year and substracting all savings. The difference is consumption, which would be taxed using either a flat or progressive rate structure.

The most fully articulated consumption tax is the Lifetime Income Tax proposed by Henry Aaron and Harvey Galper of the Brookings Institution, which would tax a person's lifetime income as it is consumed rather than as it is earned (18). The basis of the tax would be comprehensive receipts less saving. Receipts would include all wages and salaries, rent, interest, profits, dividends, transfer payments, gifts received, and inheritances. Saving would include all payments into certain qualified accounts, purchases of stocks and bonds, and purchases of real estate. Just as saving would be deducted from income, withdrawals from savings would be added. All loans would be included as receipts and all loan repayments, including principal and interest, would be deductible in computing the tax base. Inheritances and gifts received would be counted as receipts but if they were not consumed they would be just offset by an equal deduction for saving. End-of-lifetime wealth representing unexercised potential consumption of the taxpayer would be included in the tax base with an appropriate averaging provision. Thus, over the lifetime of the taxpayer, all income would be subject to taxation but only when it was consumed or when the taxpayer died. The Lifetime Income Tax would retain some features of the present income tax, including a standard deduction and personal exemptions to assure that no taxes would be levied on lower-income families, a progressive rate structure with a maximum rate of 32 percent on those with expenditures above $40,000 per year, and certain deductions to improve equity, including a deduction for large medical expenses and casualty losses. The consumption tax principle would also apply to corporations, which would calculate their tax base by adding up all receipts and deducting all business expenses, including investment in the year paid.

Two consumption tax proposals were introduced during the 98th Congress. The Progressive Consumption Tax (H.R. 5841) proposed by Congressman Heftel would implement the kind of consumption tax described by Aaron and Galper, except that the rate structure would be more progressive and it would not tax bequests as consumption by the deceased. The Broad-Based Enhanced Savings (BEST) Act (H.R. 6364, S. 3042), introduced by Senator Roth and Congressman Moore, resembles the Fair tax in that it is a broad-based income tax with a progressive rate structure. The major difference is that the BEST tax would establish a super savings account for financial assets. Contributions of up to $10,000 per year for individuals and $20,000 for couples could be deducted from taxable income and earnings would be excluded from taxation, but any withdrawals would be included in taxable income.

All three of these proposals would represent a significant departure from the present income tax. Other less radical proposals would retain the income tax but supplement it with a more modest form of consumption tax, such as a value-added tax or a national sales tax or an expanded use of excise taxes.

The most frequently mentioned reason for adopting a consumption tax is that it would increase the incentive for taxpayers to save and invest. In recent years, personal saving has hovered around 6 percent or less of disposable income, well below the level in other industrial countries, particularly Japan. This low level of savings was considered a major policy problem during the late 1970s when poor productivity growth contributed to high inflation. Critics found much of the fault for low savings in the Federal income tax. First, they argued that high marginal tax rates reduce the after-tax rate of return to saving, particularly for those upper-income taxpayers who have the greatest ability to increase their savings. Second, they argued that taxes levied on nominal rather than real gains reduce the after-tax return to saving during periods of high inflation, both for individuals and corporations. Third, they argued that the separate corporate income tax results in double-taxation of dividends and thus raises the cost of equity capital for corporations.

Numerous changes have been made in the income tax during recent years to correct this perceived anti-saving bias: eligibility for IRA's was expanded to include all wage-earners; the top 70 percent marginal tax rate on unearned income was reduced to 50 percent; the long-term capital gains exclusion was increased to 60 percent and the holding period was reduced to six months; and depreciation deductions were increased through adoption of the Accelerated Cost Recovery

System (ACRS). Nonetheless, critics of the present income tax argue that, instead of encouraging saving through tax preferences, it could be done in a more comprehensive way by exempting all savings.

Whether or not the income tax is biased against saving is an empirical question that has not been satisfactorily answered. The academic research is ambiguous. One recent study concluded:

There two ways to raise the private component of national saving through budgetary actions without losing the benefits to a large deficit: (1) cut expenditures and reduce marginal tax rates on capital income without changing the budget surplus or deficit, or (2) restructure taxes to reduce marginal tax rates on capital income without lowering total government revenues. As pointed out in chapter 3, economists are very uncertain about the likely effect of such measures on private saving behavior. The net effect on saving is ambiguous from a theoretical perspective, and the empirical evidence is not convincing on either side of the issue (19).

The fact that total private-sector saving -- including corporate saving -- has been relatively stable since the early 1950s suggests that other factors may play a much more significant role in determining savings, including income, profits, the composition of the population, interest rates, the long-term economic outlook, and attitudes. There are good reasons for eliminating many of the existing tax preferences that favor some forms of saving and investment over others, but there is no compelling reason without stronger evidence for exempting all saving from taxation. The result may be simply an unnecessary erosion of the tax base without any significant increase in the total amount saved and invested in the American economy.

More philophically, advocates of a consumption tax hold that people should be taxed on the basis of what they take out of the economy in the form of consumption rather than what they put into it in terms of work and resources that earn income. The attractiveness of this argument for the wealthy should be self-evident. For the Nation, however, this philosophy threatens to undermine our commitment to a fair and progressive tax system which levies taxes on the basis of each individual's ability to pay. Under a consumption tax, those receiving the greatest benefit from our stable government and free enterprise system would no longer be called upon to shoulder their fair burden of support for the government and the system it protects. Instead, the highest-income families could shift the burden of taxation into middle-income and lower-income families by socking large fractions of their income into tax-exempt forms of saving. The vast majority of working Americans whose incomes are just sufficient to support their families would not be so advantaged. For them, a consumption tax would become an even greater burden than the current income tax, no matter how progressive the rate schedule might be. A consumption tax would be a giant step away from our national commitment to fair and progressive taxation.

Although a consumption tax might eliminate any theoretical anti-saving bias in the present income tax, it would introduce other even more pronounced distortions into the tax system. First, the tax base would be lower than under an income tax, so tax rates would have to be higher in order to raise the same amounnt of revenues. This would increase the incentive for workers to demand compensation in the form of nontaxable fringe benefits and greatly increase the incentive to evade taxation by underreporting income. Second, a consumption tax would distort the flow of savings, because some forms of saving would be treated as consumption, and thus would be taxable, while other forms would be tax free. Orthodox consumption tax proposals would exempt only cash placed in savings accounts, stocks, bonds, and traditional investments. While these contribute to the growth of our country, so do savings that take less traditional forms, such as expenditures on education, research, child care, and health care. For these, it is impossible to draw the line between savings and consumption. Nonetheless, a tax system which rewards only financial savings will bias investors against forms of saving that may have an even higher payoff for the Nation. Third, a consumption tax would fall most heavily on taxpayers just when they are least capable of paying taxes. Students and the unemployed, who must often borrow just to maintain marginal living standards, would have to pay substantial taxes because borrowed funds would be fully included in cash receipts for the purpose of computing the consumption tax base. The elderly drawing down past savings would also be hit with a higher tax burden than under current law. Wealthy coupon-clippers and renters would face no such burden.

A consumption tax would also complicate taxation of bequests. The current tax system taxes large estates to prevent excessive accumulation of inherited wealth although much wealth, especially in smaller estates, is exempt. Under a consumption tax, wealth passed from generation to generation would permanently escape taxation so long as it was not consumed, thus permitting unlimited accumulation. Furthermore, horizontal equity in the tax code would be violated, since taxpayers with equal lifetime incomes could pay unequal amounts of tax. Both problems require that bequests be taxed in full as consumption for the deceased. The recent history of estate taxation, which saw many changes designed to reduce estate taxes, suggests that Congress would have little sympathy for the proper taxation of bequests if a consumption tax were enacted.

Adoption of a consumption tax would raise a long list of other problems. It would require a complete change in recordkeeping for both individuals and businesses. A complex transition period would be required to prevent past savings that had been taxed once under the income tax from being taxed a second time when consumed. This would be a particularly serious problem for the elderly whose savings decisions were based on the assumption that they could consume from their assets without incurring any new tax liability. A consumption tax would also cause conflicts with other countries that still tax income. Thus, even though a consumption tax might be justified on theoretical terms, the realities of a consumption tax give no sensible reasons for jetisoning the progressive income tax.

Consumption tax advocates who believe that enactment of a broad-based consumption tax is impossible have suggested that some of the tax burden can still be shifted onto consumption by piggybacking a value-added tax or national sales tax onto the existing income tax. This kind of bilevel tax plan would satisfy the President's instruction that tax reform must be revenue-neutral, while still picking up additional revenue to reduce the deficit.

The main difference between a value-added tax and

a national sales tax is in the way they would be collected. A national sales tax would be levied on goods and services at the time of final sale. A value-added tax would be levied at each stage of production, with each business computing its tax liability based on the difference between its total sales and its purchases from other business. In theory at least, the tax base would be identical for both, since the total value of sales to final consumers equals the total value added by producers. The only difference would be an administrative one.

Either tax could be a significant source of new revenues. According to a recent study by the Congressional Research Service (CRS), a broadly based national sales tax or value-added tax could have raised as much as $18.2 billion in 1984 for each one percentage point on the tax rate (20). A 5 percent tax could thus raise about $90 billion in new revenues (and more in future years) without repealing or limiting the marginal tax rate cuts enacted in 1981. Indexing and ACRS could also be preserved.

Despite any advantages, there are major problems with a national sales tax and a value-added tax. First, both would be regressive and violate the principle of ability to pay. One 1977 study cited by CRS found that a 5 percent national sales tax would amount to 3.4 percent of AGI for taxpayers in the $5,000 to $10,000 range but only 2.4 percent of AGI for those with incomes in the $30,000 to $50,000 range (21). A value-added tax would be similarly regressive. The regressivity of a national sales tax or a value-added tax could be reduced by exempting necessities or by providing a credit against the income tax that would phase out as income rises. Both expedients, however, would increase the complexity of the Federal tax system while significantly reducing the potential revenue from imposing either of these taxes as a new addition the tax code.

These taxes would also be highly vulnerable to special interests, particularly the value-added tax. Declining industries under pressure from foreign competitors will argue that an exemption from the value-added tax would enable them to compete more effectively and preserve domestic jobs. This would exempt the auto, machine tool, steel, leather, and textile industries. High-tech growth industries could also mount an attack, based on the argument that an

175

exemption would permit them to keep ahead of incipient foreign competitors. All industries producing necessities could also argue for an exemption or reduced rate in order to reduce retail prices. A national sales tax would not be so vulnerable to special interests, since it is levied at the point of final sale rather than on the producer, but arguments could still be raised for preferential rates for selected goods or services. A value-added tax or national sales tax punctured with special exemptions or preferential rates would not only erode the revenue potential, it would also be perceived as unfair by those not receiving favored treatment.

Additional pressure would be mounted during a recession, since neither a value-added tax nor a national sales tax would provide relief to businesses during a downturn. Currently, businesses that lose money during a recession pay no profits tax. However, unless they shut down, they still generate value that would be subject to the value-added tax. Thus, even in a recession with no profits, they would continue to find themselves burdened by a liability for the value-added tax. It doesn't take much imagination to foresee that this would generate intense pressure on Congress to exempt companies with no net income from the value-added tax. Again, a national sales tax would be less vulnerable to this kind of pressure. Nonetheless, because retail sales fluctuate less than incomes during a recession, neither of these taxes would contribute to the countercyclical stability of the economy.

In addition, both taxes would increase inflation. The Consumer Price Index (CPI) does not reflect increases in the income tax, but it does include increases in sales taxes. It would also reflect any price increase caused by adopting a value-added tax. This could touch off a new wage-price spiral that could only be controlled by monetary tightness and recession. Either tax would add a new level of complexity to the tax system that would require more paperwork and a new level of administration. Neither would do anything to make the tax system simpler. In fact, with a panoply of different rates for different industries or different products, the tax system would become even more complex.

In summary, neither a national sales tax nor a value-added tax is a good substitute for a simplified progressive income tax that raises adequate revenues.

IV. INCOME TAX REFORM -- SELECTED ISSUES

The three major proposals that could form the basis for tax reform in the 99th Congress -- the Bradley-Gephardt Fair tax, the Kemp-Kasten FAST tax and the Treasury simplification proposal -- all reject the notion that the tax base should be shifted from income to consumption. They are broad-based income tax systems that would repeal many of the exclusions, deductions, and credits in the current tax code and replace the present progressive rate structure with either a single flat rate tax or a simplified progressive rate. A complete list of the changes proposed by the major tax plans is provided in the Appendix to this study.

Although the three tax proposals are broadly similar, there are specific differences. Some of the proposed changes, particularly those included in the Treasury proposal, would be a matter of concern and may not represent an improvement over the present system.

1. Limit On The Value Of Deductions. Under present law, deductions and exemptions are taken at the margin against the last dollar of income. They are thus worth much more to upper-income taxpayers than to those at the bottom of the rate schedule. For example, a $1,000 deduction reduces tax liability by $500 for a taxpayer in the top 50 percent bracket but by only $110 for a taxpayer in the lowest 11 percent bracket. Preferences which are deductible at the margin are thus regressive, with the greatest benefit accruing to those at the top of the income scale. Past tax reform efforts have tried to replace deductions at the margin with credits in order to provide the same dollar benefit to all qualifying taxpayers regardless of their rate bracket. Few credits have made it into the tax system, however, and most of them are minor -- the residential energy credit, the credit for political contributions, the credit for the elderly, and the child care credit.

All three major tax reform proposals would address this inequity by repealing many deductions that are available primarily to upper-income taxpayers and by reducing the progressivity of the rate structure. This would narrow the difference in the value of deductions between taxpayers at the top and bottom of the income scale. It would also reduce the amount of income that can be sheltered through deductions. The Treasury

177

Department's tax simplification plan will continue, however, to allow taxpayers to take deductions at the margin against the last dollar of income so that, with three tax brackets and a top marginal rate of 35 percent, deductions will continue to be more valuable to those in the top bracket than to those in the bottom bracket.

Both the Fair and FAST tax proposals would go much farther toward transforming deductions into credits. The FAST tax imposes a single flat 25 percent tax rate, so each $1,000 in deductions reduces tax liability by $250 for all taxpayers regardless of income. While the Fair tax has a progressive rate structure, deductions and exemptions could be claimed only against the basic 14 percent tax rate. Deductions could not be taken against the 12 percent and 16 percent surtax rates. Thus, the Fair tax would reduce each taxpayer's liability by $140 for every $1,000 in qualifying deductions. While both the Fair and FAST tax proposals effectively transform the remaining deductions into tax credits, the Fair tax does it without foregoing a progressive tax rate structure. This limitation also makes it possible for the Fair tax to raise as much revenue as the Treasury proposal with lower tax rates.

2. **Capital Losses.** Present tax law permits net capital losses to be deducted from ordinary income, up to an annual limit of $3,000. Losses above that can be carried forward indefinitely. The annual limit on deductibility of capital losses prevents taxpayers from manipulating their assets for the sole purpose of reducing taxable income. If there were no limit on capital loss deductions, taxpayers holding large amounts of depreciated assets could realize their losses, deduct the full loss against ordinary income, and repurchase the asset after the appropriate waiting period, ending up with the same list of assets and a reduced tax liability. Since the bulk of financial assets are owned by the top 2 percent of families, according to the Federal Reserve (22), full deductibility of capital losses would be a significant new tax loophole for upper-income taxpayers. One tax expert estimates that this could cost the Federal Government as much as $4 billion annually in lost revenue (23).

The loss limit should be retained in comprehensive tax reform. We do not yet know whether the Treasury Department's tax simplification plan will propose to alter the treatment of capital losses. The FAST tax, unfortunately, would allow unlimited capital loss deductions and thus would permit upper-income taxpayers to manipulate their wealth for tax purposes. The Fair tax retains present law treatment of capital losses.

3. Depreciation. In computing taxable income, businesses should be permitted to depreciate the cost of plant, equipment, and other productive assets over their useful economic lives in such a way that taxable income accurately reflects economic profits. The present tax code fails to do this. Currently, depreciation is limited to historic cost -- i.e., the dollar cost of building a factory or the purchase price of a machine or other equipment. During periods of low inflation, historic cost depreciation is an adequate convention since it substantially reflects replacement cost as well. During periods of high inflation, however, historic cost depreciation is inadequate since it does not reflect full replacement cost, and taxable income will exceed economic profit. This raises business profit tax liabilities and reduces the expected after-tax profits on investments, thus discouraging investment.

The present ACRS shortens depreciation for tax purposes significantly below expected economic lives for virtually all business assets, in the hope that the tax benefits from early cost recovery will offset the impact of inflation on replacement costs. ACRS, however, does not uniformly shorten depreciation schedules for all assets and, as a result, some kinds of capital are now highly subsidized by the tax code while others bear a significant tax burden. These tax-induced distortions waste capital.

Of possible solutions, the fewest economic distortions would be created by a depreciation system which permitted businesses to write off the replacement cost of plant and equipment over their useful economic life. This could be done either by indexing the historic cost to an accepted capital cost index, thereby adjusting depreciation charges annually for inflation, or by discounting the anticipated annual depreciation charges and writing off the present value of the charges in the year of purchase.

The Fair tax would replace ACRS with a new method based on historic cost recovery. Under the Fair tax, equipment would be divided into six classes based on

179

the Asset Depreciation Range (ADR) lives. For example, all assets with an ADR midpoint of under five years would be placed in an asset class that would be fully depreciated over four years. Other assets would be placed in other classes, as given in the following chart:

ADR Midpoint	Class Life
Under 5	4
5.0 to 8.5	6
9.0 to 14.5	10
15 to 24	18
25 to 35	28
Over 35 and structures	40

An open-ended account would be established for each asset class and each year the taxpayer would write off a percentage of the balance in each account based on the class life and the 250 percent declining balance method. Additions to each account would be made each year for purchases of assets in that class. Subtractions would be made for dispositions of assets and for that year's depreciation deduction. Structures would be put into the sixth asset class.

This system would be much simpler than the current one since individual assets would not have to be tracked for tax purposes. It would also eliminate the current ACRS subsidy of specific assets. Nonetheless, because it is designed to approximate the present value of economic depreciation at a 10 percent discount rate, it overstates economic depreciation at low inflation rates and understates it at high inflation rates for all asset classes.

The basic depreciation system in the Fair tax could be improved by indexing the value of each asset class annually for the increase in capital prices and then permitting each class to be written off using the straight-line depreciation method. This would preserve the simplicity of the asset class innovation, keep the system unbiased among assets of different economic lives, and provide adequate correction for inflation.

The FAST tax would retain the ACRS depreciation system and thus would make no improvement over the current practice. Furthermore, for assets that are very long lived and which can change ownership, such as a factory or apartment building, the FAST tax permits full indexing of the basis in computing capital gains. When combined with ACRS, this provides a double subsidy.

The Treasury tax simplification plan would replace ACRS with a depreciation schedule that more closely conforms to economic lives. In addition, it will permit indexing of the depreciation schedules for inflation. Although special interests may protest the repeal of ACRS, it appears that the indexing provision could solve the problem of inadequate depreciation. Subject to further study, the indexing provisions in the Treasury plan could be melded with the asset class innovation in the Fair tax to provide a fair, efficient, and simple depreciation system.

All three tax proposals would repeal the investment tax credit. In periods of strong growth, the investment tax credit is a waste of money, since it rewards businesses for making investments they would likely make even without the credit. The purpose of the investment tax credit when first enacted in 1964 was to stimulate the growth of the economy by providing an incentive for business investment during a period of slack demand. It was never intended to be a permanent feature of the tax code. The investment tax credit should be repealed, although it could still be implemented occasionally during a recession or period of slow growth as part of an overall policy of fiscal stimulus.

4. Integration of the Corporate Income Tax. Since 1909, the United States has levied a tax on corporation profits. Even though the corporate income tax is even more ancient than the personal income tax, it suffers many of the same problems and needs reform just as badly. The basic problem is the erosion of the tax base resulting from numerous special tax breaks that have been enacted over the years. Today, the amount of corporate income sheltered from taxation exceeds the amount actually taxed (24). While the corporate profits tax is a significant source of Federal revenues -- $56.9 billion in Fiscal 1984 -- its contribution to receipts has slipped steadily from almost a quarter of the total during the early 1950's to just over 8.5 percent currently. The numerous special preferences in the corporate tax also misallocate resources. Investors guided more by tax consequences than economic consequences channel too many dollars into favored industries or types of capital and not enough into

181

others. The economy suffers as a result from inadequate growth of productivity and industrial capacity. With many tax preferences designed to aid existing industries, the resulting misallocation of capital impairs the ability of young, high technology companies to compete in the world market against better financed foreign competitors. Finally, the fact that large billion-dollar corporations often pay no Federal tax because of special tax preferences has contributed significantly to the feeling among taxpayers that the income tax is unfair (25).

Both the Fair tax and the FAST tax would keep the corporate profits tax as a separate but integral part of the Federal tax system. Both would reform it by repealing many of the present tax preferences and by reducing the tax rate. The list of provisions that would be repealed or revised by the Fair tax is three pages long, including the many preferences benefiting the oil, minerals, and timber industries, the investment tax credit, and the ACRS depreciation scheme. Broadening the base would permit the corporate tax to be reduced from the present 46 percent rate to 30 percent with no loss in total revenues. Corporate tax reform under the FAST tax would take much the same shape as under the Fair tax, although the investment preferences would be retained and smaller corporations would pay a reduced rate.

The Treasury Department's tax simplification plan would also broaden the base of the corporate income tax by repealing many tax preferences while reducing the tax rate to a flat 33 percent for all corporations. It would also go part of the way toward integrating the corporate income tax with the personal income tax by permitting corporations to deduct 50 percent of dividends paid when computing taxable income. Corporate tax intergation has long been a goal of business-oriented tax reformers, who argue that eliminating the current double taxation of dividends -- once by the corporate profits tax and once by the personal income tax -- would lower the cost of equity capital and increase the incentive to invest.

Despite the theoretical attractions of corporate tax integration, there are compelling reasons to retain a separate tax on corporate profits. Proponents of integration argue that corporations are inseparable from their shareholder-owners and they should be taxed as one. Nonetheless, in legal terms, corporations and their shareholders are distinct. Unlike proprietorships, where the business is legally inseparable from the owner, shareholders have limited liability for the actions of the corporation and have only limited rights in the corporation. The special rights and protections granted to corporations require that they contribute their fair share, separately from their shareholders, to the support of the government that grants those rights and protections.

The only consequence of interest in the taxation of corporate profits is an economic one -- whether or not the tax burden is too heavy -- and even there an argument can be made for a separate corporate profits tax. The corporate form of business organization permits a much greater accumulation of capital than any other form, because the investor's exposure is limited solely to the amount invested. This increased capital intensity permits corporations to achieve economies of scale and lower costs than would be possible under other forms of corporate governance. Large corporations also have greater control over their markets and can administer prices so as to achieve higher earnings. The enhanced earning power granted by the corporate form justifies a separate tax on corporate earnings. No matter what changes may be made in the personal income tax, tax reform efforts should retain the corporate profits tax, preferably as it would be revised under the Fair tax proposal.

Finally, the Treasury Department's proposal to allow a deduction for 50 percent of dividends paid would primarily benefit old-line manufacturing and service corporations while doing little to help smaller high-growth companies that plow all their earnings back into growth-producing investment. The major goal of corporate tax reform should be to reduce the waste caused by perverse tax incentives. The Treasury proposal would undermine this by channeling equity capital away from companies that reinvest their earnings into high future growth.

5. Indexation. The Federal tax system levies taxes on income and gains measured in nominal terms. It makes no distinction between real increases in income or asset values and those due solely to inflation. Real gains pose no problem under the present tax code. A taxpayer receiving a wage increase during a period of zero inflation may move into a higher tax bracket. But, after paying the additional tax, he or she will

still be better off. The same holds true for the
seller of an asset whose real value has increased. The
increase is subject to capital gains tax, but even
after the tax is paid the seller earns a real gain.

When gains are solely due to inflation, however,
the tax consequences can turn nominal gains into real
losses. If a taxpayer whose income just keeps up with
inflation moves into a higher tax bracket, the
resulting tax increase will leave less real income than
before. Of course, the taxpayer would still be better
off than with no nominal increase, but worse off than
if the increase had not been offset by inflation. The
seller of an asset whose price has gone up but has
gained no real increase in value after adjusting for
inflation is, nonetheless, still liable for capital
gains tax on the nominal increase, resulting in a real
loss. Workers and owners of capital are both made
worse off during periods of inflation by a tax system
which levies tax on nominal rather than real gains.

The value of interest income is also affected by
taxation in nominal terms. The nominal interest paid
by a borrower to a lender includes two forms of
compensation. One is the payment to the lender for
foregoing the use of his or her funds, generally
referred to as the real interest rate. The second is
the compensation to the lender for the decrease in the
value of the loan principle due to inflation. The
nominal interest rate on a loan thus includes the real
interest rate desired by the lender plus the expected
inflation rate. The entire amount of interest received
by the lender, however, is taxable, even though some
fraction of it simply represents compensation for the
declining value of the loan.

During the high inflation of the late 1970s, many
tax reform advocates suggested that the Federal tax
system should be indexed for inflation to assure that
taxes are levied only on real gains. Indexation
generally incorporated three separate proposals:

- Annual indexation of tax brackets, personal
  exemptions, and the zero-bracket amount.
  Taxpayers experiencing nominal income gains just
  equal to inflation would thus be protected
  from moving into higher tax brackets.

- Indexation of asset basis for computing capital
  gains. The nominal increase in the value of

184

an asset due solely to inflation would thus not
be taxed, and the tax would   apply only to the
real gain.

   - Annual indexation of interest income. Interest
   recipients would substract the portion of their
   interest income which reflected compensation for
   inflation, and would thus be taxed only on their
   real interest income.

The Economic Recovery Tax Act of 1981 incorporated
the first proposal. Beginning with 1985, tax brackets,
personal exemptions, and the zero-bracket amount will
be indexed to adjust for inflation during the previous
fiscal year as measured by the CPI. For example, with
inflation between September 1983 and September 1984
measuring 4.1 percent, the personal exemption will
increase for 1985 from the present $1,000 to $1,040 for
the taxpayer, spouse, and each dependent. The upper
and lower boundaries for each tax bracket will also
increase by 4.1 percent as will the zero-bracket
amount.

The benefits from this kind of indexing would be
substantially reduced by all three of the major tax
reform proposals since they would replace the highly
progressive tax rate structure of the present income
tax with either a single flat tax or a simplified
progressive rate structure with much broader brackets
and lower rates. The Fair tax would repeal indexing,
while the FAST tax would retain it for the personal
exemptions and the zero-bracket amount. Under a
simplified progressive rate structure, the benefits
from indexing the tax brackets do not justify the
costs, particularly in light of current revenue needs.
Indexation is also destabilizing over the business
cycle, with the largest tax reductions occurring during
periods of highest inflation. Equity considerations,
however, do suggest that if any part of the tax code is
indexed it should be the zero-bracket amount. This
would concentrate the benefits from tax indexing among
low-income and middle-income families that do not
itemize deductions.

The Treasury Department's tax simplification
proposal also incorporates indexation of capital basis
and interest income. This would create a major new tax
preference in the tax code that is not needed under
current economic conditions. The inflation rate has
come down substantially since the late 1970s. While

185

nominal gains and interest rates still exceed real gains and interest rates, the difference is no longer sufficient to pose an excessive burden on owners of capital assets. The much lower tax rates being proposed under the major reform plans would also reduce the tax burden levied in incomes and gains in nominal terms. Furthermore, the single major asset for the vast majority of taxpayers -- their home -- is already protected by the rollover exclusion and the $125,000 exemption for sellers over 55 years old, both of which would be retained.

Indexation of the basis of assets for computing the capital gains tax and indexation of interest income would also require a substantial amount of new recordkeeping for those receiving these forms of income and would greatly increase the complexity of computing tax liability. Interest indexation involves one further problem. Corporations and individuals can currently deduct total interest payments in computing taxable income, including that portion of the payment which simply represents compensation to the lender for the reduction in the nominal value of the loan. If lenders are permitted to index interest receipts and pay tax only on real interest earnings, borrowers would also have to adjust their interest deductions. The net result would be a shift in the tax burden from lenders to borrowers. Such a change could not be implemented without a substantial transfer in wealth or a complex set of transition rules that would simply make the tax system all the more incomprehensible to the vast majority of taxpayers.

The final problem with indexation is that it would reduce opposition to inflation. Aside from the tax consequences, inflation imposes real costs on the economy. One benefit of a tax system which levies taxes on income and gains in nominal terms, even during periods of high inflaton, is that it creates pressure on the government to control the inflation problem. Indexing makes it possible for taxpayers to adjust much more easily to inflation and would thus reduce the pressure to control it. While indexing relieves taxpayers from the costs of inflation, it does nothing to reduce the economic harm.

Indexing should thus be used for only limited purposes. Indexing of the zero-bracket amount helps protect low-income and middle-income families from being hurt by inflation since they can least afford it.

Indexing of depreciation would protect the tax system against schemes such as ACRS that create more problems than they solve. Indexing of capital basis and interest, by contrast, would greatly increase the complexity of the tax code and provide new opportunities for tax abuse.

FOOTNOTES

1. "White House Is Said to See Record Deficit of $205 Billion in Current Fiscal Year," Wall Street Journal, November 14, 1984, p.3.

2. "David Stockman: No More Big Budget Cuts," Fortune, February 6, 1984, pp. 53-55.

3. For various poll results, see Advisory Commission on Intergovernmental Relations, 1983 Changing Public Attitudes on Government and Taxes, Washington, D.C., U.S.G.P.O., 1983; and German, Mark F., "Public Opinion Polls on Government Spending, Taxes and The Budget Deficit," Library of Congress, Congressional Research Service, March 20, 1984.

4. U.S. Department of the Treasury, Internal Revenue Service, 1981 Statistics of Income, Individual Income Tax Returns, Washington, D.C., U.S.G.P.O., 1983, Table 3-3, pp. 80-82. This table shows that taxpayers at each income level pay widely different percentages of their incomes in taxes.

5. U.S. Congress, Joint Committee on Taxation, "Estimates of Federal Tax Expenditures for Fiscal Years 1984-1989," Washington, D.C., U.S.G.P.O., November 9, 1984, Table 1, pp. 9-17.

6. Musgrave, Richard A., "Tax Reform -- 1981 and After" in Economic Choices: Studies in Tax/Fiscal Policy , Washington, D.C., Center for National Policy, 1982, p.15.

7. U.S. Congress, Joint Committee on Taxation, op. cit, Table 2, pp. 18-23.

8. For details on earlier tax legislation, see Talley, Louis Alan, "Significant Federal Tax Legislation, 1970-1978," Library of Congress, Congressional Research Service, Report No.79-207E, September 21, 1979.

9. U.S. Department of the Treasury, Internal Revenue

Service, Statistics of Income Bulletin, Washington,
D.C., U.S.G.P.O., Fall 1984, Table 3, pp. 72-73.

10. Data in this section are drawn from

Riley, Dorothea, "Individual Income Tax Returns:
Selected Characteristics From the 1983 Taxpayer Usage
Study," in U.S. Department of the Treasury, Internal
Revenue Service, Statistics of Income Bulletin ,
Washington, D.C., U.S.P.G.O., Summer 1984, pp. 45-62;

Tax Notes, September 24, 1984, p. 1313; and

Wall Street Journal, October 3, 1984, p.1.

11. U.S. Congress, Joint Economic Committee, Hearings
on Fair Taxation, Washington, D.C., U.S.G.P.O., June 13
and 14, 1984.

12. Ibid.

13. U.S. Department of the Treasury, Internal Revenue
Service, Income Tax Compliance Research : Estimates for
1973-1981, Washington, D.C., U.S.G.P.O., 1983, p.9

14. Ibid., p.10.

15. See Louis Talley, op. cit.

16. Cooper, Richard N., "Overtaxed by Tax Revision,"
New York Times, September 10, 1984, p. A-21.

17. Ibid.

18. For a more thorough explanation of the Lifetime
Income Tax, see Aaron, Henry J. and Galper, Harvey, "A
Tax on Consumption, Bequests, and Gifts and Other
Strategies for Reform," in Pechman, Joseph A., ed.,
Options for Tax Reform, The Brookings Institution,
Washington, D.C., 1984, pp. 106-134.

19. Bosworth, Barry, Tax Incentives and Economic
Growth, The Brookings Institution, Washington, D.C.,
1984, pp. 182-83.

20. Bickley, James M., "National Sales Tax: Selected
Policy Issues," Library of Congress, Congressional
Research Service, Report No. 84-141E, August 17, 1984,
p.11.

21.   Ibid., p. 30.

22.   "Survey of Consumer Finances, 1983," Federal Reserve Bulletin, September 1984, p. 689.

23.   Testimony of Joseph Minarik in U.S. Congress, Joint Economic Committee, Hearings on Fair Taxation, June 13 and 14, 1984.

24.   According to the Joint Committee on Taxation, tax preferences reduced corporate income taxes by $75.2 billion during Fiscal 1984, a sum greater than corporate tax receipts of $56.9 billion. See Joint Committee on TAxation, op. cit., p. 17.

25.   McIntyre, Robert S., Corporate Income Taxes in the Reagan Years, Citizens for Tax Justice, Washington, D.C., 1984.

COMPARISON OF MAJOR TAX REFORM PROPOSALS

	Current Tax Law	Kemp-Kasten FAST	Bradley-Gephart Fair	Treasury
TAX RATES	11% to 50%	25%	14%, 26%, 30%	15%, 25%, 35%
EXEMPTIONS				
Self, Spouse	$1,000	$2,000	$1,600	$2,000
Dependents	1,000	2,000	1,000	2,000
Elderly	1,000	2,000	1,000	Credit
Blind	1,000	2,000	1,000	Credit
PERSONAL DEDUCTIONS				
Mortgage Interest	Yes	Yes	Yes	Yes
Other Personal Interest	Yes	No, except on education expenses	No	Yes, $5,000
Property Taxes	Yes	Yes	Yes	No
State and Local Income Taxes	Yes	No	Yes	No
Other Local Taxes	Yes	No	No	No
Charitable Contributions	Yes	Yes	Yes	Yes (above 2% AGI)
Medical Expenses	Yes (Amount above 5% of Adjusted Gross Income)	Yes (Amount above 10% of AGI)	Yes (Amount above 10% of AGI)	Yes (Amount above 5% of AGI)
Two-Earner Deduction	Yes (10% of lower salary)	No	No	No
OTHER INDIVIDUAL ITEMS				
Indexing Retained	Yes	Yes	No	No
Income Averaging	Yes	No	No	No

RETIREMENT					
I.R.A. Earnings	Deferred Tax	Deferred Tax	Deferred Tax	Deferred Tax	Deferred Tax
I.R.A. Deductions	Yes	Yes	Yes	YES	Yes
Keogh Earnings	Deferred Tax	Deferred Tax	Deferred Tax	Deferred Tax	Deferred Tax
Keogh Deductions	Yes	Yes	Yes	Yes	Yes
Corporate Pensions	Deferred Tax	Deferred Tax	Limited	Limited	?
Social Security	Social Security benefit exemption for low- and mode-rate-income individuals	Taxation of Social benefits is eased over current law	Keeps benefit exemption for low- and mode-rate-income individuals	Keeps benefit exemption for low- and mode-rate-income individuals	Keeps benefit exemption for low- and mode-rate-income individuals
INVESTMENTS					
Maximum Capital Gains Rate	20%	19%, then 25%	30%	30%	35%
Capital Gains Exclusion	60%	30%, then 0	0	0	0
Capital Basis	Not indexed	Indexed	Not Indexed	Indexed	Indexed
Dividend Exclusion	$100/$200	None	None	None	None
Homeowner Exclusion	Yes	Yes	Partial	None	?
General Obligation Municipal Bonds	Not taxed	Not taxed	Not taxed	Not taxed	Not taxed
Other Municipal Bonds	Not taxed	Taxed	Taxed	Taxed	Taxed
Alternative Minimum	Yes	Retained	Repealed	Repealed	Repealed
DEPRECIATION					
Investment Credit	6% to 10%	None	None	None	None
Depreciation Method	Accelerated Cost Recovery System, which allows for faster write-offs of some assets	Keeps the Accelerated Cost Recovery System	Replaces the Accelerated Cost Recovery System	Replaces the A.C.R.S. with longer depreciation periods allows assets to be depreciated using the 250% declining method	Replaces A.C.A.S.; allows asset basis to be indexed for inflation

LOWER INCOME PROVISIONS				
Earned Income Credit	Yes	Yes, modified	Retained	Retained
Child Care Credit	Yes	Repealed	Deduction	Deduction
Unemployment Compensation	Taxed over $12,000	Taxed	Taxed	Taxed
Worker's Compensation	Not taxed	Not taxed	Not taxed	Taxed
EMPLOYER PROVIDED FRINGE BENEFITS				
Health Insurance	Excluded	Benefits taxed	Included	Capped exclusive
Life Insurance	Excluded	Excluded	Included	Included
Other Statutory	Included	Included	Included	Included

Source: Tax Notes

CHAPTER 9

PRESIDENT REAGAN'S TAX REFORM

Khi V. Thai

I. INTRODUCTION

Tax reform appeared to have come to an end when the 1981 tax cut which tremendously reduced all of the federal budget revenues left little or no latitude for policy initiatives of any kind. According to its supporters, the tax cut would have stimulated the economic growth which in time would have increased public revenues and automatically eliminated the federal budget deficits. Within a year after the tax cut, however, the end of tax reform became the beginning of a period of unparalleled activity. The loss of budget revenues which was thought to be upset by high rates of economic growth has worsened federal budget deficits. The Tax Equity and Fiscal Recovery Act of 1982 and Deficit Reduction Act of 1984 have somewhat offset revenue losses caused by the 1981 tax cut and eliminated abuses and obsolete subsidies in the law. However, the size of budget deficits could not be reduced by the above efforts. Furthermore, the federal tax system still remained in a less than satisfactory condition. Thus in November 1984, after two years of research, the Treasury Department submitted to the President a tax reform proposal. Under political pressure from those who would be negatively affected by the Treasury proposal, President Reagan sent in May, 1985 a bill which contained some modifications to the U.S. Congress. Then political pressures shifted to the U.S. Congress, and consequently in early December 1985, the House Ways and Means Committee approved its own tax proposal which modified the Reagan version. Although he was not pleased with modifications made by the House Ways and Means Committee, President Reagan had to endorse this tax-revision legislation because if it failed in the House, no other comprehensive tax legislation would be considered by Congress during the Reagan Presidency. The House tax reform bill was sent to the Senate which, displeased with this tax bill, wrote another tax bill. In June, 1986, the Senate passed its own tax plan. The House of Representatives and the Senate resolved their differences through the conference committee process. The final tax version, a product of political compromise between the House and Senate, was passed by the House on September 25, 1986 and by the Senate two days later, and was promptly signed by President Reagan.

This chapter explores the need for federal tax reform; as well as summarizes the content and impacts of the Reagan tax proposal, describes political pressure against it, and finally, identifies the results of political pressure on tax reform efforts.

II. THE NEED FOR A TAX REFORM (1)

The present income tax is badly in need of fundamental simplification and reform. It is too complicated, it is unfair, and it interferes with economic choices and retards saving, investment and growth.

In a real sense, the U.S. income tax has grown without any conscious design or overall planning since it was enacted in 1913. It was originally imposed at low rates and applied to fewer than 400,000 individuals with very high incomes. The need to finance World War II and expanded non-defense expenditures turned the individual income tax into a levy paid by most Americans. Tax rates were increased during World War II, and at their peak individual income tax rates reached 94 percent. The original income tax had serious flaws, and while some of these have been corrected over time, others have grown worse. With over 90 million individual tax returns now being filed, it is important to address these problems.

It is one thing to decide to tax "income," and quite another to decide how to define taxable income. If inadequate attention is devoted to establishing a uniform and consistent definition of income, some sources and uses of income will escape tax, and others will be taxed twice, as in the United States. The result may or may not be a simple tax system, but it is certain that the tax system will contain inequities and interfere with the economic behavior of taxpayers.

---

* This section is reprinted from **"Tax Reform for Fairness, Simplicity, and Economic Growth"**, the Treasury Department Report to the President (November, 1984), pp. 1- 10.

194

The U.S. income tax is not used simply to raise revenue. Instead, it is used to subsidize a long list of economic activities through exclusions from income subject to tax, adjustments to income, business deductions unrelated to actual expenses, deferral of tax liability, deductions for personal consumption expenditures, tax credits, and preferential tax rates. In some cases, deviations from a comprehensive definition of income originated in incomplete understanding of the concept of income or in outmoded ideas about the proper fiscal relationship between the Federal Government and state and local governments. But whatever its origin, in many cases bad public policy has become accepted -- virtually enshrined -- as appropriate.

For seven decades, the Treasury Department has fought to protect Federal revenues and the fairness and economic neutrality of the tax system from those seeking to create and exploit gaps and inconsistencies in the definition of taxable income. As loopholes have been discovered or created, exploited, and then plugged, techniques of tax avoidance have become increasingly sophisticated and the complexity of the income tax has grown, in a never-ending cycle.

The resulting tax system is both unfair and needlessly complex. Moreover, it interferes with economic behavior and, thus, prevents markets from allocating economic resources to their most productive uses. Perhaps worse, the complexity and inequity of the tax system undermine taxpayer morale -- a valuable, yet fragile, national asset and a prerequisite for a tax system based on voluntary compliance.

During the past year, the Treasury Department has undertaken a thorough review of the U.S. tax system. The object has been to determine how to reduce the complexities, inequities, and economic distortions in the tax system and make it more conducive to economic growth. Although the present report was prepared internally by the Treasury Department, it draws heavily on a vast national storehouse of knowledge about the tax system and its effects on the economy. The report also reflects information, views, and concerns which the Treasury Department received from taxpayers in the course of public hearings, meetings, and discussions, and in correspondence and in more formal written statements.

195

1. The Federal Income Tax in 1954

To understand better the need for tax reform, it is useful to compare our present income tax system with the one that prevailed in the late 1950s, after enactment of the 1954 Internal Revenue Code. Though the 1954 income tax system exhibited some serious problems, it was relatively simple, it was more nearly neutral toward many economic decisions, and most citizens probably thought it was reasonably fair.

Today the American economy is far more complex than it was 30 years ago. The financial affairs of the typical American family are far more complicated than in previous generations. Ownership of both financial and nonfinancial assets is more widespread and varied. Families have a greater quantity and variety of income, both taxed and untaxed. Business transactions are more complicated, financial intermediation is more highly developed, and taxpayers are more sophisticated and better advised. We also know more about the adverse effects of taxation than 30 years ago. Therefore, it would not be desirable -- nor would it be possible -- simply to reinstate an earlier tax law that was not designed to deal with the more complex economy of the 1980s. But a useful perspective on the current need for tax reform and simplification can be gained by considering how the tax law -- and its impact on taxpayers -- has changed over the past three decades.

One important defect of the 1954 income tax was a schedule of marginal rates that reached 91 percent for a small number of taxpayers. Besides creating severe disincentives for saving, investment, and work effort, the confiscatory rates may have spawned many of the vexing tax avoidance schemes that now riddle the income tax. But the advantages of the earlier income tax were also manifest. Virtually all taxpayers below the top 10 percent of the income distribution paid tax at an essentially uniform marginal rate of about 20 percent. Only at the very top of the income distribution did rates become steeply progressive. The income tax was still being used primarily to raise public revenues, and not to guide households and private business enterprises into a multitude of activities --some of dubious value--through preferential tax treatment. With notable exceptions, the income tax was levied on a base that included most income. The erosion of that base by a multitude of exclusions, adjustments, deductions, and credits not required to measure income accurately had not reached its present stage.

Compared to today, the 1954 income tax was simpler, more neutral, and fairer, in many respects. Perhaps as importantly, it was probably seen to be fair by most taxpayers, and the perception of fairness helped maintain the voluntary compliance so crucial to the American system of taxation.

2. The Decline in Simplicity

In 1954 the income tax was simpler for most taxpayers, in part because incomes were lower and the financial affairs of most families were simpler. There was little need for most taxpayers to work through a variety of complicated forms --and even more complicated instructions --to determine eligibility for a particular tax benefit. Only 25 percent of taxpayers itemized deductions in 1955, compared to 35 percent in 1982. Thus, fewer taxpayers found it necessary to save receipts verifying a multitude of expenditures accorded tax-preferred status. There was also little need to engage the services of a tax professional to file an individual income tax return. Tax planning -- the rearrangement of one's economic affairs to minimize taxes -- was the concern of only a few. Most taxpayers did not even feel the need to consider the tax consequences of major decisions, much less everyday transactions.

Today the proliferation and expansion of exclusions, adjustments to income, deductions, and credits create a major burden of paperwork and make part-time bookkeepers of many Americans. At present, about 100 different Federal tax forms are used by individuals. Many decisions -- for example, whether and how to make a charitable contribution, whether to participate in insurance plans offered by an employer, and whether to contribute to a political party -- all have tax consequences. Ordinary citizens are confronted with the alternatives of using a professional tax preparer, becoming knowledgeable in arcane tax law, running afoul of the tax administration, or possible passing up available tax benefits. Today, over 40 percent of all individual income tax returns -- and some 60 percent of all long forms (form 1040s) --are prepared by paid professionals. So-called tax shelters, once known only to the wealthy, are now attracting increasing numbers of middle-income Americans, many of whom do not have access to sophisticated tax advice and

197

are misled by the misrepresentations of unscrupulous promoters of illegal shelters, often with disastrous effects. Legislative response to the tax shelter problem over the last 15 years has involved a patchwork of solutions that has generally increased the complexity of the tax system without correcting the underlying causes of tax shelters.

3. Erosion of the Tax Base

In 1954, the income tax did favor certain economic activities over others. For example, even then, tax experts criticized the fact that income from oil and gas properties, interest on state and local securities, and appreciation on capital assets were accorded preferential tax treatment. These "loopholes," as they were called, created inequities and distorted the use of the Nation's resources. By comparison, most interest, dividend, and labor income was taxed in full, and few forms of personal expenditure were tax deductible. The most important itemized deductions were for state and local taxes, charitable contributions, interest payments, and medical expenses; some of these had valid or easily understood justifications.

The last three decades have seen enormous erosion of the tax base. Compensation has increasingly taken the form of tax-free fringe benefits and legally taxable "perks" that many taxpayers improperly treat as tax-exempt. Interest on bonds issued by state and local governments has long been tax exempt, but recently these governments have increasingly used tax-exempt bonds to finance private investments. The investment tax credit greatly reduces the effective tax rate on income generated by business equipment, and accelerated depreciation and the deduction for interest expense combine to eliminate most taxes on income from debt-financed investments in real estate. In extreme cases these and other features of the tax law create losses for tax purposes that can be used to shelter other income. Exclusions, itemized deductions, and the deduction value of credits offset about 34 percent of personal income in 1982, as opposed to only 18 percent in 1954.

4. Economic Distortions

The lack of a comprehensive income tax base has two obvious and important adverse effects on the ability of the marketplace to allocate capital and labor to their most productive uses. First, the smaller the tax base, the higher tax rates must be to raise a given amount of revenue. High tax rates discourage saving and investment, stifle work effort, retard invention and innovation, encourage unproductive investment in tax shelters, and needlessly reduce the Nation's standard of living and growth rate.

Second, tax-preferred activities are favored relative to others, and tax law, rather than the market, becomes the primary force in determining how economic resources are used. Over the years, the tax system has come to exert a pervasive influence on the behavior of private decision-makers. The resulting tax-induced distortions in the use of labor and capital and in consumer choices have severe costs in terms of lower productivity, lost production, and reduced consumer satisfaction.

The existing taxation of capital and business income is particularly non-neutral. It favors capital-intensive industries over others, such as services. The tax system favors industries that are unusually dependent on equipment over those -- such as wholesale and retail trade -- that rely more heavily on other forms of capital, including inventories and structures. High technology companies are put at a particular disadvantage. Since they do not require large capital investments that benefit from preferential tax treatment they bear the full brunt of high tax rates. A tax system that interferes less with market forces in the determination of what business should produce -- and how -- would be more conducive to productive investment and economic growth.

5. Inequities

Erosion of the tax base also creates inequities. Most obviously, it is unfair that two households with equal incomes should pay different amounts of tax, simply because one receives or spends its income in ways that are tax-preferred. There is, for example, no reason that employees should be allowed to escape tax on fringe benefits and entertainment provided by their employers, while others must buy the same benefits and entertainment with after-tax dollars. Even at moderate income levels, taxpayers with similar incomes can incur tax liabilities that differ by thousands of dollars. Moreover, gaps in the tax base create inequities across

199

income classes, as well as within income classes. Some of the most important tax preferences -- those that give rise to tax shelters -- benefit primarily those with high incomes.

6. Unfair Treatment of the Family

Thirty years ago the personal exemption for the taxpayer, spouse, and each dependent was $600, and there was a standard deduction of 10 percent of adjusted gross income, up to $1,000. Thus a family of four would pay no tax until income exceeded $2,675. Even though the personal exemption is now $1,000 and a larger "zero-bracket amount" has replaced the standard deduction, inflation has resulted in a substantial decline in the real value of the "tax-free amount," the level of income at which tax is first paid. Some families with incomes below the poverty level have become subject to tax. Tax burdens have increased relatively more for large families with many dependents than for other taxpayers.

The tax law was designed for a society in which dependents are generally present as part of a family with both parents present. Some groups with greater-than-average proportions of poor families, such as the elderly and the disabled, receive special tax treatment, but this treatment is often arbitrary and random, and depends on the source of the income, not on the need of the family. Until recently, the working poor have almost always been excluded from such special treatment. The special burdens faced by many single heads of households -- especially those caring for dependents and trying to work at the same time -- have been addressed inadequately.

7. Inflation and the Income Tax

The U.S. income tax was not designed to be immune from inflation. Thus when inflation accelerated in the 1970s, taxpayers with constant real incomes were pushed into progressively higher tax brackets. The proportion of income paid to the government increased, even when real income did not, and higher tax rates created serious disincentives. Historically, "bracket creep," as this effect is called, could only be offset by periodic congressional action to increase the personal exemption, zero-bracket amount (ZBA), and bracket limits. But bracket creep sensitized the public to the problem of high and rising tax rates, and the Economic

Recovery Tax Act of 1981 made a major step in tax reform by reducing tax rates and curing bracket creep. Even though many taxpayers are still subject to needlessly high marginal tax rates, the personal exemption, ZBA, and bracket limits will be indexed, starting in 1985. However, another important cause of inflation-induced tax increases remains uncorrected.

During inflationary times, taxes are collected on totally fictitious income. Capital gains taxes are paid when the prices of assets merely rise with inflation. Business firms are not allowed tax-free recovery of their real capital investments in inventories and depreciable assets. Moreover, high interest rates that merely reflect expected inflation overstate the real income of recipients of interest and inflate deductions for real interest expense.

The interaction of inflation and taxes creates further inequities and distortions. The overstatement of real interest income and deductions arbitrarily increases the tax burden on savers and rewards borrowers. Resource allocation is distorted by effective tax rates on some types of capital income that can easily exceed 100 percent. During the 1970s, the combination of high rates of inflation and a tax system that was not inflation-proof caused an increase in the tax-induced bias in favor of investment in owner-occupied housing; this probably aggravated the shortage of funds for business capital formation.

The combination of lower rates of inflation, the Accelerated Cost Recovery System of depreciation, and the lower tax rates on long-term capital gains have relieved some of the problem. Even so, the present tax system does not accurately measure real income from business or capital under most circumstances. Moreover, the tax treatment of business inventories and of debtors and creditors remains dependent on the rate of inflation.

8. The Rise of Tax Shelters

The well-advertised boom in the tax shelter industry in recent years has had particularly adverse effects. Some shelters involve little more than thinly veiled, if sophisticated, tax fraud. But even perfectly legal tax shelters distort the allocation of scarce capital because they produce highly visible inequities in taxation. Perhaps most importantly of all, they

201

undermine taxpayer confidence in the integrity and fairness of the tax system. Tax shelter losses typically result from a combination of current deductions for future expenses, deferral of taxable income, and conversion of ordinary income to preferentially taxed long-term capital gains. Thus, shelters allow taxpayers to defer tax liability far into the future. Tax deferral is equivalent to an interest-free loan from the Federal Government.

Recent data on tax returns of partnerships, a commonly used vehicle for tax shelters, indicate the nature and magnitude of the problem. In 1981 partnerships operating in the United States reported aggregate losses in excess of aggregate profits. This is not a cyclical phenomenon; partnership losses have increased steadily, relative to profits, for two decades. (See Figure 1-1.) Yet there is no reason to believe that Americans are losing more and more money each year by investing in these enterprises. Rather, many partnership investments are profitable on an after-tax basis, because they generate accounting losses that can be used to reduce or eliminate tax on other income (that is, to shelter other income from tax). But many shelter activities that offer attractive after-tax yields have little social value, as evidenced by before-tax yields that are low and sometimes even negative.

Partnerships in two industries that are favorites with tax shelter investors --oil and gas and real estate -- are a case in point. In 1982, of the $60 billion in aggregate losses reported by all partnerships, $31.6 billion in aggregate losses reported by all partnerships, $31.6 billion were attributable to losses reported by oil and gas and real estate partnerships, even though partnerships reporting losses in these two industries had a positive net cash flow of $7.6 billion.

Between 1963 and 1982, the number of taxpayers who claimed partnership losses on their individual returns increased by 400 percent, from 412,000 to 2.1 million, even though the total number of individual tax returns filed during the same period increased by only 50 percent. As a result of this growth in tax shelter activity, there has been a significant erosion in the base of the Federal income tax, particularly among taxpayers with the highest incomes. In 1983, partnership losses claimed by individual taxpayers may have

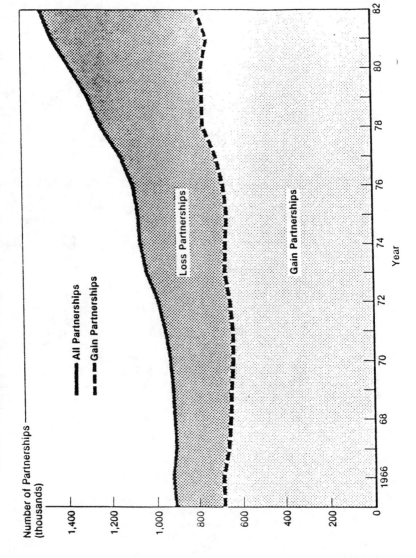

GROWTH IN PARTNERSHIPS, 1965—1982

Number of Partnerships
(thousands)

All Partnerships
Gain Partnerships

Loss Partnerships

Gain Partnerships

1966   68   70   72   74   76   78   80   82

Year

203

sheltered as much as $35 billion of individual income from taxation. An estimated 82 percent of this total ($28.6 billion in partnership losses) was reported by taxpayers whose gross income before losses was $100,000 or more, and 60 percent ($21.0 billion) was reported by taxpayers with gross income before losses in excess of $250,000. By comparison, these groups reported 9 percent and 4 percent, respectively, of all gross income before losses reported by individuals.

A sample of taxpayer returns illustrates quite strikingly the way in which tax shelter accounting losses can be used to shelter substantial amounts of income from tax. A group of 88 taxpayers who held interests in certain non-abusive tax shelters -- shelters whose legitimacy was not being questioned by the Internal Revenue Service-- were chosen for statistical analysis. Though this sample was not selected scientifically, there is no reason to believe it is not representative; certainly it indicates the nature of the problem.

Taxpayers in this sample reported positive income -- that is gross income before losses --of $17 million, or an average of $193,000. On average, each of these taxpayers owned interests in 6 partnerships, and a total of $6.4 million in net partnership losses was reported on the 88 returns. When these losses are added to other business and investment-related losses of almost $8.7 million, the taxpayers in the sample reported gross income of only $1.9 million. Thus, accounting losses from tax shelter partnerships reduced the gross income of taxpayers in the sample by almost 40 percent, and other losses reduced income by an additonal 49 percent (See Table 1-1). The taxable income of these individuals was further reduced by adjustments to gross income and by itemized deductions.

Of the 88 returns sampled, 19 returns, with an average gross income before loss (positive income) of $243,710, reported a total income tax payment of $500 or less; 37 returns, with an average gross income before loss of $172,113 reported a total tax payment of $6,000 or less. By comparison, a typical family of four, with positive income of $45,000, but no tax shelter losses, would pay $6,272 in taxes. The extent to which tax shelter losses can be used to dramatically reduce tax liabilities is further documented by estimates from the 1983 Treasury tax model which show that 9,000 taxpayers with gross incomes before losses

Table 1-1

How Tax Shelter Losses Reduce Gross Income*

(Sample of 88 Individual Income Tax Returns of Tax-Shelter Partners)

Gross Income Before Loss Class	Number of Returns	Total Gross Income Before Losses	Total Net Partnership Losses	Total Other Losses**	Gross Income After Losses
Less than $60,000	22	$ 590,435	$ -278,805	$ -120,136	$ 191,494
$60,000 - $100,000 ...	20	1,634,839	-204,311	-260,361	1,170,166
$100,000 - $200,000 ..	17	2,499,210	-993,585	-709,124	796,502
$200,000 or more	19	12,311,199	-4,667,042	-7,848,097	-203,940
Total ..	88				
Average		$ 193,587	$ -69,815	$ -101,565	$ 22,207

Office of the Secretary of the Treasury   October 30, 1984
    Office of Tax Analysis

* Calculations are from a sample of 88 individual income tax returns secured from four IRS Service Centers. Taxpayers filing these returns have investments in tax shelter partnerships that have previously been classified by an experienced examiner and accepted as nonabusive.

** Other losses include items such as nonpartnership business losses, partnership losses carried from prior tax years, and net capital losses.

of $250,000 or more paid no tax as a direct result of partnership losses, while 59,000 taxpayers with that much positive income were able to reduce their tax payments by at least one-half.

9. The Decline in Taxpayer Morale

The United States has long been proud of the "taxpayer morale" of its citizens -- the willingness to pay voluntarily the income taxes necessary to finance government activities. Taxpayer morale ultimately depends, however, on the belief that taxes are fair. If the basis for this belief comes under suspicion, voluntary compliance with the tax laws is jeopardized. Thus, the perceived lack of fairness of the income tax may be as important as actual complexities, economic distortions, and inequities. Taxpayers resent paying substantially more tax than their neighbors who have equal or higher incomes. This is true even if the neighbor reduces taxes through commonly available and perfectly legal exclusions, adjustments, deductions, and credits, rather than by questionable or illegal means. Many witnesses at tax reform hearings the Treasury Department held throughout the country during June 1984 emphasized that tax should be collected on virtually all income, with little regard to how the income is earned or spent. Taxation can be thought to be unfair because the basic tax structure is defective, as well as because taxpayers who do not comply with the law are not penalized. The proliferation and publicity of tax shelters has a particularly pernicious effect on taxpayer morale.

III. CONTENT AND IMPACTS OF THE REAGAN TAX REVOLUTION

The shortcomings of the federal tax system as described above can be corrected only by overhauling the current tax system. President Reagan has put his political prestige on the line to win reform plan. The Reagan tax reform, if enacted, would offer lower tax rates to individuals and businesses in exchange for the elimination of a variety of deductions and exclusions. As mentioned in Section II of this chapter, the basic principle of the Reagan tax reform is to encourage work, savings, and investment as well as to make the tax system fairer and simpler. The tax reform is limited, however, by the current structural budget deficits of the federal government which cannot absorb further budget revenue losses. This constraint leads to a zero-sum game in the politics of tax reform:

there are losers and gainers in this game. In order to protect losses caused by tax reform, interest groups have mobilized their financial and political strengths to protect their interests. This section will summarize the Reagan tax reform proposal and its impacts on taxpayers and corporations, describe the activities of interest groups regarding this proposal and compared these important tax proposals.

A. Impacts of Reagan Tax Reform

1. Impacts on Individuals

The Reagan tax plan would collapse the present 15 tax brackets ranging from 11 to 50 percent, into three brackets with lower rates of 15, 25 and 35 percent, and would double the personal exemption to $2,000. However, it would eliminate or reduce a variety of deductions and exclusions.

a. Lowering Tax Rates

As a result, every income earner would benefit from the lowering of tax rates: at least 2 million people at or near the poverty level would be removed from the tax rolls, and working married couples would pay less taxes. According to the Treasury Department's estimates, the Reagan plan would reduce taxes of 59 percent of families earning from $10,000 to $15,000, 64 percent of those in the $15,000-to-$20,000-income bracket, 65 percent in the $20,000-to-$50,000 range and 71 percent of those earning more than $200,000 (U.S. News & World Report: 22).

Most of the losers are found in the middle, upper-middle and some higher-income classes. Again, the Treasury Department estimated that 28 percent of families earning $30,000 to $50,000 would pay higher taxes, as would 22 percent of the $50,000-to-$100,000 group and 28 percent of the $100,000-to-$200,000-income class. Two-earner families would suffer the loss of the special deduction -- 10 percent, or up to $3,000 of the lower-paid spouse's earnings as enacted in 1981 to ease the tax penalty on married workers. Workers would pay tax on employer-paid health-insurance premiums and other fringe benefits, but would gain in child-care credit. But jobless workers would have to pay tax on the full compensation they receive while out of work if their total income is above $18,000 for married or above $12,000 for single. Disabled workers also would

207

face tax for the first time on their compensation. But veterans' benefits would remain tax-free.

Lower-income elderly, blind and disabled would come out slightly ahead, higher-income elderly slightly behind. But the special credit for the lower-income elderly, blind and disabled would be made more generous. There would be no change in Social Security taxes.

b. Eliminating or Reducing Tax Deductions and Exemptions

Home mortgage interest deductions would be allowed by the Reagan tax plan for only a principal residence, which would be worthless due to lower tax rates. Deductions for interest paid on credit cards and other personal loans would be restricted. Tax-deferred annual contributions to individual retirement accounts (IRAs) would be expanded to $4,000 for single-income couples, but tax-deferred contributions that workers make to employer-sponsored 401(K) retirement plans would be reduced.

The rules for all types of retirement-savings plans would be made more consistent and also toughened to discourage the early withdrawal of funds. Employers that terminate an over-funded pension plan would face an extra 10 percent levy on assets they retrieve.

Deductions for state and local government taxes such as property taxes, sales taxes, and personal income taxes would be eliminated. No tax deductions would be permitted for prize awards for artistic, professional, civic and other achievements.

All miscellaneous and employee business expenses, fully deductible under the current law, would be lumped into a single category deductible only in excess of 1 percent of adjusted gross income.

2. Impacts on Investors

The Reagan tax plan would reward risk-taking investors by lowering taxes for:

- profits from the sale of stocks or other assets held more than six months. Investors would pay taxes on only 50 percent of such profit, but with the proposed top personal tax rate of 35 percent, that means they would pay a maximum of 17.5 percent instead of a higher rate of 20 percent under the current tax system.

- shared dividends. Corporations would be rewarded for paying dividends through a tax deduction for 10 percent of the payments they make. Recipients of dividends also gain through low personal income tax rates although they lose the exclusion from tax for the first $100 of dividends received by an individual and $200 by a couple filing jointly.

The Reagan tax plan, however, would reduce or eliminate loopholes by:

- taxing insurance policy-holders at least part of the yearly increase in cash value of new whole-life insurance policies. In an exception, holders of variable life insurance policies would not be taxed on cash buildup. This is a boost for one of the insurance industry's newest products: deferred annuities.

- eliminating companies' tax credit for giving stocks to workers through employee-stock-ownership plans.

- limiting cash or other income-producing assets transferred by parents to their children with the idea of saving tax by having investment earnings on the assets taxed at the child's low tax rate.

- curtailing the use of so-called Clifford trusts, by which a parent can shift income-earning assets to a child for 10 years and then get the assets back.

- limiting tax savings from many limited-partnership tax shelters. New real-estate programs, for example, prevent investors from claiming tax losses greater than the amount of cash investment.

Also affecting partnerships is the new general limit on deducting interest expenses.

In general, closing tax write-offs and other breaks for investment which is enhanced by lower individual taxes blocks high-income persons from paying little or no tax.

3. Impacts on Business

Pledging to encourage economic growth rather than to increase tax revenues, President Reagan recommended a reduction in the top corporate tax rate to 33 percent from 46 percent. High-tech growth corporations, service companies, venture-capital firms, retailers and wholesalers should benefit most from the reduction.

However, large manufacturing corporations, which have used rapid depreciation and investment credits under the current tax law, might see their tax rate rise because the Reagan tax plan would eliminate or reduce a variety of tax breaks by:

- eliminating investment tax credit. This would hurt the so-called "old-line smokestack" industries such as steel, aluminum, paper, machine tools, machinery and transportation which invest heavily in plants and equipments to conduct their businesses.

- reducing the speed of tax write-offs for the depreciation of the equipment and property. For example, depreciation is stretched from five to seven years for general machinery, from 18 to 28 years for commercial construction. Also, a tax credit of up to 25 percent of the cost of rehabilitating old or historic buildings would be abolished. However, to offset the negative effects of the longer write-off periods, the cost on which depreciation is based would be adjusted upward annually for inflation.

- reducing deductions for business meals and eliminating all deductions now allowed for business conventions and seminars held aboard cruise ships and for entertaining customers and clients at sporting events, theaters, and country clubs. This would hurt restaurant, hotel, travel and other entertainment industries.

- eliminating the percentage-depletion allowance for large oil and gas producers but this allowance would be retained for small producers.

- eliminating deductions allowed under the current law for bad debts and interest on borrowings to carry tax-exempt bonds. Banks, savings and loans, other thrifts, as well as credit unions with assets of more than 5 million dollars would pay more taxes due to the loss of their tax-exempt status.

- repealing a special 20 percent deduction now
  allowed life-insurance companies and limiting the
  deduction they can take for reserves, as well as
  other deductions.

- repealing farmers' income averaging of investment
  tax credit and capital gains on depreciable
  property.

- repealing tax exemptions for bonds issued by state
  and local governments to help finance private
  projects. In addition to loss of federal
  deductibility for local taxes, this tax measure
  would hinder state and local governments efforts
  in luring industrial development.

   In general, the Reagan tax plan would bring about
other major changes in the way the economy and
society function. It penalizes high-tax states such as
New Jersey, Maryland, Massachusetts, Minnesota, New
York, Wisconsin and California to the advantage of low-
tax states; and deprives the banking, mining, timber,
oil and gas, life-insurance and commercial real-estate
industries of special tax breaks. But it favors the
regional economies of the South and Southwest in the
competition with the Northeast and Midwest; rewards
high-tech and service industries at the expense of
"smokestack" manufacturers; and benefits venture-
capital firms but tightening up on tax-shelter
promoters.

B. Political Pressure Against the Reagan Tax Reform

   Unanimity is rare in the American public policy
making process. This is particularly true in the
federal tax reform due to several reasons. First of
all, policymakers disagree over values. Some think
that tax equality should be most important, thus
support a more progressive tax system; this means that
wealthy individuals should pay a higher tax rate while
poor individuals should pay a lower percentage. Some
others believe that a good tax policy should be able to
spur economic growth, and support a tax system which
gives incentives to savings and investments. Moreover,
it is difficult to measure the full consequences of a
policy decision. A classic example is the window tax
enacted in England in 1696. At that time, the
government did not have a good base to determine
taxable income. The window tax base was considered as a
good measure of ability to pay because wealthy

individuals had houses with more windows than those of poor individuals. A consequence beyond the intention of policy makers was that dark houses with few windows were built to avoid tax. Similarly, it is difficult to measure the full consequences of tax measures such as impacts of elimination of certain tax deductions or exemptions on the industry and local state, regional and national economy.

Finally, policy makers disagree about what the consequences of a government policy will be. Would tax breaks given to wealthy individuals, for instance, be used for savings and investments?

Facing uncertainty about the consequences of policies they make, lawmakers are subject to pressure of interest groups and their constituents. As mentioned in Chapter 3, fiscal bias exists among lawmakers due to their concern about being reelected by voters. Among other things, they vote under the pressure of their voters and interest groups at home.

Since the Treasury Department's proposed tax reform plan was submitted to President Reagan, the lobbying efforts of every interest group have followed its evolution. It is unfair to say that the modifications President Reagan made in the treasury tax plan sent the "wrong signal" to interest groups and that "they whetted the appetite of every interest group for keeping its cherished tax breaks" as stated by The New Republic (June 17, 85: 7). With or without modifications made by President Reagan, it is a common practice in the American policy making process that interest groups involved in all stages of the evolution of any legislation, from the time the bill was initiated to the time it would be passed by Congress. Students of interest groups may find that the interest groups' showdown over the Reagan tax reform is one of the strongest in the U.S. history because the tax reform will affect every single individual, industry and state and local government.

Interest groups and their political action committees have used, among other pressures, their monetary power of contributions to sway policy makers to their side. In the first six months of 1985, members of the House Ways and Means and the Senate Finance Committees, who comprise 10.5 percent of Congress, collected 23.5 percent or $3.5 million of the $15 million given by political action committees. This $15 million political contribution is three times greater in the first six months of 1983, a comparable non-election-year period (Congressional Quarterly Weekly Report, 1985: 1806).

Leading the charge against key elements in the Reagan tax reform plan were advocates for state and local governments, insurance industry, organized labor, and many other groups. The proposed abolishment of federal tax deductions for state and local taxes was opposed by organizations that form one of the most effective lobbies including the National Governors Association, National Conference of State Legislatures and the 1.1-million-member American Federation of State, County and Municipal Employees. To convince lawmakers, they argued that this abolishment could throw their budgets into disarray, force reduced public services and cause affluent and middle-income taxpayers to move elsewhere.

Immediately after the treasury tax reform plan was sent to President Reagan, the insurance industry launched a 2-million-dollar public-relations drive to preserve its tax status by sending 1 million cards and letters to Congress, running TV advertisements in 62 cities and producing a short film titled "The Worst Little Horror Story in Taxes" (U.S. News & World Report, June 10, 1985: 31). As a result, a tax group-life insurance recommended in the Treasury reform plan was dropped in the Reagan tax plan.

The 13.7 million member AFL-CIO sent hundreds of thousands of postcards to key legislators, and held regional conferences of union leaders across the country to plan strategy how to gain media attention. As a result, major modifications in workers' benefits were made in tax plans following the treasury proposal.

Under the pressure of representatives of the industry, including the Independent Petroleum Association of America, the percentage-depletion allowance for small drillers' the immediate write-off of intangible drilling costs proposed in the Treasury proposal were preserved in the Reagan tax bill.

Fearing erosion of home values caused by proposed abolition of property-tax deductions and limitation on mortgage-interest deductions for second homes, and changes in rules relating to depreciation of commercial and industrial buildings, real estate industry

213

lobbyists relied heavily on traditional strengths -- a broad, locally influential membership and a reputation for contributing liberally to congressional campaigns. Modifications were made regarding limitation on mortgage interest deductions for second houses. The 18-million-member American Association of Retired Persons and other senior citizens' groups have been fighting to save tax breaks important to the elderly, including deductions for state and local taxes and the double exemption for persons 65 and over. The National Association of Independent Colleges and Universities is among opponents of tax plans to limit charitable deductions only to those who itemize returns by arguing that education could be deprived of billions in gifts and services.

Added to activities of interest groups described above are other groups of industry and professionals including restaurants, motels and teachers.

Not all taxpayers, however, oppose the Reagan tax reform. The poor and venture capitalists benefit from it through lower tax rates. Advocates for these interests supported it but have little organized influence on Congress.

C. President Reagan Tax Reform: A Compromise Outcome?

The American government is characterized by its responsiveness. It responds to the need for a major tax reform; but it also responds to the pressure of a variety of interest groups and political parties which are hurt by the reform or do not gain as much as they expect. Consequently, starting from the Treasury proposal drawn from long held economic theories of both liberal and conservative tax scholars, President Reagan, the House Ways and Means Committee and the Senate Finance Committee sacrificed conceptual purity to accommodate political interests. Representative Dan Rostenkowski, Chairman of the House Ways and Means Committee, stated: "We have not written a perfect law. Perhaps a faculty of scholars could do a better job. A group of ideologies could have provided greater consistency. But politics is an imperfect process" (New York Times, November 25, 1985: 10).

As shown in Appendix A, some tax deductions and exclusions for intangible oil drilling costs, capital gains, some exemptions for credit union, and taxes deferred for life insurance investment income and annuity income which were eliminated in the Treasury proposal, were modified in the Reagan tax bill. The House Ways and Means Committee, facing pressure from constituents and influenced by their political party's ideology, rewrote the Reagan tax plan to:

- provide more tax relief for lower- and middle-income taxpayers and preserve a series of special tax breaks popular among middle-class constituents, such as the deductions for state and local taxes and vacation-home mortgage interest;

- retain current special tax treatment for small business, credit unions, small and medium-size banks, small timber producers, farmers, property owners, state and local governments and charitable organizations; and

- increase tax rates for capital gain to 36 percent from 33 percent proposed by President Reagan and the Treasury, and add a higher 38 percent tax rate on the top of three personal income tax brackets proposed by President Reagan.

Dissatisfied with the House Ways and Means Committee's tax reform proposal, the Senate Finance Committee controlled by conservative Republicans came up with its own tax plan which would, among other things, provided more tax savings for high-income tax-payers, and reduce tax rates for capital gain from 36 percent voted by the House to 33 percent as proposed by President Reagan and the Treasury (see Appendix A). On June 24, 1986, the Senate, on a 97- 3 vote, approved its tax plan and sent it to conference with the House to resolve the differences between the two tax bills. After a summer of discussions, members of the Conference Committee, chaired by Representative Dan Rostenkowski, finally produced a compromise tax bill on August 16, 1986 and sent it to the House of Representatives. The bill was passed by the House on September 25, 1986 and the Senate on September 27, and was signed by President Reagan on October 22, 1986.

Tracing the chronology of efforts leading to the 1986 tax reform discloses a lot about the power of President Reagan in framing a public debate on his own terms. He made tax reform the highest legislative priority of his second term and made his tax reform proposal as a "white hat issue" which was hard for legislators to oppose openly. As stated by House

215

Minority leader Robert H. Michel, it would be politically devasting for the Republican party if President's
tax reform failed for several reasons. Republicans who
adhere to the theory that high levels of taxation
inhibit investment endorsed the bill because of its low
tax rates. Moreover, they found it politically advanta-
geous to support as a way to dispel the notion that
they belonged to the party of big business (New York
Times, September 28, 1986: 34).

Democrats were also in a difficult political
situation. House Speaker Thomas P. O'Neill Jr. stated
that if House Democrats blocked the tax bill, they
would give President Reagan "a club to hit" them over
the head with until the November, 1986 election. It was
to their advantage to join President Reagan in what was
a traditional Democratic stance against tax loopholes.
The Democrats felt that they would be tarnished as the
party of special interests if they opposed the tax
reform (New York Times, September 28, 1986: 38).

Despite the perceived political advantages of both
Republicans and Democrats in supporting the Reagan tax
reform, the tax bill has had many narrow escapes. It
almost collapsed in Fall 1985 in the House Ways and
Means Committeee, only to be revised through old-
fashioned political horse trading by Dan Rostenkowski,
chairman of the Committee. Then when the bill reached
the House floor, it was almost killed when Republicans
mounted a surprise procedural attack. President Reagan
saved the bill with powerful arm-twisting and
extraordinary lobbying trip to Capitol Hill.

As a result of political compromise, the new tax
law differed in many ways from President Reagan's
original blueprint. For instance, his proposed personal
income tax rates of 15 percent, 25 percent, ang 35
percent were changed to 15 percent and 25 percent; and
his proposed corporate tax rate of 33 percent was
changed to 34 percent.

In general, the new tax law drastically reduces
income tax rates for individuals and corporations and
eliminates or reduces hundreds of deductions and other
tax advantages. Some major provisions are mentioned
below.

D. SOME MAJOR PROVISIONS OF THE NEW TAX LAW

Most taxpayers and corporations will get an

average tax cut of 6.1 percent and more than 6 million taxpayers now on the tax rolls will pay no tax due to lower tax rates, higher tax exemptions and standard deductions (See Appendix A).

1. **Lower Tax Rates.** In 1987, tax rates will range from 11 percent of taxable income to 38.5 percent. After that, there will be two tax rates of 15 and 28 percent, and a third, hidden rate of 33 percent. Capital gains will be taxed as ordinary income; this means a lower tax rate for investors. Several million taxpayers, including those with income between $30,000 and $40,000, will pay more tax.

2. **Increased Personal Exemptions.** Each dependent will have a tax exemption of $1,900 in 1987, $1,950 in 1988, $2,000 in 1990 and will be adjusted for inflation afterward. When taxable income exceeds $71,900 for couples and $43,150 for singles, exemptions will be gradually reduced in accordance with increase in earnings. Blind and elderly lose their extra exemptions allowed by the old tax code.

3. **Increased Standard Deductions.** Taxpayers who do not itemize deductions will get some relief. In 1988, couples get $5,000, singles $3,000, heads of household $4,400, and blind or elderly $600 extra per spouse if married and $750 if single. Annual inflation adjustments will be made to standard deductions afterward.

4. **Repealed Itemized Deductions.** The new tax law repeals deductions for state and local sales taxes, interest on consumer credits such as credit cards and car loans, special deductions for two-income earners. Except for some investments in oil and gas, most passive investment losses, generated by big depreciation deductions, could not be used to shield wages from taxation.

5. **Corporate Taxes.** Top corporate tax rate of 46 percent will drop to 34 percent. Small businesses will pay as little as 15 percent. However, credit for investment will be repealed and depreciation will be less generous for buildings and more beneficial for most equipments.

V. CONCLUDING REMARKS

The new tax law will have a variety of impacts on

217

federal budget deficits and the economy in addition to individual taxpayers and corporations. The pressure of spending cuts in efforts to reduce budget deficits coupled with the pressure of interest groups against these cuts makes revenue raising alternatives necessary. The possibility of plugging tax loopholes and revamping the tax code is one way besides raising taxes to increase budget revenues. However, increase in revenue through repealed tax loopholes is offset by decrease in revenue through lower tax rates. The end result of the new tax law will make federal budget-deficit targets required by the Gramm-Rudman law difficult to be met.

How will the new tax law affect the economy? It is not easy to assess this impact. By repealing the investment tax credit, a major job-creating incentive for most of the last two decades, by shifting $120 billion in taxes from individuals to corporations in the next five years, and by reducing depreciation allowance, the new tax law would reduce the incentives for business expansion which could lead to a weaker economy. However, by lowering individual taxes, it would increase work incentives and expand the consumption market. Apparently, the new tax law will push the economy toward consumption and away from investment as it transfers the tax burden from individuals to businesses.

While its impact on the economic growth is uncertain, the new tax law reflects a shift toward the laissez-faire philosophy rather than using the tax code to push certain social and economic goals. Instead of being driven by tax incentives written over the years to encourage activities lawmakers perceived as economically or socially beneficial, individuals and corporations will be guided by the marketplace.

Major Provisions of Three Tax Reform Proposals

	Current Law	Reagan Plan	House Bill	Senate Bill
Individual Tax Rates	11-50 percent (14 brackets)	15,25 and 35 percent	15,25,35 and 38 percent	15 and 27 percent (lower rate would be phased out for high-income taxpayers)
Personal Exemption	$1,080(1986)	$2,000	$2,000 for non-itemizers;$1,500 for itemizers	$2,000 for low-and middle-income taxpayers (exemption would be phased out for high-income taxpayers)
Corporate Tax Rates	15-40 percent on first $100,000 of income; 46 percent thereafter	33 percent;lower rates for income below $75,000	15-30 percent up to $75,000; 36 percent above $75,000	33 percent; same as House bill for income below $75,000
Interest Payments	Deductions for home mortgage and non-business interest	Unlimited deduction for primary residences; additional interest deductions capped at $5,000	Unlimited deduction for mortgages on first and second residences; additional deduction of $10,000 ($20,000 for joint returns)plus the value of a taxpayer's investment income	Unlimited deduction for mortgages on first and second residences; no consumer interest deduction; interest paid on borrowing to produce investment income would be deductible equal to the value of the investment earnings
Health Benefits	Employer-paid health premiums not taxed; medical expenses deductible if more than 5 percent of adjusted gross income	First $10 a month in employer-paid premiums for individuals ($25 for families) taxed as income; retain existing law for medical deductions	Retain existing law on taxation of health benefits and medical deductions	Retain existing law on taxation of health benefits; medical expenses would be deductible to the extent they exceed 9 percent of adjusted gross income

Charitable Donations	Deductible	Full deductions for itemizers; none for non-itemizers	No change for itemizers; non-itemizers could deduct amount above $100	Full deductions for itemizers; none for non-itemizers
State and Local Taxes	Deductible	Deduction eliminated	No change from existing law	Income, real estate and personal property taxes would be deductible; 60 percent of sales taxes above amount of state income taxes would be deductible
Depreciation	Recovery periods of 3-19 years with accelerated write-off	More generous write-off over 4-28 years; value adjusted for inflation	Recovery periods of 3-30 years; partially indexed for inflation	Retain current system of rapid write-offs, permitting larger write-offs for most property over longer periods
Capital Gains	60 percent exclusion; top effective rate of 20 percent	Top effective rate of 17.5 percent, but assets eligible would be limited	42 percent exclusion; top effective rate of 22 percent	Special exclusion repealed; taxed at same rates as regular income
Investment Tax Credit	6-10 percent	Repealed	Repealed	Repealed
Oil and Gas	Allow percentage depletion, and expensing of intangible drilling costs	Repeal oil depletion allowance for all but small wells; keep "intangible" drilling breaks, but subject to minimum tax	Repeal percentage depletion allowance for all but small wells; allow expensing of intangible drilling costs for non-producing wells; 26-month write-off for producing wells	No change from existing law for percentage depletion allowance or intangible drilling costs
Business Expenses	Deductible	Deduction for entertainment repealed; limit on meals	Deduction of 80 percent of business meals and 80 percent of entertainment costs	Similar to House for meals and entertainment; most miscellaneous deductions eliminated

PART IV

BUDGET DEFICIT-REDUCING MEASURES:

A SYSTEM PERSPECTIVE

CHAPTER 10

RESTRUCTURING THE FEDERAL BUDGETING
AND ACCOUNTING SYSTEM*

U.S.
3226
5410

Charles A. Bowsher

The 1980s have been years of unprecedented growth
in the nation's budget deficit. Current projections
indicate that deficits will continue to increase if
present policies are continued, and consensus is
growing that this would create ever increasing risks
for economic stability and growth. The response to
this consensus will involve an enormous challenge to
federal managers.

Revenue increases, spending cuts, or both, are the
only available ways of correcting current and future
imbalances in the nation's budget. Most reform
proposals focus on the need to restructure our current
program priorities and tax policy. They are often
described as longer term measures. But I suspect that
effects of the budget problem on federal managers will
be much more immediate.

In civilian agencies, managers will face
increasing pressures to cut programs and to reduce
costs. In the Department of Defense, they will face
equally great demands to assure that the rapid growth
is managed effectively and that increased defense
resources are translated into increased defense
capability. Timely and reliable program and financial
information are critical to successful management under
these circumstances. However, our current financial
management structure and supporting systems are not
capable of coping with the demands which must be placed
on them if managers are to meet their responsibilities.
We must begin now to modernize the federal government's
financial management structure and put the systems into
place that will serve the needs of the public and the
government.

I. FINANCIAL MANAGEMENT ISSUES

---

* This chapter is reprinted from Public Administration
Review, Vol 45, No. 1 (January/February, 1985), pp. 176
- 184.

1. Consistent and Reliable Financial Information Is Essential for Good Management

The activities of the federal government are massive in comparison to those of any other nation or industry. For example, over $2 billion is spent daily to keep the government operating. Controlling such an immense operation requires accurate and timely information so that difficult policy and management decisions are made before they are too late. However, today's financial reports do not provide a clear picture of government activities. In many cases they are so untimely or irrelevant (or both) that they are useless as a basis for managerial decision-making.

A clear example of this problem is the lack of consistency in the way the federal budget is prepared versus the way expenditures and revenues are accounted for and reported. Budgets are requested and justified in terms of programs and projects, such as infant health care or claims for flood control. Accounting and other financial reports, however, often focus on appropriations and categories of expense, such as travel or personnel, without relating them to the particular programs or projects for which the funding was requested and approved.

Illustration 1

**Illustration of budgeting/Accounting Mismatch:
A Major Medical Care Account**

Budget System Reporting Categories

- Maintenance and operation of facilities
- Contract services
- Grants for state services
- Civilian health program

Accounting System Reporting Categories

- Personnel compensation
- Communications, utilities, rent and other
- Other services
- Supplies and materials

Managing the government efficiently also requires reliable and timely management reporting that compares expectations with actual performance. The current federal financial structure focuses management's attention on obligation and outlay reporting that seldom compares budgeted with actual financial data. While both obligations and outlays are important, neither is a consistently reliable measure of the actual resources consumed in carrying out government programs. Obligation-basis reporting is essential in monitoring the extent to which agencies are making commitments for future payments. Cash-basis reporting is essential in managing fiscal, debt, and credit policies. However, reporting that compares the resources actually consumed to provide an output with those budgeted to achieve the desired results would provide managers with a better basis for decision-making.

Budgeting and accounting should should be on the same basis and use the same reporting categories so that meaningful management reports can be produced, measuring actual results against plans. An integrated budgeting and accounting system that focuses on the resources used or consumed to achieve program results will help to assure that the costs of activities are consistently recorded across government. Such a system could compare and report the estimated and actual costs of operations, organizatins, programs, and projects.

Among the benefits to the federal government of adopting such a system would be:

- The ability to compare planned with actual use of resources;

- Reliable project status reporting;

- If desired, the ability to establish user fees for government services that fully cover the cost of those services;

- The ability to compare activities of similar operations across the government;

- More accurate budget estimates based on actual past program and project costs;

- The ability to measure the input of resources and the output of performance;

- Greater assurance that financial transactions are not

225

artificially moved from one fiscal year to another; and

- Increased accountability for the management of public funds.

2. Project Reporting Helps Management to Focus on Specific Activities.

Project reporting provides specialized reports to monitor and control specific activities, such as construction of capital assets or development of major weapons systems. This form of reporting is lacking or is not always complete or consistent with existing federal financial systems. The Department of Defense Selected Acquisition Reports (SARs), reporting on the status of major weapons systems, illustrate the need for improved project reporting. For example, in the December 1982 SARs:

- The $20.1 billion baseline SAR estimate for the B-1 bomber excluded more than $1 billion in costs, such as flight simulators for pilot training, that were clearly part of the program.

- The estimate for the Army's Bradley Fighting Vehicle showed an illusory decrease of $679 million in ammunition cost. This amount was substracted because SARs do not include ammunition costs unless the ammunition is unique to a specific weapon system. In this case, the Army had decided to buy the same ammunition for the Bradley and the Light Infantry Vehicle.

- Though they are built by the same contractor, two different inflation estimates were used for the Navy's Tomahawk Missile and the Air Force's Ground Launched Cruise Missile. Since the December SARs must tie to the president's budget, it is evident that the budget requests for these two systems were based on imcompatible assumptions.

The SARs are provided to Congress quarterly. They were created by the Defense Department in 1969 because its management systems, which focused on obligations, did not provide needed information on costs, production rates, and technical performance. Though useful, the SARs have three major limitations. First, the SARs rely on contractor and other information that does not necessarily tie to the accounting systems of the

Department of Defense and can be reconciled to the budget only in December.

Second, information on the same weapons systems may be reported differently from one year to the next, and the changes are not always clearly explained. The SAR of December 31, 1982, for example, reported the Trident II submarine as a new weapon system even though the only difference between it and the Trident I was the type of missile it would carry. This had the effect of disrupting the historical data on what is essentially the same weapon system.

Finally, the information in the SARs is not consistent with that in other budget documents provided to Congress. According to the Congressional Budget Office, cost estimates in the December 31, 1982, SAR for 13 systems excluded at least $40.8 billion in program costs reported elsewhere.

According to the Congressional Budget Office, cost estimates in the December 31, 1982 SAR (Selected Acquisition Reports for 13 (defense) systems excluded at least $40.8 billion in program costs reported elsewhere.

From this discussion, it should be obvious that the SARs have serious weaknesses as a project reporting system. Those deficiencies must be corrected if the current defense building is to be managed effectively and public support for that building is to be sustained. The problem, however, is not limited to the defense program. Many civilian agencies also undertake large projects, and the project reporting systems in many cases are just as inadequate or maybe worse than the SAR system.

Clear, summary project reports of the type displayed below would make it much easier for members of Congress and executive branch policy officials, as well as program managers, to quickly determine the status of projects - civilian or military - and explore further the causes of any increased cost estimates and schedule slippages. They would have information about a project's expected cost, how this compares to previous estimates, how much money has been spent, what it has been used for, and what has been accomplished.

227

3. **Performance** Information Can Assist Program and Budget Evaluation

A management system that measures only financial resources is incomplete. An effective system also measures what is produced using these resources. Assessing government accomplishments requires measuring employee and program performance. Though the size and complexity of the government make it difficult, developing effective performance measurement systems is clearly possible. Output measures are already in place for large parts of the government. Many of the measures need to be improved - and most of all they need to be used - but their existence demonstrates the feasibility of the approach.

A well-developed financial management structure should include performance information that can be used for both day-to-day management and policy and budgeting decisions. An effective system of measuring program performance requires:

- agreeing on objectives and relevant measures of accomplishment;

- systematically collecting reliable, consistent, and comparable information on costs and accomplishments; and

- supplying that information routinely for use in management, planning, programming, and budgeting.

Strong performance monitoring systems can answer many routine questions about program performance. Consider, for instance, a program whose goal is to immunize children against certain childhood diseases (e.g., mumps, polio). A reliable system of performance indicators would provide information on the level of resources and effort devoted to each program site, the number of eligible children being served, the number of immunizations administered, and the cost per immunization. The incidence of these diseases in children could also be monitored.

Even the best systems, however, cannot answer all important questions about program effects and policy alternatives. Therefore, a modern structure of financial management should include a systematic way to identify questions that warrant special analysis. In our example, we may notice that at several sites there

228

is a precipitous drop in the number of children being immunized. But our indicators give little clue as to why this should be so. A study could be undertaken to determine the reason for the drop and the appropriate actions to take.

Such special studies can provide decision makers with important additional information about program performance. But it is equally important that these studies be designed so that their results can be integrated with the information produced by the regular performance and financial reports. The results can then be used to help identify both future resource and program needs and ways of improving the routine performance measures in use.

4. Planning for Capital Investments Must Be Strengthened

Federal capital investment activity is managed through numerous agencies, programs, and funding sources. No structured approach exists to make capital investment decisions, and no policy mechanism is in the place to assess capital investment priorities for the government as a whole. The lack of visibility for investment decisions, coupled with a budget and accounting approach which treats capital spending as if it were the same as spending for current operations, creates what some consider to be a systematic bias against capital investment.

The needed visibility of capital budgeting within the unified budget could be achieved by displaying capital investment activities separately.Thus, each major functional category in the budget (e.g., national defense, energy, agriculture) might include an operating component and a capital investment component.

The capital component could include new investments in capital assets, whether acquired directly by the federal government or through loans and grants to state and local governments. The several capital components could be combined to represent the federal government's capital budget. The operating component would include salaries, utilities, contracted services, and other expenses not related to investment, as well as depreciation expenses if applicable.

This separation of capital and operating expenditures within the unified budget would:

229

Illustration 2

A Sample Project Report Construction Project

Project Status of 10/3/83

	Planned Cost	Actual Cost To Date	Estimate to Complete	Total Cost to Complete	Increase(+) Decrease(-)	Months Under (-) Over (+)
Research and Development	16	20	0	20	+4	+2
Testing and Evaluation	4	3	0	3	-1	
Design	10	11	0	11	+1	+1
Procurement	70	10	65	75	+5	+2
	100	44	65	109	+9	

Funding Status as of 10/3/83

			Obligations		
	Appropriation				
Number	Description	Date	Amount	Amount	Unobligated
XXXX	Research and Development Testing and Evaluation (FY 82)	10/81	20	20	0
XXXX	Research and Development Testing and Evaluation (FY Supplemental)	2/82	3	3	0
XXXX	Construction (FY 83)	10/82	10	10	0
XXXX	Construction (FY 83 Supplemental)	4/83	1	1	0
XXXX	Construction (FY 84)	10/83	70	35	35
	Totals		104	69	35
	Current Estimate		109		
	Increase (+)/Decrease (-)		+5		

230

- elevate the visibility of capital investment decisions;

- facilitate the development of replacement planning; and

- allow a comparison of the long-term costs and benefits of capital investments across budget functions.

Federal managers have long complained about a perceived bias against productivity enhancing capital investment. The approach suggested here could help to eliminate any such bias. It has many of the advantages of a separate capital budget. At the same time, it maintains the integrity of the unified budget, an essential defense against manipulating the definition of capital investment.

5. Planning and Programming Can Improve Decision Making on Major Policy Issues

Sound financial management requires a process that focuses attention on major policy issues and alternatives and their probable future consequences. To be effective, the process needs information on the actual costs and benefits of prior decisions. Increasingly, the major problems facing the nation defy short-term, narrowly focused solutions. "With rising health care costs and an aging population, for example, managing the costs of Medicare requires both a long-term strategy and consideration of the interaction of Medicare with other health programs, such as Medicaid, and with private health insurance programs."

The federal government currently has few of the necessary pieces of such a process. Often, top management attention to policy or legislative issues is unstructured, divorced from actual experience, focused on individual programs, and concerned only with the next year or two. Budgeting remains the dominant financial management process and the focus of decision makers' attention. The budget process tends to operate as a separate system that ignores or "crowds out" information from both agency planning and program offices and the accounting system. Consequently, products developed in these two phases are not used well in the budgetary process. Yet sound budgeting and sound financial management depend both on the analysis

231

of future trends and program needs (planning/ programming) and on past performance (accounting). No single process should dominate.

A structured planning and programming process can help identify solutions to major long-term problems, such as financial health care. The cornerstone of this concept is the use of a formal, analytical process for considering the medium - and long-term implications for current decisions. To be successful, the planning and programming structure must be an integral part of financial management decision-making, as it is in the Defense Department. When the planning, programming, and budgeting system (PPBS) was tried by civilian agencies in the late 1960s, it failed in part because it was added to, and often competed with, existing systems and processes, rather than being built into the basic structure of financial management.

A well-developed, modern, government-wide structure of planning and programming would highlight the major policy and program options available to decision makers together with their likely benefits and costs. Making these decisions in a more systematic way would reduce some of the pressure on the budget process. It would also enable Congress, the president, and agency officials to focus their policy deliberations more systematically on the major issues facing the nation.

The inadequacies of the planning and programming elements of the decision process have serious, but often unrecognized, implications for managers. It is in these stages where program goals and strategies are examined and expectations are set. If these expectations are poorly conceived or imcompatible, or if the budget process ignores them, it is the manager who must cope with the resulting ambiguity and explain the failure to achieve expected results. Thus, the manager has a very real stake in developing an effective planning and programming system.

Illustration 3

Effective Planning and Programming

Major Elements

- A mechanism to identify, evaluate, and select realistic goals and strategies for addressing major issues.

- A multi-year view for those programs where sound choices cannot be made using the one-year budget horizon.

- A program structure that relates the costs of programs to the out-puts (results, benefits) produced or missions served.

- The ability to apply modern analytic techniques in assessing issues and alternatives.

- A means to aggregate program costs by major activity area and agency as well as government-wide.

- Feedback mechanisms that reliably, consistently, and systematically develop and provide useful program performance information and analyses to those who need it.

Major Benefits

- Assist officials to focus on the fundamental questions of what the government should be doing and how best to accomplish it.

- Encourage longer term thinking and permit more realistic multi-year financial planning for agencies and the government as a whole.

- Provide an essential analytic framework for decision-making and a better basis for evaluating the benefits and costs of alternatives.

- Facilitate choices among alternative goals, missions, strategies, and programs.

- Help assure that programs are affordable and balanced given national priorities.

- Enable officials to learn about the results of past decisions and apply this knowledge more effectively when future program decisions are made.

233

6. Full Disclosure of All Costs and Liabilities Is Necessary for Adequate Planning and Budgeting

Congress and the executive branch must be fully aware of all the government's financial commitments to adequately manage and oversee its activities. Today the federal budget does not include all governmental activities, nor does it disclose all costs of those activities that do appear in the budget. In addition, financial reports do not fully disclose the government's financial committments. For example, the government's liability for retirement benefits represents a major commitment of future federal resources. A recent report estimated the unfunded portion of retirement benefits to be several hundred billion dollars. But the budget only partially recognizers retirement benefits being earned by today's civilian employees, while those of military personnel were not recognized at all until Congress changed the law in the Department of Defense Authorization Act of 1984. The comprehensiveness of the budget will be further reduced if the current plan to move Social Security retirement and disability funds off the budget in 1993 is implemented.

The Federal Financing Bank had $106.9 billion in off-budget loans outstanding in 1983 and issued some $32 billion in new loans in 1982. In addition, costs of direct loans, such as loan write-offs and interest subsidies, are not routinely disclosed to decision makers. Anticipated write-offs, such as those for foreign military sales and many loan programs, are often not recognized in the budget or the accounting systems. The cost of interest subsidies is often buried as part of the interest on the public debt. Thus, decision makers may be misled into assuming that programs are less expensive than they are.

Loan guarantees are another case where the government's financial condition is not fully disclosed. Contingent liabilities should be accurately measured and incorporated into the government's financial reports.

To avoid the risk of inappropriately mortgaging the future, decision makers should recognize the long-term consequences of current benefit and loan programs. Budget documents, financial statements, and reports received by Congress and the executive branch should

Illustration 4

Total Unfunded Civil & Military Retirement Costs

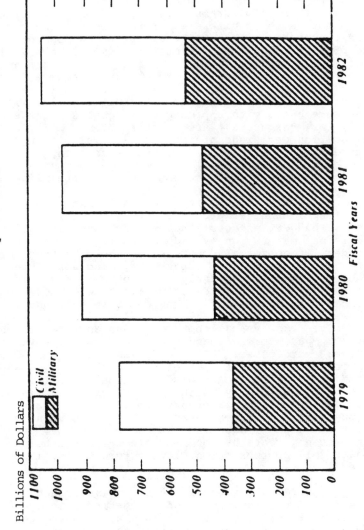

fully disclose the financial position of the government and reflect all costs of government activities.

In the short run, it is often tempting for program managers and policy officials to seek to hide the true costs of their programs. It may appear that doing so allows them to acquire greater resources in support of their objectives than would otherwise be possible. That temptation should be resisted for two reasons. First, the results will come back to haunt the manager and the program itself when the true costs are eventually disclosed, as they surely will be. Second, if this sort of distortion is allowed, other managers also will play the same game, with unpredictable results. Managers, as well as taxpayers, are better served if resource allocation decisions are made on a level playing field, where numbers mean what they appear to mean.

7. The Federal Budget Process Could Be Streamlined

Reliable, timely information is indispensable to an effective budget process. However, equally important is a budget process that focus the attention of decision makers on available choices. The current budget processes of Congress and the executive branch are unduly detailed, repetitive, and work-intensive. These processes urgently need to be simplified and streamlined so that decision makers can more easily concentrate on the budget choices that confront them.

Over the years, both Congress and the executive branch have made changes designed to improve their budget processes. The Congressional Budget and Impoundment Control Act of 1974 created an essential framework for Congress to set national priorities. But the act did this by adding to the existing machinery for authorization, appropriation, and tax legislation. Though it devotes an ever greater proportion of its time to budget issues and the budget process, Congress in recent years has been unable to pass a budget and enact all appropriations laws before the beginning of the fiscal year.

Improvements tied in the executive branch - e.g., planning, programming, and budgeting; management by objective; zero-base budgeting - also have generally been added to existing systems and processes. As a result, both Congress and the executive branch are faced with burdensome processes marked by repetitious detail that obscures, rather than highlights, budget

Off-Budget Loans Held By The Federal Financing Bank

Billions of Dollars

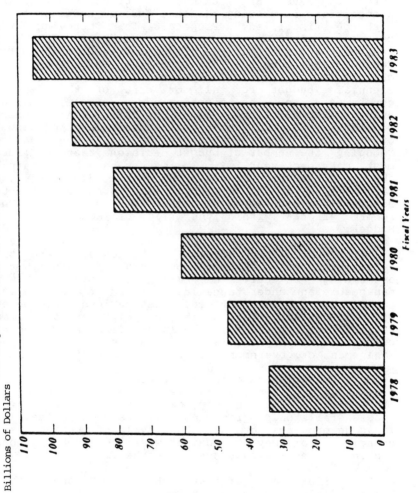

choices.

Budget execution, like budget preparation, has grown more detailed and complex. Managerial flexibility and efficiency is increasingly limited by the growing number of constraints on the uses of funds imposed by both Congress and executive branch officials. Recognition is growing that the federal budget process must be simplified. Proposals for improving the congressional budget process have come from both within Congress and such outside groups as the Committee for Economic Development. Those proposals include selected changes in congressional organization and procedures; a biennial budget for all or part of the federal government; and the adoption of a single, omnibus budget, appropriations and tax bill. All these proposals have the common goal of reducing the number of layers in the congressional budget process and/or reducing the number of budget decisions that Congress must make each year. Similar issues have been raised about the executive branch process, as indicated by the 1983 National Academy of Public Administration report, **Deregulation of Government Management** and by continuing reform efforts within the Office of Management and Budget.

Proposals for reform in both Congress and the executive branch should be judged against the overriding objective of making the process more manageable and understandable. Members of Congress and top executive branch officials must be less encumbered with unnecessary detail so they can give more attention to major policy issues, the long-term consequences of current budgetary decisions, and the oversight and management of government programs and agencies.

If these reform efforts succeed, the implications for managers will be substantial. Much of the burden of the present, inordinately complex budget formulation process falls on program managers, as does the task of managing programs for which the levels of funding keep changing from day to day or week to week as one continuing resolution succeeds another.

8. Good Financial Information Requires Strong Accounting, Auditing, and Reporting

The importance of good financial information underscores the need for well-designed, integrated budgeting and accounting systems. Because current systems are not integrated, budgets are frequently developed without reliable information on what has occurred. This often leads to unrealistic budget planning and difficulty in controlling budget execution. Reforms are needed to strengthen how the government accounts for financial resources and to improve the financial information used by Congress and the executive branch. The consistent application of comprehensive accounting principles and standards by all agencies would ensure comparability of financial data throughout the government. Then, financial data would reflect differences in fact, rather than differences in the accounting treatment of the same facts.

Consistent, comparable data from integrated financial systems is essential for preparing government-wide financial statements. These statements can supplement budgeting and accounting information by giving an overall picture of the financial health of the government that is not available elsewhere. They could also disclose the cumulative financial effect of decisions on the nation's resources and provide early warning signals to policy makers. Many organizations, such as publicly owned corporations, are required to present comprehensive financial reports to the public. Just as shareholders expect management to report the financial position of their companies, so taxpayers should hear about the financial position of their government. Many state and local governments are moving toward this practice, partially influenced by federal reporting requirements for revenue sharing and other grant programs.

Auditing introduces discipline to the financial reporting process by confirming the accuracy and reliability of the information in financial statements. Financial auditing enhances the oversight of programs by providing a better basis for selecting areas for program audit and evaluation. Auditing is also essential to any program to strengthen internal controls. The Federal Manager's Financial Integrity Act of 1982 represents important progress. This act requires each executive agency to report annually on its compliance with internal control standards prescribed by the comptroller general and on its plans for correcting problems.

As with other elements of a strong financial

Illustration 6

The Cost of Processing Federal Payroll Checks Varies Widely

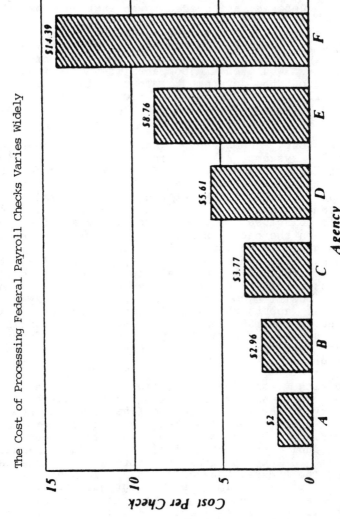

management structure, federal managers have a stake in the quality of public financial reporting on their programs. Taxpayers have shown their skepticism about the efficiency and effectiveness with which their tax dollars are being spent. Publishing audited financial statements-accompanied by corrections of any deficiencies they reveal - can make a major contribution to restoring confidence in our governmental institutions.

9. Modern Financial Systems Are Needed to Make Improvements

Federal decision makers are working with financial management systems that were designed for a bygone era. Many of the gaps, inconsistencies, inefficiencies, and wide disparities in quality previously discussed are the result of these antiquated systems. According to a recent presidential study commission, much of the government's data processing technology is out-of-date, and senior officials of the government have no practical means of collecting summarized management information on a government-wide basis.

Current financial management systems also are inefficient. For example, a recent GAO study revealed that the average cost to issue a federal payroll check varies from about $2 to $14, depending on what payroll system is used.

Agency efforts to update obsolete equipment for their financial management systems often do not take full advantage of improved technology. Frequently, agencies acquire new hardware without redesigning their systems to fully exploit the capabilities of the new equipment. Some agencies (such as the Air Force, the Department of Agriculture, the Department of Commerce, and the Veterans Administration) have tried to modernize and consolidate their systems. But accomplishments are limited by the need to interact with antiquated systems elsewhere.

Two basic approaches may be used to improve current systems. One is to redesign existing systems without altering the basic roles and missions of agencies involved in federal financial management. This approach will yield new systems and equipment. But it will not achieve the most efficient operations.

A second approach might be to revise the basic

241

structure of financial management by locating a few (20 or so) processing centers in the cabinet departments and major agencies to handle both disbursements and financial accounting. Other federal agencies could share common systems for related activities, allowing substantial savings in development and operating costs. The result would be higher productivity in federal financial management operations and more timely, compatible, and reliable financial information.

Consistent, comparable information from the individual agency systems should flow into a central system that is capable of routinely summarizing, consolidating, and reporting relevant information to top policy makers in the executive branch, members of Congress, and the public on a timely basis.

II. PUTTING IN PLACE A MODERN FINANCIAL MANAGEMENT STRUCTURE

Recognition is growing that federal financial management must be modernized. Many efforts are now underway to improve financial management systems and reporting, including projects in the Departments of State, Treasury, and Commerce, as well as the government-wide initiatives of "Reform '88." Congress is considering several proposals for reform as well. The challenge is to integrate these efforts into a broader strategy for comprehensive overhaul of the structure. This can lead to the creation of a more modern, efficient, responsive, and reliable financial mangagement structure to support decision making and management in both Congress and the executive branch.

Many of the benefits that could be achieved through a modern structure of financial management already exist in the integrated financial management systems of progressive state and local government. Such a structure can be built for the federal government, but it will not emerge by accident, nor can it be created through isolated efforts in a few agencies. Building the structure will require the design and installation of new systems over an extended period. Coordination of new and existing system development activities can yield major benefits at little additional cost. An equally important investment must be made in the people who implement and operate the system. They must be recruited more carefully, trained more thoroughly, and offered a more attractive career path.

242

Organizational realignments will be needed. Financial operations should be consolidated into more efficient units that use modern technology. Responsibilities for interagency policy making should be clearly assigned. Finally, all actions must be coordinated to serve the needs of the government as a whole. Because developing a new system is likely to overlap several presidential administrations, it will require firm commitment, clearly identified leadership responsibility, and continuity of purpose. These key ingredients, however, can only exist if supported by a broad and stable bipartisan consensus - including Congress and the executive branch.

A modern structure for managing federal government finances will not cause the budget deficit to disappear, nor will it make difficult budget decisions easy. However, structural and systems improvements can help to ensure that policy makers, executive branch officials, and federal managers receive timely, viable, relevant, and consistent information with which to make those decisions.

CHAPTER 11

PERSPECTIVES ON PROPOSALS FOR BUDGET PROCESS REFORM*

Donald W. Moran**

1. The Continuing Appetite for Process Reform

The Federal "budget process," as embodied in the rules and procedures that the Congress established for itself under the Budget Control & Impoundment Act of 1974, has been a fertile ground for "reform" movements since its inception.

Itself enacted as a "reform" measure, the Act attempted to provide the Congress with a method for ordering its own deliberations to reconcile policy priorities within an overall fiscal policy framework. In attempting such a reconciliation, the Congress for the first time imposed upon itself the same sort of optimalization problem to which the Executive Branch had been subjected since the enactment of the Budget & Accounting Act of 1922.

While perhaps surprising to students of public policy, students of human psychology could have easily predicted that the tensions generated within the deliberative machinery thus established would bring as much pressure to bear on the walls of the process as on the subject matter. The world of practical politics is the unending search for the moving middle. In evaluating the budget process, we must keep in mind that the broad reach of the current Federal enterprise offers a range of "middles" to choose from. The linear arithmetic sum of consensus compromises on tax policy, defense and social welfare policy is not, in general, the locus of the middle on fiscal policy matters. The budget process, then, has never been a means of subduing excruciating political problems; rather, is has perforce become the mechanism by which the Congress annually selects the excruciating political problems it will endure for yet another year.

5. From the General to the Particular

---

*   This chapter is reprinted from <u>National Tax Journal</u>, Vol 37, No. 3 (1984), pp. 377 - 84.

I am not suggesting that this irreconcilable dilemma materialized instantaneously in 1974. Quite the contrary: the process itself was established to cope with just this problem. It was hoped that an annual debate on fiscal policy priorities, quantified in specific programmatic terms, could at least give order to what had been, until that time, a process of fiscal policymaking by default.

In large measure, the Budget Act, and the processes established under it, have achieved the goal of making aggregate fiscal policy issues the central organizing theme of budgetary debate. Despite the strains and stresses, in every year since its inception, the process has in fact put members of both bodies on the record in favor of a comprehensive set of decisions. While few have had unreserved praise for the **policy outcome** of these deliberations, it is nevertheless important to note that fiscal policy, as well as program funding decisions, is now being made annually in a more or less coherent process.

The interesting questions, then, do not center on whether the budget process "works" - but rather on whether our perceptions of the **consequences of its present workings** imply invidious biases which **can be corrected** through procedural **reform.**

In assessing these issues, I draw primarily from my own conclusions developed over the years I have dealt with these questions in both the Legislative and Executive Branches. As a general rule, the Administration has taken no position with respect to proposals for changes in what are, in the main, internal Congressional procedures. In what follows, then, the views expressed are my own, and should not be interpreted as an expression of Administration policy with respect to Congressional budget reform.

3. The Range of Process Reform Proposal

Throughout this paper, I will concentrate on proposals to reform **Congressional** budget procedures In doing so, I do not mean to suggest that whatever difficulties the Nation faces in budgeting can be ascribed to defective Congressional procedure. There are a number of ways in which the way the President's budget is drafted and presented profoundly affects the outcome of Congressional budgetary deliberations. Similarly, the heavy role of the Executive Branch in budgetary execution cannot be ignored in assessing the efficacy of Federal fiscal control mechanisms.

Yet the structure of our Constitution makes the nexus between the Congress and the President in the legislative process established under Article I the primary locus of budgetary policymaking. The present ground rules for the legislative process, as it relates to budgetary matters, are embodied in Congressional, rather than Executive Branch procedures. In assessing the Federal Government's capacity for effective budget decision-making, therefore, I believe it is proper to zero in on the way the Congressional budget process works to advance-or frustrate-the ability of our multi-Branch political system to come to terms with policy optimalization problems.

While no one typology is satisfactory, I believe that the universe of process reform proposals can be divided into three broad categories:

I. SCOPE OF THE BUDGET PROCESS

Proposals to expand the breadth of the budgetary net have been with us since the inception of the process. Given the rising share of Federal activity, particularly in credit programs, outside the formal structure of the Unified Budget, those who promote comprehensiveness of budgetary treatment have long argued for new measures to ensure that these "non-budget" items are considered, either by bringing on-budget the off-budget financing activities of the Federal Financing Bank, or in more explicit controls on obligation levels for direct loans and loan guarantees.

While we have not achieved either theoretical or practical perfection in these areas, I believe that considerable progress has been made in taking account of non-budget items. Since 1980, we have had a formal credit budget allocating direct and guaranteed lending activities by function. Similarly, we have made real progress in reducing the size of the off-budget spending problem. In FY 1981, off-budget outlays peaked at $21.0 billion, or 3.2 percent of on-budget outlays. In FY 1983, just two years later, off-budget outlays had fallen to $12.4 billion, despite the fact that the Congress had moved the Strategic Petroleum Reserve procurement account ($1.641 billion in FY 1983) off-budget during FY 1982. If adjusted for this shift, FY 1981 off-budget program levels as a share of on-budget outlays were cut to 1.4 percent of on-budget outlays, or by 58 percent.

In all, while continued vigilance is needed, particularly in establishing credit budget ceilings with working programmatic bite, I do not look to budget process reforms, per se, as the necessary solution to these problems.

An apposite point in this regard is the simple observation that, within the walls of the existing budgeting system, there is already a bias for chronic deficit finance.

Academic students of budgeting have long ago concluded that the budgetary practices of industrialized countries are essentially "incremental" in nature (1). While models of "zero based budgeting" have been in vogue from time to time-most recently during the Carter Administration as a theory of Presidential budget formulation-the operating reality has always been that budget decisions have been perceived by policymakers as the additive outcome of increments (and decrements) to prior year policy (22).

This model served the system well when the divergence between revenues and outlays was a minor percentage of both aggregate totals. Small percentage adjustments in program levels and revenue structure could produce rough fiscal balance without major political shocks to the system.

Beginning in the late 1960s, however, projections of unending real economic growth led participants in the process to turn their attention to spending the "fiscal dividend" that would accrue from boundless prosperity. As budget decision-making was oriented more and more toward structural fiscal balance rather than literal fiscal balance, incremental policy decisions produced outcomes that, due to cyclical factors, moved the realm of "politically feasible" revenue and spending policy further and further apart (3). Hence, each cyclical swing moved the budgetary posture relentlessly toward chronic deficit finance. The table below summarizes this trend.

In Fiscal Year 1983, outlays exceeded revenues by 32.5 percent. Clearly, imbalances of this magnitude are outside the range of incremental policy adjustments. This basic understanding informs the Administration's support for fundamental changes in the way in which fiscal policy requirements are cast. Absent exogenous constraints on the system-in the form of Constitutional requirements carrying a strong presumption of fiscal balance-no amount of changes in budget decision rules will overcome the incapacity of "business-as-usual" fiscal incrementalism to lead us toward fiscal restraint. It seems to me that this problem should be dealt with before considering proposals to expand the application of the existing machinery.

ON-BUDGET DEFICIT AS A SHARE OF GNP:
CYCLICAL PEAKS AND TROUGHS

	68-70	71-74	76-79	83-??
Trough	3.0%	2.2%	4.0%	6.1%
Peak	0.3%	0.3%	1.2%	?

Source: Budget of the United States Government, 1985, p.9-60.

1. Timing Issues

Considerable interest has been expressed in timing questions of two types-proposals for multi-year budgeting, and proposals for biennial budgeting.

In actual practice, we may be as far down the road toward multi-year decision-making as it is reasonable or feasible to go. Presidential budget submissions presently project both current services and Presidential policy for a five-year period (in the case of the FY 1985 budget, from 1985-89). Current Congressional practice embodies three-year budget resolutions, with reconciliation instructions cast on the premise that entitlement changes will be assessed on the basis of three-year projections of the impact of law changes.

The only part of the process that is not multi-annual in character at the present time is the annual appropriations process. It has been argued that moving to biennial appropriations would both ease the

Congressional workload, and provide the opportunity for greater restraint, as agencies can juggle the program obligations patterns to stay within appropriated levels more easily given the "headroom" of two years worth of budget authority.

Given the experience with multiple supplemental appropriations actions in our present annual system to cover unanticipated needs and changes in funding policies within the year, however, it is unclear whether moving to two-year appropriations would do anything other than exacerbate the trend toward supplemental appropriations funding. The table on the following page summarizes the experince of the last two years. This history should at least give us pause as we evaluate the desirability of moving to a two-year cycle. Further efforts to expand the multi-year character of the budget development and enforcement process, in and of themselves, do not appear to offer substantial new benefits.

2. Budget Enforcement Mechanisms- The Most Promising Area for Study

In my view, the most promising area for further attention is at first blush a technical one-the way in which the broad and narrow policy decisions made in the budget process are translated into concrete legislative actions to enforce the implicit policy of the budget resolution.

This conclusion is drawn from the premise that the expectations that Members of Congress and the President have about the "reality" of decisions made in the budget resolution process explains a significant amount of both Congressional and Executive Branch behavior relative to the Resolution itself. For many years before 1981 the Budget Resolution was often viewed by the participants as a largely symbolic exercise, a shadowboxing effort designed to provide high political drama prefatory to the real legislative work of authorizing legislation and appropriations.

Few students of the process would argue with notion that interest in the budget process rose to new heights once the 1981 experience demonstrated that policies made in the budget process actually mattered. If the resolution of policy disputes in the Budget Resolution process becomes the "final word" on legislation, then the Budget Resolution debate becomes

SUPPLEMENTAL APPROPRIATIONS
AS A SHARE OF TOTAL APPROPRIATIONS
FY   1983-1984

Fiscal Year	Amount ($ billions)	%of Total
Fiscal Year 1983		
Initial Appropriations	511.7	91.8%
Second Continuing Res.	21.7	3.9%
1983 Jobs Bill	16.9	3.0%
1983 Pay Supplemental	0.8	0.1%
1983 Program Supplemental	6.4	1.1%
Total	557.5	100.0%
Fiscal Year 1984		
Initial Appropriations	552.8	96.3%
Second Continuing Res.	12.0	2.1%
Fall, 1983 Supplemental	0.2	neg.
First 1984 Supplemental	8.8	1.5%
Second 1984 Supplenental	0.4	0.1%
Total, FY 1984 to 5/14/84	574.2	100.0%

Source: Office   of Management & budget,   Central Budget
Management System

the vehicle for actually hashing out policy priorities.
This   is   really   nothing other   than   saying   that   the
budget process, in this case, becomes the sort of forum
envisioned   by the architects of the Budget Act.

In short,   if the process as seen as   binding,   it
will   attract   to the debate those actors who   must   be
attracted   to the debate if the final outcome is   going
to   be perceived as a consensus expression of budgetary
policy. As I will discuss in more detail later, failure
to   attract all facets of the real legislative   process
to   the budgetary debate will rob the final   Resolution
outcome   of   the   ethos   necessary to   preserving   the
Resolution as a meaningful fiscal blueprint.

3. Restoring the Legislative Franchise

As   I   see it,   the major budget   process   problem

needing attention in the next few years is the failure of the process to fully enfranchise the real legislative machinery of the Congress in the process.

In 1981, the Omnibus Reconciliation Act became, with a few notable exceptions, the **entire legislative program** for the First Session of the Ninety-Seventh Congress. The way in which the final product was crafted, particularly in the House, gave rise to the view that the budget process was poised to completely consume the regular order of legislative development, disenfranchising the Authorizing Committees from control over their own legislation.

In 1982, it was the Appropriations Committees' turn to conclude that the formal appropriations allocation methodology applied under Section 302 of the Budget Act had taken over their world. With the President using the allocations established under Section 302(b) allocations to Appropriations Subcommittees as a standard to judge Appropriations legislation, appropriators somewhat justifiably concluded that the rest of the legislative world was acting as if appropriations bills for FY 1983 had **already been presumptively written** as part of the crosswalk of the functional detail in the Budget Resolution to the Appropriations Committees under Section 302(a).

This perceived disenfranchisement was, in my opinion, the proximate cause of the breakdown in the budget process during 1983. It is true that substantial arguments about policy differences on questions of taxes, defense spending and domestic programs would have made Congressional/Executive consensus on these questions difficult to reach, at best. Yet the internal mistrust of the process that had developed by that point made many key legislative players reluctant to even **sit down at the table,** for fear of having the prerogatives subsumed in broader notions of the general good. The result is that the finally-enacted Congressional product, in addition to lacking Administration support, also lacked **internal legitimacy in the Congress.** In such an environment, the enforcement legislation implied by the Resolution's reconciliation instructions **never had a chance.**

4. The 1984 Situation

If viewed in this context, the President's call

for a so-called "down payment" on needed budgetary legislation takes on even more meaning than simply the generalized notion that forward momentum is desirable. By asking the Congress to take up and pass those items about which **legislative consensus existed**, the Administration was effectively signalling its desire to reenfranchise the existing legislative machinery of the Congress in the budgetary debate.

As of the date of this writing, it appears that that machinery is once again in motion. Without explicit formal direction, key authorizing legislation has moved in both Houses, and it appears likely that significant budget-related legislation, above and beyond that envisioned in the FY 1984 reconciliation process, may be enacted into law this year.

5. Implications for Budget Process Reform

Regardless of the outcome of this particular undertaking, however, there are lessons to be learned from the last three budget cycles that point toward a profitable redirection of emphasis in our budgetary machinery.

6. The Central Role of Legislation

If concrete legislative activity - in the form of changes in authorizing legislation or the enactment of appropriations bills-is the underlying aim of the budget process, then the process should be tailored to the end.

The existing "reconciliation" machinery, in theory, fits this model well. By calling for measurable action by identified legislative committees, it establishes both a **timetable for legislative action** and **a standard by which the legislative product** of **committees can be judged.** The recommendation, by many observers, that the reconciliation process should be more widely applied is testimony to the workability of this approach in achieving end results.

As we have seen over the last eighteen months, however, process design alone is not sufficient to produce the expected outcome. In the FY 1984 budget process, reconciliation instructions were crafted on the basis of policy assumptions about changes in cost-of-living allowances (COLAs), Federal pay, revenue-raising legislation, and medicare reform.

253

Legislation on the first two questions (COLAs and pay), reflected and underlying legislative consensus on the need for restraint in these two areas. While the legislation bogged down in the latter part of the Ninety-Eighth Congress' First Session, this was due in large part to efforts to maintain linkage between these issues and the more troublesome questions of tax policy and medicare, about which there was far less underlying consensus.

When finally delinked this spring, H.R. 4169, the COLA/pay bill, passed quickly, and has been enacted into law. As of this writing, however, legislation implementing tax and medicare changes is still struggling toward enactment.

The lesson I draw from this is that when the Budget Resolution debate is used to highlight the need for consensus on concrete legislative changes, it works fairly well, creating an environment where assumed legislation can be more or less easily enacted.

In the case of revenue and medicare questions, however, the Budget Resolution debate centered on numerical policy change targets rather than concrete policy choices. As a result, the subsequent legislative process has had to struggle with the underlying policy problems without benefit of prior consensus. In the absence of such underlying policy agreement, it is very unlikely that the final legislative product of these deliberations will closely match the budgetary targets assumed in either last year's Resolution, or whatever Resolution is finally agreed to this year.

To summarize, then, I believe the budget process works best when it is substantively legislative in character. If the policy debate in the Budget Resolution context is viewed as concrete and real, then the collective decisions embodied in that product can be easily translated into implementing legislation. On the other hand, if the debate is general, dealing with vague targets and global policy questions, then the ensuing legislative process has no anchor upon which to produce acceptable implementing legislation.

As the deliberative nature of the process changes from debate on line item amendments toward a debate about competing packages, there is an ever-greater tendency toward generality rather than legislative specificity. In 1981, the package approach worked largely because the legislative alternatives offered in the Reconciliation process tracked closely to the policy detail underlying the alternative budget packages offered in the **budget process.** In particular, the so-called Gramm-Latta package adopted in the House prevailed, in my view, because the underlying policy assumptions had already been adopted, as a package, during the preceding debate on the First Concurrent Resolution for Fiscal Year 1982.

II. THE APPROPRIATIONS PROBLEM

Viewed in this light, it is easy to understand the difficulties involved in dealing with discretionary annual appropriations in the budget process.

While the formal translation mechanism provided in the budget Committee "crosswalk" of the Budget Resolution to Appropriations committee allocations under the Section 302 process is supposed to perform this function, it is unsatisfactory for a number of reasons. First, the implications of choosing specific functional detail in the Budget Resolution are generally little known, and almost never debated when the Budget Resolution is under consideration.

Under the theory underlying the crosswalk exercise, it is technically possible to translate the resolution functional detail into a set of thirteen line-item appropriations bills. Yet such translations are **not available** to Members of either House when the Resolution is under debate. As a result, the final "302(a) allocations" prepared by CBO under Budget Committee staff guidance and provided to the Appropriations Committee after the Resolution Conference Report has been agreed to have **absolutely no legislative legitimacy,** except perhaps as a binding total at the level of **total discretionary appropriations.** As a result, the 302(b) allocations of this total to each Subcommittee by the Committee leadership often bear **very little relation** to the functional detail agreed to in the Budget Resolution.

In such an environment, it should be no wonder that Appropriations Committee Members behave assuming that their line-item policy decisions are **completely unconstrained** by the Budget Resolution Process. If anything, the scorekeeping rules of the Budget Committees and the Administration subsequently used to evaluate each bill become **technical obstacles to be circumvented** rather than guideposts to implementing the prior intent of Congress.

Again, lacking coherent debate about real legislation in the appropriations area during the budget process, the task of translating between the fiscal policy assumed in the Budget Resolution and the all-important appropriations cycle becomes impossible.

III. TWO POSSIBLE ROUTES TO REFORM

It seems to me that there are two different approaches that could be taken to the problem of imbuing the budget resolution process with greater legislative legitimacy.

The first, while of questionable practicability, would simply be to transform the process into a concrete legislative package. Rather than producing a Concurrent Resolution embodying aggregate fiscal targets, functional assumptions, credit totals and reconciliation instructions, one could simply, in theory, have the Budget Committee produce an omnibus reconciliation and appropriations Joint Resolution. Introduced and referred to the appropriate Committees under expedited procedures, it could be brought to the floor in the summer, debated in splendid detail over a period of weeks, and conferenced in pieces before September 30. Being a Joint, rather than Concurrent Resolution, it would require the President's signature to become law. Once signed by the President, however, there would be no need for follow-on legislation.

Such an approach, of course, runs the risk of producing legislative bottlenecks of staggering proportions. The art of logrolling, moreover, would be raised to Olympian heights, as all legislative accomodations needed for the year would have to be loaded onto the only train leaving the station. Without authority for a line item veto, the President (and, almost certainly, the taxpayers) would be at the mercy of whatever fine print found its way to the drafting table. In all, while such an approach would be a conceptually clean method of resolving the legislative legitimacy problem, we would soon suffer problems of a different order.

The second approach, while less conceptually tidy, would simply be to reorder the structure of the First

Concurrent Resolution itself to cast the debate along legislative lines. Rather than debating functional totals for spending and credit, the Congress could instead debate explicit legislative targets for each Committee (or group of related Committees) based on an assessment of the reports that Committees are now required to file (albeit in perfunctory fashion under current practice) with the Budget Committees by March 15.

In practice, an analogue to this approach has been in operation for over two years on an informal basis. In the so-called "Gang of 17" negotiations between the Administration and Congressional leaders early in 1982, the decision format was based on large clusters of different issues each having different legislative enforcement implications. For example, rather than debating functional totals (e.g., "Health" or "Energy"), the discussants worked on producing consensus on changes in the baseline for categories such as "Discretionary Domestic Appropriatins" and "Means-Tested Entitlements."

While that negotiation failed to produce a line-item consensus, it did set the stage for subsequent agreement on a compromise First Concurrent Resolution later in the year, after all alternatives failed. Few have reported happiness with the policy outcome of that subsequent process. Yet the impetus for legislative action was clear.

In each ensuing budget process (FY 1984 and FY 1985), Congressional debate on differing alternatives has been cast in terms of just such a legislatively-oriented decision typology. When voting on the floor, Members have had summaries produced along the lines discussed above, comparing and contrasting the various alternatives in just such a way.

To date, there have been few instances where such a decomposition of the budget has been supported with sufficient clarity about underlying line-item policy detail to form the basis for a subsequent legislative consensus. Yet the recently announced "Rose Garden Agreement" between the Administration and Republican leaders in the Congress does carry such underlying assumptions. Rather than relying on vague targets in each category, it tracks in large measure actual legislation which is now moving in the Congress, and carries concrete, known assumptions about levels for defense and non-defense appropriations. In all, if agreed to in **either** a budget resolution or legislative context, it forms the basis for predictable legislative outcomes. In my view, it serves as a model for the sort of legislatively-oriented policy specifications needed to ensure the enforceability of budget Resolution policy choices.

IV. THE REAL SUBSTANCE OF REFORM

While I have concentrated on structure and process questions, the real purpose underlying this discussion has been to highlight the importance of getting the legislative agenda out onto the table early in the game. This degree of specificity serves, in my view, two essential purposes. First, of course, it establishes a public standard about which Members can publicly debate. If adopted, subsequent implementing legislation could be (except for rearguard actions by affected parties) largely non-controversial. If changes are wrought or measures dropped, it would nevertheless force a necessary "truth in packaging" discipline.

The second, and most important function, however, is simply that it attracts key Congressional power centers to the aggregate fiscal debate, forcing consensus building over policy as a means of achieving consensus on aggregate fiscal policy. The great dilemma of our times, budgetarily speaking, is that all the things the political system wants to do, taken in isolation, do not add up to an aggregate fiscal policy we can long tolerate. In my mind, it is no longer possible to avoid this problem. Until the annual debate about fiscal policy becomes a debate about concrete, difficult policy choices, it will continue to be of little utility in solving our pressing fiscal problems.

FOOTNOTES

** Any views expressed herein are those of the author and should not be ascribed to either the Office of Management & Budget or the Reagan Administration as an expression of policy.

1. Excellent comparative work is in progress on these questions under the auspices of the OECD "Study on the Capacity to Budget."

2. See "The Budget Message of the President" for Fiscal Year 1979, **The Budget of the United States**

Government, 1979.

3. See, for example, the "Budget Message of the President" for Fiscal Year, 1973, The Budget of the United States Government, 1973.

CHAPTER 12

A LINE-ITEM VETO FOR THE AMERICAN PRESIDENT

Thomas D. Lynch, Ph.D.
Professor, School of Public Administration
Florida Atlantic University

I. INRODUCTION

This chapter contains an argument for adopting an amendment to the U.S. Constitution which would give the President the power to line-item veto budget related legislation. The nation has been experiencing large yearly deficit budgets which have added significantly to the national debt. The Congress and the President argue the other institution is responsible, and the problem gets worse each year. Reform proposals have been welcome by the public with a balanced budget amendment being approved by many state legislators. Unfortunately, all the serious reforms have flaws which would create even greater problems than the current situation. Most agree that there is a problem, but there is not a consensus on the solution.

A reform, that has received support from both liberals and conservatives, is the line-item veto which is used in 43 of the 50 states. The form of the veto can vary significantly as illustrated in the various states. This chapter advances one variation which meets the unique needs of the federal government. The reform is designed to break the epolitical stalemate between the Congress and the President without abandoning the concept of "separation of powers" so central to the American system of government. In fact, if the budget is in balance, the line-item veto power would not even exist. The concept is simple: the President can line-item veto various sections of the budget and related bills to get the next fiscal year's budget balanced. If Congress disagrees, it can override the President by a 3/5 vote in each chamber. The President is given the responsibility to get the budget in balance and the Congress maintains the ultimate power of legislative control if they can act with a 3/5 super majority.

The development of this chapter is to (1) present the need, (2) state the suggested reform, (3) state the likely negative arguments and the refutations to those arguments, and (4) summarize the chapter.

261

This type of development is conventional and has the advantage of answering the following questions:

* Is there a need and what is the nature of that need?
* What can and should be done to meet that need?
* What type of concerns should be appreciated in evaluating this proposal so that the pros and cons can be intelligently addressed?

II. THE NEED

1. Support for the Line Item Veto

Senator Edward M. Kennedy and President Ronald Reagan both support a Presidential line-item veto reform. Other supporters include former President Jimmy Carter, business leader J. Peter Grace, most Presidents since the Civil War, Senators Joseph Biden, Alan Dixon, Robert Dole, and William Proxmire, Congressman Jack Kemp, economist Milton Friedman, the Wall Street Journal, the Washington Times, former U.S. Office of Management and Budget directors including David Stockman, the U.S. Chamber of Commerce, Mayor Diane Feinstein, political scientist Clinton Rossiter, U.S. Conference of Mayors, and many others. On July 23, 1985, Senator Kennedy wrote:

> "The budget process is in shambles, the deficit is out of control, and Congress is part of the problem. Congress has too much control over the purse, and the President has too little." 1/

In President Reagan's 1984 State of the Union message, he supported the line-item veto with these words:

> "Some 43 of our 50 states grant their governors the right to veto individual items in appropriation bills without having to veto the entire bill. California is one of those 43 states. As Governor, I found this "line-item veto" was a powerful tool against wasteful or extravagant spending. It works in 43 states. Let us put it to work in Washington for all the people." 2/

Over 100 years ago the astute British observer James Bryce said:

"Such an amendment is desired by enlightened
men, because it would enable the Executive
to do its duty by the country in defeating
many petty jobs which are now smuggled into
these (appropriation) bills, without losing
the supplies necessary for public service
which the bills provide. Small as the change
seems, its adoption would cure one of the
defects due to the absence of ministers from
Congress, and save the nation millions of
dollars a year, by diminishing wasteful
expenditure on local purposes." 3/

Beside past Presidents and scholars, the American
public also favors the item veto. In the first opinion
polls on the subject in 1945, 57 percent favored it
and thirty years later 69 percent favored it. Table 1
presents the poll results from 1945 to 1983. Moreover,
solid support is found among Americans of diverse age,
region, and partisan background as noted in Table 2.

TABLE 1:
PUBLIC SUPPORT FOR THE ITEM VETO CONCEPT

The pollsters asked essentially the following question:
"At the present time, when Congress passes a bill,
the President cannot veto part of that bill but must
accept it in full or veto it. Do you think this should
be changed so that a President can veto some items in
a bill without vetoing the entire bill?"

Year	Favor	Oppose	No Opinion
1945	57%	14%	29%
1953	63	24	13
1957	61	26	13
1975	69	20	11
1978	70	19	19
1981	64	24	12
1983	67	25	8

Source: George H. Gallup, The Gallup Poll: Public
Opinion. (Wilmington, Delaware: Scholarly Resources,
1984), pp. 239 - 240.

PUBLIC SUPPORT AND OPPOSITION TO THE ITEM VETO CONCEPT
by education, age, and region, and partisan affiliation

Background Profile Data	Favor	Oppose	No Opinion
By Education			
College	64%	30%	6%
High School	68	21	11
Grade School	47	27	26
By Age			
18 - 29	64	26	10
30 - 49	68	22	10
50 and over	60	25	15
By Region			
East	63	29	12
Midwest	67	23	10
South	58	27	15
West	71	22	7
By Partisanship			
Republicans	72	19	6
Indep./Unaffiliated	68	23	9
Democrats	63	29	14

Source: George Gallup, The Gallup Poll: Public
Opinion. (Wilmington, Delaware: Scholarly Resources,
1982), pp. 248 - 249.

2. Checks, Balances and the Veto

The framers of the U.S. Constitution created a
checks and balances interplay in order to make and
enforce policy decisions in the national government.
All three branches must cooperate but also check the
other. For example, the law making power was given to
Congress but the President can veto any law and the
courts can interpret the law. Article 1, Section 7
says:

> "Every Bill which shall have passed the House
> of Representatives and the Senate, shall,
> before it becomes a law, be presented to the
> President of the United States; If he shall
> approve he shall sign it, but if not he
> shall return it . . ."

Congress by a two-thirds vote in each house may choose
to override the President's veto and the bill shall
become law.

The general veto was used sparingly by our first Presidents but some later Presidents used it extensively. George Washington used it twice and both John Adams and Thomas Jefferson vetoed no bills. Subsequent other Presidents (such as Grover Cleveland, Franklin D. Roosevelt and Gerald Ford) have used this power extensively. 4/

As an instrument of fiscal constraint, the general veto power has not been successful. For example, President Reagan has seldom vetoed fiscal measures despite his fiscal conservatism. Members of Congress almost routinely add amounts to existing programs and even add new programs. They do this to bills involving essential programs and projects they know the President cannot veto for fear that his own programs and projects will not make it through the congressional process again. The normal appropriation bill is massive, complicated, and unwieldy. Thus, a general veto is not a practical tool in most situations.

If the President does veto, then there is no appropriations bill and a continuing resolution must be used or a major part of government comes to a halt. Today, a continuing resolution is used much like a regular appropriation bill. Thus, a Congressional /Presidential game of chicken exists with each branch seeking the other to meet its demands or the government goes without any money causing massive hardships to the people. Although such games exist, they demonstrate the weakness rather than the viability of the general veto as applied to the appropriation process. The Wall Street Journal says "The existing veto, which can shut down several departments at once, has become pointlessly destructive. It is obsolete." 5/

3. Flawed Constitution

The social invention of James Madison and the other framers of the Constitution created a remarkable fundamental law which has served the United States of America extremely well for over two hundred years. Nevertheless, it was not perfect and the current budget/deficit crisis is one example of that imperfection. Another imperfection was permitting slavery which significantly contributed to this nation's only civil war. That error was corrected by the 13th, 14th, and 15th amendments to the Constitution. Now, another amendment is necessary to correct a more subtle error in Madison's remarkable understanding of the workings of human institutions of power.

Chart 1 illustrates that since World War II the federal government has not been balancing its budget. The yearly deficit has become the normal occurrence. This is not necessarily a problem if the nation is expanding its gross national product and its tax system is not strained by interest payments for the national debt. Since somewhat before the Reagan election in 1980, the yearly deficit has started increasing at an alarming rate.

CHART 1:

YEARLY FEDERAL DEFICIT

Source: Congressional Budget Office, "The Economic and Budget Outlook: Fiscal Years 1987 – 1991." Appendix D.

As Charts 2 and 3 indicate, the problem has become increasingly significant in terms of both the yearly interest payment on the debt and the gross national product. Chart 2 shows the yearly growth in the interest payment on the federal debt from 1962 to 1985. The growth, from 1962 to 1972, in the interest

CHART 2 :

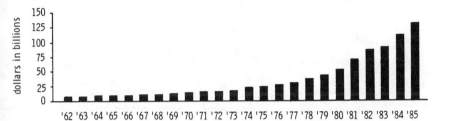

YEARLY INTEREST PAYMENT ON FEDERAL DEBT

Source: Congressional Budget Office, "The Economic and Budget
Outlook: Fiscal Years 1987 - 1991." Appendix D.

CHART 3 :

DEBT HELD BY PUBLIC

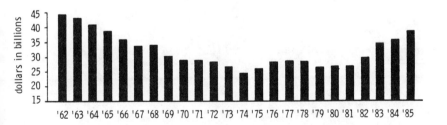

percent of GNP

Source: Congressional Budget Office, "The Economic and Budget
Outlook: Fiscal Years 1987 - 1991." Appendix D.

payment is modest. From 1973 to 1978, the growth is significant. From 1978 to 1985, it is remarkable. Chart 3 shows the federal debt held by the public as a percent of the gross national product. As a percent of the national economy, the relative debt was getting progressively less until about 1970 when it leveled off. Starting in 1982, it started growing, which is most unusual as that type of growth normally only occurs in periods of major war.

As Chart 4 indicates, the payment on interest is becoming an increasing portion of the yearly total outlay for the federal government. This probably is the most disturbing trend as it shows the mounting negative impact of the large yearly federal deficits. More and more discretionary money must go to interest payments rather than other purposes such as domestic programs and defense.

CHART 4 :
INTEREST PAYMENT ON DEBT

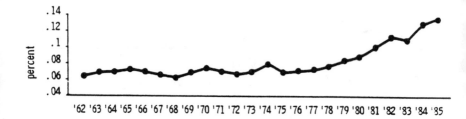

as total percent of total outlay

Source: Congressional Budget Office, "The Economic and Budget Outlook: Fiscal Years 1987 - 1991." Appendix D.

The nation's leaders decided to cut taxes and increase expenditures primarily for defense purposes. One chamber of the Congress was controlled by one political party - the Democrats - and the other chamber was controlled by the President's party - the Republicans. This plus the increased activities and importance of interest groups (those same groups which Madison called "necessary evils") led to an environment which resulted in yearly massive deficits.

Saying "no" to specific programs has become politically very difficult for persons who wish to continue in office. Also many programs have been established whose budget cannot be controlled by means of budget and appropriation decisions. The Democratic controlled House does not wish massive cut backs in domestic programs and the Senate tends to side with a President who wishes lower taxes and higher spending on defense. Thus, the wish lists adds-up to massive yearly deficits with the necessary cuts not being politically sound. A political stalemate exists with each group being able to defend much of their programs but unable to reach an accord that makes a balanced or near balanced budget possible.

The Constitutional drafting challenge is to break the stalemate without significantly altering the arrangements of powers among the major political institutions. The concern for tyranny by an overly strong executive should be no less today than two hundred years ago. But government fundamentally flawed, so that it can not deal with basic decisions, can lead to rebellion or other acts which prevent its primary function of deciding national policy through peaceful means. The current stalemate might disappear with a different political arrangement of political actors, but it would reappear when those forces were realigned in the same manner. Thus, Constitutional revision is needed.

A simple reform, used by 43 of 50 states, is the line-item veto. A very specific line-item veto provision is advocated in this chapter. It is designed to meet the specific needs for revision of the Constitution and is meant to be accomplished within the larger intent of the founders.

4.Impoundments as a Line-Item Veto

A de facto Presidential budget line-item veto

without a Congressional override provision existed until 1974. It was called _impoundment_. For example, President Grant signed a rivers and harbors appropriations bill but refused to spend money for a few projects he considered of a purely private or local interest. This extra-constitutional Presidential power had no legal basis, but it was used to stop spending when wars came to an end or for managerial or efficiency purposes.

Congress generally but sometimes reluctantly went along with Presidential impoundments until the late 1960s and early 1970s. Then, President Richard Nixon withheld funds to substitute his policy for that of the Congress. Not surprisingly, Congressional leaders felt he was acting unconstitutionally in that his actions were done without (1) Constitutional or legal authority, (2) notice to the Congress when an impoundment was taken, and (3) no opportunity was given Congress to override his policy position as was done traditionally with vetoes. In every court case which challenged President Nixon's use of impoundment, the third branch of government overturned his policy impoundments.

Impoundment powers still exist but they are now legitimate and can be done under important controlled circumstances. Title X of the Impoundment Control Act of 1974 established two types of impoundments: _deferrals_ and _recisions_. In both cases, the President must notify Congress of the impoundment and the Controller General monitors the process. If the President does not comply, then the Controller General notifies Congress. If the Executive Branch refuses to comply, the Controller General can bring the matter to the federal court. With the federal court system ruling against the President and the Constitution requiring the President to uphold the law, the Congress would be in a position to impeach the President.

The deferral and recision provisions work differently. Under the deferral provision, a President can delay spending for any period up to the end of the fiscal year. But either chamber of Congress can disapprove by resolution and the President must spend the money. Under the recision provision, a President can cancel expenditures but both chambers must approve the recision. _7/_

In 1983, the Supreme Court ruled in <u>Immigration</u> and <u>Naturalization</u> <u>Service</u> v. <u>Chadha</u> that a one-house legislative veto was unconstitutional. Thus, Congress can only defer by passing a law which itself can be vetoed by the President. Senator Hatfield has observed that there is now a <u>de facto</u> line-item veto. It does not apply to money tied to a short-term spending deadline, but Senator Hatfield is correct for money which is authorized for several years or indefinately.

In practice under David Stockman Directorship of the Office of Management and Budget (OMB), the possibility was never tested because Stockman wished to avoid a move to rewrite the Budget Act. The latest Director of the OMB, James C. Miller III, took a different view and has used the policy deferrals extensively. Not surprisingly, Congressmen, such as Vic Fazio (D - Calif.) were upset. Thus, a suit was filed which called for the President's impoundment powers to be declared void because Congress did not intent them to be used in their present manner. They won at the District Court level, but it is likely to be appealed to the Supreme Court. To add confusion to an already confusing situation, the Balanced Budget Act of 1985 has made passing supplemental spending bills more difficult, thus partly defeating an established mechanism Congress used to overturn deferrals. <u>6/</u>

Thus, the President does have a weak line-item veto. The strongest aspects of the veto power are not likely to stand a court challenge. The net effect is to have a line-item veto which can be overridden by a much easier standard than exists for most American government chief executives.

III. THE PROPOSED AMENDMENT

1. The Intention

Exhibit 1 presents the language of the proposed amendment to the U.S. Constitution. This section explains the amendment and the purpose of its various provisions.

The intent of the amendment is to break the political stalemate that has resulted in massive yearly federal budget deficits. The concept is rather simple. If there is a federal deficit budget passed by Congress, then the President can use the line-item

EXHIBIT 1:
PROPOSED LINE-ITEM CONSTITUTIONAL AMENDMENT

1. The Congress shall pass a Budget Bill and all related authorization and appropriation bills seventy-five (75) days prior to the beginning of the forthcoming fiscal year which shows the next fiscal year's operating and capital budget totals. The Budget Bill must include for the forthcoming fiscal year total estimated (a) accrued and likely actual revenues including all receipts, (b) all accrued and actual obligations and expenditures, (c) unfunded liabilities, (d) contingent liabilities, and (e) all loan proceeds. All sections of authorization and appropriation bills inconsistent with the Budget Bill are null and void. No elected person in the Congress or Executive Branch shall receive any federal government compensation unless and until the Budget Bill and all related authorization and appropriation bills have become law.

2. If Congress does not pass the Budget Bill and all related authorization and appropriation bills in a timely manner or the President determines the Budget Bill will result in either (a) total accrued expenses less major capital items is greater than the total of all accrued revenues and receipts less bond proceeds, or (b) total expenditures on major capital items does not equal loan proceeds, then the President shall declare in a message to Congress that the budget is unbalanced and he can use his line-item veto power as defined in Section 4 of this amendment. If Congress overrides this Declaration by a 2/3 vote in each chamber within fourteen (14) days after the Declaration message to Congress, the Presidential Declaration takes no effect.

3. Except to make interest and principal payments on the national debt and meet employment obligations to federal employees, the Congress cannot authorize, make contracts, or appropriate monies beyond one year. The Congress can declare its intention to make monies available for specific programs and projects beyond one year, but it does not carry the force of law.

4. If there is a Presidential Unbalanced Budget Declaration and Congress does not override it, the President has the power for thirty (30) days after the Congress has an opportunity to override the Declaration to strike any legislative authorization or appropriation language in a duly passed congressional

bill as well as substitute lower amounts so long as those changes are likely to reduce federal expenditures in the current or next fiscal year and are consistent with section 3 in this amendment. Each of these Presidential decisions can be overridden individually or collectively by a 3/5 vote of each chamber. Any changes not overridden in thirty (30) days after the President has notified the Congress in writing of the line-item veto carries the full force of law.

5. Congress shall make all laws necessary for the full implementation of this amendment.

veto power for thirty days to make the necessary cuts. The Congress is then given the opportunity for thirty days to override that decision by a 3/5 override vote in each chamber. This would mean that the President could use this power to assure a balanced or near balanced budget. If he does not choose to do so, then he becomes politically responsible for that decision and he can not blame the Congress except in those areas where they overrode his decision.

This proposed amendment is designed carefully to minimize any lessening of legislative power as extra power is given the President only to cut expenditures under certain conditions. The President can only use the line-item veto power to cut expenditures if the Congress had not passed the budget in a timely manner or the bill resulted in an unbalanced budget. Even then, if Congress asserted itself, it could by 2/3 vote within fourteen days not grant that extra power to the President. If that occurred, the responsibility of an unbalanced budget would fall clearly to the leadership of the Congress.

Even if the President used his line-item veto power, the Congress could act with a 3/5 majority in each chamber within thirty days to override the President's decision. The three-fifths margin was patterned after the Nebraska constitution which had a two-third override requirement and reduced it to a three-fifths. 8/ The intention is to avoid stalemate and place a standard slightly higher than a simple majority to override cost cutting measures. Congressional overrides are possible only when the Congress can actas a strong unified unit. Under such conditions, stalemate would not exist and then Congressional intent should dominate.

This proposed amendment was crafted to permit a President to veto more than discretionary federal spending associated with current federal budgets and appropriations acts. Without the third clause, only a small portion of yearly budget expenditures would be subject to line-item veto. For example, the Congressional Budget Office (CBO) estimated that in 1985 only $2.9 of $925 billion would be subject to a line-item veto. Chart 5 uses a House Budget Committee report that is based on a Congressional Budget Office estimates. Major cuts are only possible if the President can cut defense, social security, entitlement programs, multi-year grants and contracts, and others.

Interest payments are excluded because to do otherwise
would increase interest costs. Employee retirement
benefits are excluded because such commitments are
traditional for employers.

Because of the amendment, the President would be
in a position to pick and chose where to make cuts
across a very broad spectrum of federal programs.
Thus, he could avoid across-the-board-cuts which create
irrational policy and preclude good management. Almost
all programs and projects would be subject to possible
cut or elimination in the line-item veto
process. Without the third clause, this amendment would
not be effective at balancing the budget as pointed out
in Chart 5.

CHART 5:

OPEN TO LINE - ITEM VETO

dollars in billions

1985 Expenditures

	Net Interest Payments	$116
	Social Security	$189
	Medicare and Medicade	$98
	Other Mandatory Programs	$92
	Prior Year Obligations	$100
	Untouched Defense Spending	$155

Note: Chart uses 1985 expenditure data and assumes line-item veto
only applies to appropriations.

Source: 1985 Congressional Budget Office Report prepared for the
House Budget Committee.

---

2. Other Important Provision

Beyond the intentions to eliminate the political stalemate which has so radically increased the national debt, the proposed amendment has several other important elements. It:
* requires the President to notify the Congress of the line-item veto,
* provides a Congressional possibility to attempt to override the vetoes individually or collectively,
* establishes a thirty (30) day limit for Congress to override the vetoes, and
* provides a strong incentive to members of Congress to pass the budget in a timely manner,
* gives a line-item veto power which includes striking language and reducing numbers but excludes any non-budget related vetoes,
* avoids technical issues such as "what is a balanced budget" and "when is a forecast correct",
* does not tie the budget decision to any technical concept such as <u>gross</u> <u>national</u> <u>product</u>,
* encourages the use of capital budgeting,
* stresses the importance of unfunded liabilities,
* uses the accrual concept of accounting,
* gives Congress the power to tailor laws to implement this amendment.

The above points will be discussed.

1. Presidential Notification Requirement

Presidents prior to 1974 had a practice of not notifying Congress of their impoundments. Not surprisingly a provision of the 1974 legislation required such notice. The Congress cannot carry out its function if it is unaware of major policy decisions made by the President. The proposed amendment requires the President to notify the Congress of any line-item veto. In all likelihood, Congress would enact legislation detailing how that was to be done.

2. Individual or Collective Congressional Override

The Congress has thirty (30) days to react to the President's line-item veto. Individual attempts to override all the detail line-items vetoes may be impractical. Thus, Congress is given the flexibility to package the override attempts as they wish.

3. Thirty (30) Day Limits

The delays in the deliberative process can be used to establish policy. Thirty days is considered to be an adequate time given that the President and Congress already are familiar with the detail of the budget and related bills. The line-item vetoes would be addressed to number reductions and language changes in substantive and appropriations bills which lead to budget reductions. Without a deadline, the political actors wishing to stall would have a significant advantage to the detriment of proper government administration.

4. Incentive to Pass Timely Budgets

Administering a government budget when you are uncertain of the amount you have to spend during the year is a major handicap to federal bureaucrats. However, they normally must face this condition because Congress rarely passes the budget in a timely manner. In some cases, Congress even fails to pass the stop gap continuing resolution. This has meant that occasionally some government employees have had to borrow money to pay their rent or buy their food until Congress decided to pass the necessary appropriation legislation to pay their employees. Ironically, such behavior would not be tolerated by the government if it were done in the private sector. The political stalemate between the two chambers and the President tend to make timely passage of budget / appropriation bills nearly impossible. This makes continuing resolutions necessary and leads to late and even non-passage of appropriations bills.

The amendment has two incentives built into it to encourage timely passage of the budget bill: (1) A provision which says no elected Congressional or Executive Branch employee can receive his or her pay check or other compensation unless and until the budget is passed. (2) Untimely passage of the budget bill is reason in itself for the President to declare an unbalanced budget exists and that he can use the line-item veto power. Occasions might arise when Congress feels it can not pass a timely budget bill, but a personal and institutional price would be paid for that decision. Now, there is no penalty.

The use of deadlines is also an important means to insure timely actions on the budget related legislation. Congress must pass the budget act seventy

five (75) days before the beginning of the fiscal
year. This is to give fourteen (14) days to Congress
to decided to override the Declaration, thirty (30)
days for the President to exercise the line-item veto,
and another thirty (30) days for the Congress to
override those vetoes. Assuming the President acts
promptly in his line-item veto declaration, this would
mean the budget and related bills would be passed
prior to the beginning of the new fiscal year.

5. Striking Language and Reducing Numbers

The amendment uses the concept of an amendatory
partial veto similar to the one used in the state of
Washington. This veto can be used to achieve a
substantive or policy changes. 9/ Also, it applies to
the monetary provisions of almost any bill as well as
appropriations bills. 10/ Budgeting is policy and
cutting programs is a policy change. Given that can-
didates for large cuts in the federal budget must come
from monetary provisions of substantive (authorizing)
legislation, this amendatory partial veto power is
critical. Only with it can sufficient size cuts be
made.

As a curb on unnecessary policy cuts, the amendment does say the veto power can be used only for
budget reductions. Obviously, major controversies can
expect to occur with a partial veto that can substantially alter legislation. But, that is the nature of
politics. Note that safeguards have been designed to
protect the separation of powers concept, but this
would alter the power relationship somewhat between
the President and Congress.

6. Avoid Technical Issues

Framing an amendment addressed to achieving more
responsible federal government budgeting must include
technical terms which could lead to complex legal
disputes that put the whole process in question. The
recommended approach avoids having the technical
definition of terms halt the use of the line-item
veto. The President uses his definition and decides to
declare a budget unbalance. Congress then can decide
to do nothing or challenge the decision by a 2/3
override vote in both chambers. Certainly, their would
be arguments over the terms, but the ultimate use of
that extra Presidential power will not rest on any
court interpretation of those terms.

Under this amendment, there would be technical issues and court disputes, but they would not threaten the use of the line-item veto itself. The use of accrual accounting terminology would be subject to professional disagreement between the two branches. However, institutional means of solving such disputes have been in place for several years already.

7. Capital Budgeting

A common practice in many nations, state governments, local governments, and private companies is to use a capital budget normally in connection with a five year or longer capital improvement program. This amendment does not mandate this reform, but it does refer to "less major capital items" and "loan proceeds". Also, the basis used to determine the existence of an unbalanced budget includes language designed to encourage the use of loan proceeds tied to major capital items.

This language does not require the federal government to use a capital budget but it is encouraged by the language. Given the large national debt, many years would be necessary to get it into proper proportions without causing undue hardships on the people. In that time, major capital items would be less than loan proceeds because portions of those proceeds would pay for other programs and expenses. However, the implicit goal would be to have loan proceeds equal major capital items.

8. Unfunded and Contingent Liability

The federal government has an extensive contingent liability and a significant unfunded liability which is largely ignored. In a private company, such a practice would not be acceptable. We keep track of these figures in the private sector because they represent a potential major expense which could cause significant financial problems for the company. The federal government is not in the same position as a private company because it does have taxing power. Nevertheless, contingent and unfunded liability should be a major concern as it limits the future budget decision options. By including a reference to this concept in the amendment, hopefully this will make Congressional and Executive leaders more sensitive to this important matter.

279

9. Accrual Concept

The concepts of accrual accounting are largely accepted in the private sector and increasingly accepted in the public sector. Certainly the nature of government means that not all the concepts of accrual accounting are relevant to the federal government. In the accrual method of accounting, revenues are recorded when they are earned or billed and expenditures are recorded when they are obligated. In the cash method, income is recorded when it is received and expenditures are recorded when they are paid. The accrual method permits better accountability, but cash positions still must be maintained carefully to avoid any cash flow embarrassments. The use of these terms in the proposed amendment is to encourage their use by the Congress and the President.

IV. NEGATIVE ARGUMENTS AND REFUTATION

1. The Negative Position

Although there are many supporters of the line-item veto reform, there are also significant opponents and reasoned arguments against the amendment. This particular version of the line-item veto has not been tested in public debate, but the concept has been subject to close examination. This section of the chapter will raise the various negative arguments against the reform based on an examination of the literature. This section will also refute those negative arguments.

The list of opponents to the reform include such notable people as (1) most leaders in Congress including Senators Mark Hatfield, John Stennis, Robert Byrd, Charles Mathias and Representatives James Wright and Mickey Edwards, (2) important interest groups like Common Cause and the AFL-CIO, (3) media people and groups including David Broader, the New York Times, the Washington Post, the Philadelphia Inquirer, and (4) scholars including Arthur M. Schlesinger, Jr., James Sundquist, Louis Fisher, Rodger Davidson, and Allen Schick. To that list of scholars must be added Thomas E. Cronin who, with Jeffrey J. Weill, authored an excellent paper for the 1985 national American Political Science Association conference. Although that paper argues against the Presidential line-items veto, the author of this chapter used it extensively in preparing this and the Cronin/ Weill paper is strongly recom-

mended for persons trying to get a balanced view on
this public issue. The title of the Cronin and Weill
paper is "An Item Veto For The President?: An Analysis
of Its Merits, Assumptions, and Demerits Or An Essay On
An Idea Whose Time Shouldn't Come". 11/

The author of this chapter may be somewhat pre-
sumptuous in listing the negative arguments because
this particular version of the reform is new and
anticipating all the arguments is a difficult task.
Therefore, sins of omission may exist, but as the
public debate continues subsequent revisions of this
chapter will attempt to address the serious negative
arguments as they arise. The list of negative arguments
follows and following that list is a more detailed
explanation of each argument and a refutation of it:
* The real reason why there are continuous yearly
    budget deficits is due to an inability of the
    political leaders to tackle the tax system, the
    subsidy system, the entitlements, military
    spending including procurement, and the govern-
    ment pension system.
* Presidents already have the tools to get a balanced
    budget and the fact they don't use them indi-
    cates that another tool would not make any
    difference.
* The line-item veto would be a partisan tool that
    could actually increase federal spending and
    make the Congress irresponsible as they would
    tend to "pass the buck" on hard political deci-
    sions to the President.
* Because a President has the line-item veto power
    does not mean that it will result in a balanced
    budget. Presidents, including Reagan, are not
    inclined to use this type of veto on most
    projects and programs. President's get essen-
    tially the budgets they propose so it is
    disingenuous to believe that the line-item veto
    would result in anything different.
* An item-veto can only be exercised on discretionary
    federal spending which is not enough to bring
    the budget in balance in any particular year.
* The line-item veto at the state level is a partisan
    instrument and has not been a remarkable weapon
    to curb deficit spending.
* The reform would upset the separation of power
    between the Congress and the President.

* This power would strengthen the power of the
    bureaucrats in the White House and the Office of

Management and Budget.
* This reform is not needed because the Congress
  passed the a Balanced Budget Act in 1985 which
  is solving the problem.

The above list of arguments is grouped into four
sets: (1) The proposed reform is misdirected. (2) The
reform will not work. (3) the reform will work, but
create other evils of a worse nature. And (4) The most
recent attempts to resolve the problem are working and
no other reforms are needed. The grouping will be used
to systematically examine each argument.

2. Misdirected Reform

Is the proposed reform misdirected? Is the real
reason there is a continuing yearly massive budget
deficit because of failed leadership? Does the
President already have the tools to solve the problem
and adding one more tool will not stop a failure of
will or inability.

Almost all agree that the national tradition of
large unbalanced budgets is a serious problem which is
not being resolved. Maybe the cynics are correct! All
we need is new leadership, but the elected process
gave us this leadership and there is no reason to
assume that it will do much better in subsequent
elections. James Madison wanted the nation's leaders
to be statesmen, but he recognized that they would
occasionally fall below our highest expectations.

A successful political process must assume more
normal human traits and try to compensate for them.
Certainly, the lessening strength of the political
parties and increasing strength of interest groups has
contributed to the current situation. Members of
Congress know that unless they can pass-the-buck on
hot issues that they can become the political target
of any number of special interest groups. They know
that saying "no" in general may be good politics, but
saying "no" to appropriations important to key people
in their districts and states is political suicide.
Thus, politicians can be in favor of balanced budgets,
but against specific cuts which together prevent the
budget from being balanced.

The President can and also does play the political
game of "having it both ways". The President supports
every balanced budget idea, but seeks no tax increase

and a major increase in defense spending. His proposal is an unbalanced budget as is the final Congressional version. But the Congressional version is likely to be significantly different then the President's version. Congress will not cut domestic programs as radically as the President proposes or those members will not be re-elected. They seek smaller cuts for domestic programs and some compromise from the President on added taxes and less money for defense. The result is a political stalemate which makes timely passage of appropriations almost impossible, an unlikely environment for compromise because of the political cost, and more continuing resolutions rather than appropriation legislation. The process is part of the problem and expecting extraordinary leadership is not reasonable.

The President does have important tools to deal with Congress. He can propose a balanced budget. He can and does work with Congress as they prepare legislation. He does have the general veto. He can use the legal modified impoundment powers provide in the 1974 Budget Act. This current and subsequent Presidents can end the budget crisis. He can merely agree to raise taxes and not raise defense spending. But remember President Reagan won by 49 states and clearly won on the basis of no tax increase and high sums for defense. He should not have to abandon his policy position any more than a liberal Democrat who believes in more money for domestic programs and less for defense.

The system should allow positions to be taken without resulting in political stalemate. Proposing a budget, working with Congress, and vetoing appropriation bills has not and will not be adequate under the current set of conditions facing this nation. Each political actor is wiser to accept stalemate and get reelected than to be statesmen like Madison wished. The Constitution is a brilliant invention which needs a little fine tuning after 200 years.

3. Reform Not Working

Is all this talk of a line-item veto raising false hopes because it cannot or will not lead to balanced budgets? Will it just enter the bag of political tricks which result in increased funding to satisfy log rolling gambits? Will the President follow the lead of the nations' governors and use the line-item veto for partisan negotiations and not deficit reductions? Is it an ineffective tool because it can only focus on the relatively small discretionary funds decided upon in the appropriation process?

The passage of a new amendment will not change the character of the type of person the American people select as President. Yes, the President will probably use the threat of a line-item veto to get his pet projects through the Congressional process. Yes, legislators will also bargain among themselves in attempts to get the necessary 3/5 vote to override a line-item veto. In others words, politics will continue and adapt itself to the process change.

The amendment does not guarantee that a President would use the new power to reach a balance budget. However, the new power clearly makes "passing the buck" to Congress very difficult because the responsibility would rest with him and he would have the power to exercise that responsibility. A reasonable guess is that a President would use the power to phase down the national debt in such a way as to avoid unnecessary economic hardship to the country that a quick return to a balance budget would generate. A conservative President would take his cuts out of domestic programs, but recall that such a President would be elected by the people and such cuts would be clearly his responsibility.

Scholars have carefully examined the use of line-item veto power by the nation's governors. They found that the veto was used primarily as a tool of partisan politics and infrequently used to reduce budgets in the various states. Fiscal restraint is not necessarily correlated with the line-item veto.12/ The false conclusion reached is that such a power would not be effective for a President.

The logical failure is not realizing that 49 of 50 states also have a balance budget constitutional requirement and rarely is that requirement seriously breached at the state level. In other words, governors do not have to use the line-item veto power in an extensive manner because the state budgets are either balanced or nearly balanced. The mere existence of that power plus the balance budget requirement means that a radical use of line-item veto is not necessary. Probably after a few years with the amendment, the President would not be able to use the power for that purpose as well because the Congress would pass balanced budget.

Would the amendment be strengthen with a balanced budget requirement? No, because the federal government will have to take some time to correct the deficit problem and that same government must be given the flexibility to meet unexpected challenges such as war and economic crisis. The federal government is not in the same position as the state governments, but it can benefit from some of the same tools used effectively at the state level.

Interestingly, the budget process of the United States of America has evolved with much of the real budget making decisions falling outside the traditional budget/appropriation process. Clearly, any debt incurred must be paid and the yearly budget item for interest payment is largely <u>pro</u> <u>forma</u>. Also, individuals working for the federal government as soldiers or civil servants have retirement and other benefits associated with their employment. Again, the total amount for veteran benefits and other federal retirement can not be controlled in the budget process.

Those obligations are extensive but small compared to the entitlement programs and multi-year contract and loan authority granted the various federal agencies. Those agencies follow the law and say that if a farmer, a person seeking welfare, or other eligible person or group wishes federal money then they are entitled to that money. It is not a grant but an entitlement in which the federal government must find the money. There is no budget decision. Also, defense and other agencies normally contract many years into the future for their projects and that multiple year budget implication is not weighted in a proper budget context. The federal government must simply pay without considering that decision in the context of the larger yearly budget decision. Without section 3 in the amendment, the new line-item veto power would be as ineffective as the present system.

With today's budget system, the real decision on budgets is in the language of the authorization bills which have established the entitlement programs and multi-year contracting. The solution is to follow the example of many state and local government. They do not allow for more than one year obligations except for payment on their debt and retirement payments to their former employees. This will create procurement challenges for career public employees, but it should be relatively simple for Congress because they only have to pass that which they already agreed upon in the past.

The amendment does give the power to Congress to state its none binding intention. That should be adequate for possible multi-year purposes. Remember, Congress can revise its entitlement programs and there are never any iron clad future year federal obligations even now. This merely gives the President the power to alter them to effect budget reductions. Obviously, politically popular programs would not be subject to cuts or only small cuts. Some programs, which are financed by special obligated revenues such as highways, probably would not even be cut as their dedicated revenues could meet their needs.

The proposed amendment would give the President the power to act.

4. Create Worse Evils

Would this amendment create a whole new set of serious problems for the nation? Would it upset James Madison's separation of powers in such a manner that Executive would become to powerful? Would it really give power not to the President but to his Office of Management and Budget bureaucrats?

A reading of the Federalist Papers helps one appreciate the logic and the influence of political theory on the creation of the Constitution. James Madison did believe in social contract theory and he was concerned about establishing a government that had a stronger executive than in the old Articles of Confederation. He and the others were also concerned about the potential tyranny of the President. The separation of powers doctrine has served the nation well.

Would the proposed amendment significantly shift the relationship such that the essential purpose of the doctrine was lost? Actually, the Constitution created three powerful political institutions which interact in the formulation of policy and its execution. This proposal merely continues that interaction without disrupting its primary purpose.

This amendment would somewhat strengthen a President especially a fiscally conservative President. But safeguards are built in to permit Congress to assert itself when it can act as a unified unit. In fact the veto power only exist if Congress does not pass a balanced budget. Realistically over the next five to ten years, the President is likely to have the line-item veto power until the budget is balanced as a normal occurrence.

This reform is merely an extension of the veto concept found already in the Constitution and the notion of a line-item veto for the chief executive is actually the norm in the U.S. This is not a radical change, but it is a change which would shift the responsibility to balance the budget to the President if Congress failed to do so. If the President went too far in the collective minds of the Congress, it would have the power to veto his specific decisions by a 3/5 veto in each chamber. The complex system of checks and balances would be maintained under this proposal, but the checks and balances would be altered in a manner quite consistent with American political reform tradition.

In the nation's capital of the 1980's, staff to the Congress and to the President are often significant actors themselves even though they act and speak for elected officials. In preparing to line-item veto a budget and related bills, clearly the President of the United States would not be in a position to do all the detail work associated with such a task. He would use a staff and that staff is likely to be the Office of Management and Budget. Thus, budget examiners would have a second opportunity to recommend budget cuts after the budget bill is passed.

Some members of Congress, who also use large staffs (e.g., the General Accounting Office, CBO, and various committees' professional staffs) themselves, object to the influence of these civil servants on the President. To think that a trillion dollar budget could be analyzed and decided upon by a single person or committee is beyond reasonable expectation. Of course staff will be important in both the Congress and the Executive Office of the President. Naturally, a President will be the one responsible for the vetoes and he would be wise to insure his staff understands his policy and properly aids him.

5. Gramm-Rudman Non-Solution

The Gramm-Rudman-Hollings Act (also called the Balanced Budget Act of 1985) has been somewhat effective in its first year, but it will fail as it is fundamentally flawed. 13/ The act requires that the deficit be reduced by $36 billion a year until it vanishes in 1991. This is to be done by:
* setting yearly deficit total deficit targets,
* using an across-the-board sequestration process if the Congress does not meet the yearly targets, and
* tightening up on the procedural rules related to the budget process.

The act ran into immediate difficulty with a question about its constitutionality. A court case brought by Alan Morrison (a Ralph Nader lawyer) and Representative Mike Synar (D - Oklahoma) questioned the constitutionality of the new law. The Supreme Court ruled that assigning an executive function to the controller general (a legislative official) violated the separation of powers concept of the Constitution. This left the law operative only because it has a back-up provision. This provision requires the Congressional Budget Office (CBO) and the Office of Management and Budget (OMB) to both estimate the deficit. The two estimates are averaged and the Congress votes to certify the deficit findings. Congress could decide not to certify the findings. If Congress did so, it would be saying either the deficit did not exist or it failed to decide on the extent of that deficit. Both are certainly possible given the conflict between the two chambers and the relative low congressional regard for estimates done by OMB.

If Congress certifies the deficit problem, it has 45 days to accomplish the necessary reduction of spending, increasing taxes, or both. If it fails to act or acts but cannot overcome a Presidential veto of its decision, then automatic spending reductions take place following a formula established in the law. 14/ The formula merely calls for an across-the-board cut with major exemptions in debt service and social security. Thus, both domestic and military programs would be cut in an arbitrary manner. Of course this procedure is established in law and Congress could void the whole process by amending the law at any time. The threat of across-the-board cuts with its irrational implications is the game of chicken sanction which is meant to force both the Congress and the President to act responsibly.

Such threats do not always work.

One pleasant fact to report is that the revisions to congressional procedure related to the budget seem to be resulting in great Congressional budget discipline particularly in the Senate. A Senate rule says that any legislation, amendment, or budget resolution is out of order if it would breach the Balanced Budget Act's deficit ceiling. Thus, to add money over the ceiling is almost impossible because any Senator could kill it by merely raising a point of order. Under the rule, the only way a program can get more money is for the proponent of additional funding to also propose cutbacks equal to or greater than the additions. This rule is only applicable if the yearly figures are over the ceiling, but Congress tends to work right up to or even over the deficit ceiling.

The result of the new procedural rules is that Congressional budgeting decisions are a zero-sum game. If a congressman wishes to suggest additional appropriations, the suggestion must include specific suggestions for cuts equal to or exceeding the extra appropriation amount. This discourages action because additional political enemies are made when cuts are proposed. Politically achieving support for more money and specific cutbacks is very difficult. Thus, there is a whole new way that budgets are decided upon in the Senate. Budget Committees now have more leverage and more budget discipline exists in Congress. Supplemental appropriation bills, in particular, have become more difficult to pass as they must also be deficit neutral. 15/

On the surface, the Balanced Budget Act seems sound, but it is fundamentally flawed. The act is based on the assumption that it will take a budget reduction of $36 billion a year until the deficit is reached in 1991. The act is based on projections of the deficit and not on reality; this is important assumption brings us to an unfortunate but likely chain of events. The most noted fact about federal budget and deficit forecasting is that it is always wrong and often significantly wrong. Unfortunately, forecasts are always wrong by underestimating the yearly budget deficit. Traditionally, the OMB estimate is off more than the CBO counterpart estimate. If the economy makes unforeseen shifts, the projects are off not in the magnitude of $32 billion but as high as $95 or more billion. As the time for final budget decisions draw near, Congress and the President can normally manipulate enough to find $10 billion without altering policy significantly. When the numbers reach the level of $32 billion or higher, then difficult cutting decisions must be made or the across-the-board cuts come into effect.

In the years following the 1986 revised tax law, the revenue forecasting accuracy in the federal government should reach an all time low. Although the radical tax shifts should net to a revenue neutral situation if the policy makers are correct, the consequences are not that predictable. The changes could result in additional revenue. A more reasonable assumption is that the army of accountants and tax lawyers will have some unanticipated victories resulting in lower taxes for their clients and less revenue for the federal government. This coupled with the reasonable likelihood of a slowing economy could mean substantially less federal revenue without a lessening demand for federal expenditures.

At some point in the near future, the real deficit and the target deficit assumptions in the act will not only be different but the real numbers will be significantly higher. The only way to remedy the problem will be to rewrite the law with a mechanism to update the deficit targets that were not placed in the original law. Congress will then start an annual charade of updating the targets much like they annually update the limit placed on the national debt. Much is said at that annual "ceremony" of the debt ceiling but realistically Congress must raise the debt limit because there is no other choice. In all likelihood, a parallel "ceremony" will exist on raising the deficit ceilings.

This divergence of reality and Congressional fiction has already begun. The forecasting agencies of OMB and CBO cling to an optimistic view of economic growth. Given that such a view makes it easier to meet the immediate deficit ceilings of this year's budget, such optimistic forecasting is not surprising. However, when reality proves the forecasters wrong, then the next year's deficit ceiling becomes politically impossible to meet. Something would have to give and the most likely candidate would be the ceilings in the Balanced Budget Act. The brutality of large across-the-board cuts makes that option practically and politically impossible. The Balanced Budget Act will be another failed attempt to control the national deficit.

A definitive declaration that the Balanced Budget Act will fail is premature. However, this author cannot be optimistic about the likely success of this noble attempt.

. SUMMARY

The argument has been made that the U.S. Constitution should be amended to include a line-item veto power for the President in order to bring greater responsibility to the federal government budget process. Few argue that the current yearly massive unbalanced budgets are desirable. Most agree with the American public that this type of irresponsible decision making must stop. Some argue that it is a failure of leadership. This chapter argues the evolved political process makes it almost impossible for politicians who wish to be reelected to behave in statesmen-like manner. The problem is the process.

The founders of the republic wrote a Constitution based on their extensive experience with government, an excellent understanding of political theory, and an appreciation for the strengthens and weaknesses of political leaders. Not surprising their efforts need an occasional fine tuning as recommended here.

They believed in a separation of powers with a veto power given the President. Over time the general veto power has become a relatively ineffective device in dealing with budget related issues. The extra-legal impoundment provision was a line-item veto; but in its legalization in 1974, its strength as a viable Presidential tool was diminished significantly. By creating a viable line-item veto power, the political stalemate could be ended and the nation would be better served. In the spirit of the men such as James Madison, the Congress must have a means to override such vetoes and the proposal creates such a means.

The proposed amendment has the following key provisions:
* it only becomes a viable Presidential power when the President in a message to Congress says either Congress failed to pass a timely budget bill or that bill is unbalanced,
* the President can line-item veto not only appropriations bills but other legislation which

effects yearly budget levels, and
* Congressional safeguards are built into the process
  because the Congress can deny the Pesident the
  the line-item veto power with a 2/3 vote in each
  chamber and can override any line-item veto with
  a 3/5 vote.

The proposed amendment has several other advantages because it:
* creates an implicit Congressional goal to have a
  balanced and timely budget or the President will
  be given extra powers in his relationship with
  Congress,
* gives a real sanction to elected officials to pass
  timely budgets or not be paid,
* encourages Congress to use the capital budget,
  contingent liability, unfunded liability, and
  accrual concepts which have proven very successful in the private sector and in many governments,
* avoids legal challenges on technical terms which
  could be used to ruin its effectiveness,
* provides requirements for notifications to Congress
  by the President in order to avoid unknown veto,
  and
* uses deadlines like thirty (30) days to prevent
  political stalling which would unnecessarily
  harm government administrative practices.

In summary, the proposed amendment to the Constitution would solve the contemporary unbalanced budget
problem but still provide flexibility to meet national
crises when they arise. The proposal focuses on ending
political stalemate on the yearly budget question and
ends "buck passing" by focusing responsibility on the
President. In keeping with the spirit of men like James
Madison, the proposal does not end "separation of
powers" but merely expands upon the approach. The
President would be responsible, but the Congress has
the ultimate responsibility if they chose to override
the President by a 3/5 vote. The essential balance of
power remains, but the stalemate is broken.

ENDNOTES

1. Cronin, Thomas E. and Jeffrey J. Weill. "An Item
Veto For the American President?" paper presented at
the American Political Science Association meeting in
New Orleans, August 29-31, 1985. p. 1 and Appendix C.

292

2. Reagan, Ronald. State of the Union Message. January 25, 1984. Weekly Compilation of Presidential Documents. V. 20. January 30, 1984. p. 90.

3. Bryce, James. The American Commonwealth. 3d ed. New York: Macmillan and Co., 1893. p. 214.

4. Cronin and Weill. p. 2.

5. "Veto the Veto," Wall Street Journal, editorial, February 7, 1985. p. 34.

6. Rauch, Jonathan, "Power of the Purse", National Journal. 5/24/86. pp. 1259 - 1261.

7. Cronin and Weill. p. 17.

8. Nebraska Constitution, Article IV. Paragraph 7.

9. Burke, Timothy P. "The Partial Veto Power: Legislation by the Governor." Washington State Law Review. V. 49. February, 1974. p. 608.

10. Cascade Telephone Co. vs. State Tax Commission. 176 Washington 616 (1934); State ex rel. Ruoff vs. Rosellini. 55 Washington 2d 555 (1960).

11. Cronin and Weill, Appendix C.

12. Abney, Glenn and Thomas R. Lauth. "The Line -Item Veto in the States: An Instrument for Fiscal Restraint or An Instrument for Partisanship?" Public Administration Review. V. 45. May/June 1985. pp. 372 - 377. Also Robert C. Moe. "Prospects For The Item Veto At the Federal Level: Lessons From the States". Paper presented at the 1985 American Political Science Association in New Orleans.

13. Much of this section of the chapter draws upon Jonathan Rauch, "The Edge of the Abyss". National Journal. 9/6/86. pp. 2117 - 2120.

14. Gramm, Phil. "Deficit Dilemma Squarely Faced", Miami Herald. July 26, 1986. p. 25A.

15. See endnote 6.

OTHER REFERENCES

Louis Fisher. "The Item Veto: The Risks of Emulating the States". paper presented at the American Political Science Association meeting in New Orleans, August 29-31, 1985.

Thomas D. Lynch. Public Budgeting in America. Second Edition. Englewood Cliffs, N.J., Prentice Hall, N.J., 1985.

Alan Murray. "Government's System of Accounting Comes Under Rising Criticism". Wall Street Journal. February 3, 1985.